80 DAYS JOURNEY
with the DESERT FATHERS

SAINT SHENOUDA PRESS

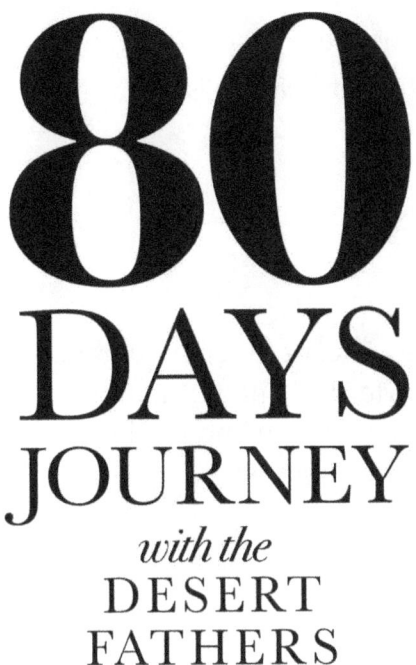

80 DAYS JOURNEY
with the DESERT FATHERS

By: Palladius Bishop of Helenepolis

ST SHENOUDA PRESS
SYDNEY, AUSTRALIA
2024

80 Days Journey with the Desert Fathers
By: Palladius Bishop of Helenpolis

COPYRIGHT © 2024
St. Shenouda Press

All rights reserved. Except for brief quotations in critical publications or reviews, no part of this book may be reproduced in any manner without prior written permission from the publisher.

ST SHENOUDA PRESS
8419 Putty Rd,
Putty, NSW, 2330
Sydney, Australia

www.stshenoudapress.com

ISBN 13: 978-0-6457704-7-6

Cover Design:

Mina Rizkalla
www.minarizkalla.com.au

Introduction

IN THIS BOOK ARE WRITTEN THE EXCELLENT DEEDS and the marvellous lives of the holy and blessed Fathers, who took upon themselves the yoke of solitary life, and who made themselves to be remote from the world, and who lived in the desert. They wished to live wholly the heavenly life, and to travel on the road which leads to the kingdom of heaven. Let us emulate their example and endeavour to do with all our might what they did! Together with these we commemorate also the marvellous women who led their lives in the Divine Spirit, who with a brave mind brought to an end the strife of the labours of spiritual excellence, according to the Divine manifestation and love, for they wished to lay hold upon their souls, and to bind upon their heads the crown of holiness.

I will first of all commit the weight of the matter to the Providence of God. And I will, with all diligence, make use of the prayers of the holy Fathers, so that I may be able to mount up as upon wings to the place where their contests were waged, and may tell the story briefly of those athletes, who though young became great and divine men who did valiantly and who triumphed in the works and deeds of spiritual excellence. I will also relate the histories of those blessed women who were adorned with the fair attire of the monastic life, and who attained to pre-eminence in divine labours. Some of these divine persons of whom I am about to tell the story, I was held to be worthy to see face to face. Concerning the heavenly lives of the others who died in the contest of the fear of God, I have learned from the athletes of Christ, who were arrayed in God.

Through very many cities, villages, caves and holes in the earth, and in the tabernacles which the monks had in the desert for a distance as far as a man could walk, I have for sake of the labour of the fear of God, have set down in writing with exactness the things which I have seen. I have also made known to you in this book the things which I have heard from the Holy Fathers concerning the triumphs of great men, and concerning the women who for the sake of the hope which is in Christ performed mighty works which were above nature, and I have sent it to your hearing which loves divine words. Oh you Lausus who are triumphant among men, and who arose among the friends of God, and who are the ornaments of this believing and God-fearing kingdom, and are the true friend and servant of God,

DAY 01

Abba Isidore

By the help of our Lord I will, therefore, begin to write for you, O Lausus the histories of the holy Fathers, and I will omit nothing concerning them which I will not make known in my discourse, neither the histories of those who lived in cities, nor of those who lived in villages or in caves, nor of those who became famous in the desert. No, I will even add to my discourse the histories of those who lived among the general assembly of a community, for no special country or place in which they lived and in which they perfected the life of ascetic excellence needs to be sought out, for everywhere they led the pure life and conversation of chastity and integrity, and performed the deeds of the simple mind in which, through the help of Christ, they did and fulfilled the lives and deeds of angels.

At first, when I went to Alexandria in the second consulship of the Emperor Theodosius the Great, who now because of the orthodoxy of his faith in Christ sojourns with the angels, I met in the city a wonderful man who was adorned in every respect with the most beautiful qualities of speech, and knowledge, and life and conversation, whose name was Isidore. He was a priest and was the overseer (i.e. manager or secretary) of the hospital of the church of Alexandria, and it was said of him that in his early youth he had lived in a monastery in the desert, and that he triumphed in the contest of ascetic life. I saw, moreover, his cell in the mountain of Nitria. I met him when he was seventy years of age, and when he had lived fifteen years longer he departed from this world. Now to the end of his life this holy man never put on either a linen tunic or even a head-covering; he never washed, and he never ate flesh, and he never ate a full meal seated comfortably at a table; and yet, through Divine grace, his body shone.

He possessed a sound and healthy body, and he was, by the grace of Christ, so fully endowed with strength that those who beheld him and who did not know him would not be persuaded that he lived a life of self-denial, and they thought and said that he must lead a life of great luxury and that he must eat abundantly of rich meats. If I were to undertake to declare the marvellous character of his life and deeds, and wished to recount the excellence of his soul, and to make manifest every fact concerning them, all time would not suffice for me to declare them, nor would paper suffice for me to write them. For this man was so lovingly merciful and so full of peace that, by the reason of orthodoxy of his faith in Christ, even his enemies who did not believe were put to shame by him, from his early youth up, and at his good deeds and at the abundance. His graciousness was put to the blush; for he was gracious to every man.

He possessed the gift of the spirit and the knowledge of the Holy Scriptures, and the comprehension of divine learning, and he kept the commandments so strictly that at noon, the time when the brethren were accustomed to take their food, the mind of this holy man was carried away as it were in a slumber, and the greater number of the brethren were marvelling at his example and knowledge, and many, many times they tried to persuade him to relate to them the things which he saw, and entreated him to tell them concerning the marvellous state which had come upon him, but he could not be persuaded to do so. Finally, he was constrained by the power of their love, and he answered and said to them, "My mind departed and was carried away by contemplation, and I was snatched away by the similitude of a thought, and I was fed with the food of glory, which, however, it is impossible for me to describe."

I knew this man, and on several occasions he burst into tears at the table; and when I asked him, "What is the cause of these tears?" He said to me, "I am ashamed of myself because, being a rational being, I eat the food of an irrational creature; I desire to live in paradise, where I should enjoy the food which is imperishable. For although we have received that power which is from Christ, yet am I drawn to partake of the food which perish would partake of the food which is spiritual, and I would that I were in the paradise of delights in the dominion which God has given to me; and behold I am eating the food of the beasts."

To this man were known all the members of the Roman Senate and the freeborn women of the nobles of Rome, because in former times he had gone with Bishop Athanasius to that city, and he had also been there with the holy man Bishop Demetrius. Isidore, having great riches, and wanting nothing, was accustomed to give abundantly and without sparing to the poor and needy. When he had ended his days and came to die, he made no will whatever; and he left no money to any man, and he left nothing to his brethren. To his sisters who were virgins he also left nothing, and he made no provision at all for them, but committed them to the care of Christ, saying, "He who created you will provide for your living and also whatsoever things of which you have need, even as He has provided for me." With his sisters was a company of about seventy sisters.

When I had come to him to be his disciple, and I was persuading him to hold me worthy of the rank of those who lived in a monastery, being in the vigour of my early manhood and needing not the word only but also the labour of the body, and severe physical exercises, even like the young unbroken animal, I begged him to teach me his beautiful way of life and to let me dwell by myself, for I was heedful of nothing, being in the vigour of my early manhood, and I had no great need of doctrine, but only to learn to subdue the passions of the flesh. Then, like a good teacher, he took me outside the city to a place which was six miles distant, and in which there was restful solitude, and he handed me over to an anchorite whose name was Dorotheos.

DAY 02

Dorotheos of Thebes

DOROTHEOS OF THEBES' LIFE WAS ONE OF SPIRITUAL EXCELLENCE. He had lived in a cave for sixty years. He commanded me to live with him, and to lead a life of self-denial with him for a period of three years, so that the passions of the flesh might leave me. For the blessed Isidore knew that blessed old man, and he knew that his life was stern and severe, and he admonished me, saying, "When you have completed this period of three years, return to me for the remainder of the doctrine of spiritual knowledge." But I was unable to fulfill these three years with him, on account of a severe illness into which I fell, and so I departed from Dorotheos before the end of the period, and I returned to him that had brought me out, and entered his abode that I might learn the doctrine of the spirit.

The life of Dorotheos was one of exceedingly hard toil, and the manner of it was severe, and his food was meager and wretched, for he lived on dry bread. And he used to go round about in the desert by the side of the sea the whole day long in the heat of the noonday sun and collect stones with which he built cells, which he used to give to the brethren who were unable to build cells for themselves; and he used to finish one cell each year. One day I said to the holy man, "Father, why work you thus in your old age? For you will kill your body in all this heat." He said to me, "I kill it lest it should kill me." He used to eat one small bread cake, which weighed about six ounces, each day, and a little bundle of green herbs; and he drank water by measure. What then? I know not. As God is my witness I never saw this man stretch out his legs and lie down as men are accustomed to do; and he never slept upon a bed of palm leaves, or upon anything else, but he used to work the whole night long weaving baskets made of palm leaves to provide himself with the daily bread which he required and food.

I imagined at first that he used to work in this manner because I was present, and then I thought, "Perhaps it is only for my sake, and to show me how to perform such severe labors, that he does this." So I made enquiries of many of those who had been his disciples and who were then living by themselves and were emulating his spiritual excellencies, and I also asked others of his disciples who were living by his side if in very truth he always labored in this wise, and they said to me, "He has held to this practice from his youth up, and he has never been in the habit of sleeping according to what is right. In the daytime he never sleeps willingly, but sometimes when he is working with his hands, or when he is eating, he closes his eyes and is snatched away by slumber. "As he sits working he eats, and unless slumber overcomes him suddenly he would never sleep at all. Many times he is overcome by slumber while he is eating, and the morsel of bread falls out of his mouth because he is overcome by drowsiness." And when from time to time I used to urge him to sit down, or to throw himself upon a mat of palm leaves and to rest a little, he would answer me saying in a grieved manner, "If you are able to persuade the angels to sleep, then you will be able to persuade me."

One day, towards the ninth hour, Dorotheos sent me to the fountain from which he drank water to fetch him some water, so that he might eat his meal, for he used to eat about this time, and when I had gone there I chanced to see a viper going down the well; and because of my fear I was unable to fill the pitcher with water, and I went back to him, and said to him, "O father, we shall die, for I have seen a viper going down into the water." When he heard these words he laughed reverently, and constrained himself, and he lifted up his face and looked at me not a little time, and he shook his head, and said to me, "If it were to happen that Satan had the power to show you in every fountain an asp, or again to cast into them vipers, or serpents, or tortoises, or any other kinds of venomous reptiles, would you be able to do without drinking water entirely?" When he had said these words to me, he went out and departed to the fountain and drew water, and brought it back. Having made the sign of the Cross over it he straightaway drank there from before he ate anything. He constrained me to drink and said to me, "Where the seal of the Cross is, the wickedness of Satan has no power to do harm."

This blessed man Isidore, the overseer of the hospital in Alexandria, related to me the following story, which is worthy of record, and he heard it from the blessed Anthony where he lived with him in the desert in the days of Emperor Maximinus, the prosecutor.

DAY 03

The Virgin Potamiaena

THERE WAS A CERTAIN YOUNG VIRGIN CALLED POTAMIAENA who was exceedingly beautiful and was a Christian. She was the handmaiden of a certain worldly man who was given over to a life of pleasure, and she lived in very great luxury, and her master flattered her greatly, wishing to destroy her. Being unable to bring her into subjection to his will, he at length was seized with madness, and he became furiously angry with her and delivered her over to a certain prefect who lived at that time in Alexandria (i.e. Basilides), saying, "She is a Christian, and she reviles the government and utters blasphemies against the Emperor."

He promised to give him much money saying, "If she can be persuaded to do my will, keep her for me without disgrace and punishment, but if she persists in her obstinacy of heart, punish her with every kind of torture you please, and do not let her live to laugh at me and at my luxurious way of life." When they brought the valiant woman before the throne of the judges, she was greatly moved, but she was not persuaded; and the prefect tortured the body of the virgin of Christ with many different kinds of tortures. Then again after these things he thought out a crafty plan and invented a method of punishment by torture which was as follows. He commanded them to bring a huge cauldron which was full of pitch and to light a fierce fire under it, and when the pitch was melted and was boiling, the judge cried to her, saying, "Go and submit yourself to the will of your lord, and know you if you do not do this thing, you shall straightaway fall into this cauldron." When she heard this, she sealed her soul, and answered and said, "You judge with iniquity, O judge, for you command me to become subject to fornication. I am the handmaiden of Christ, and it is right that I should stand before His throne without blemish."

When the judge heard this, he was straightaway greatly troubled and filled with wrath, and he commanded them to bring her and to cast her into the cauldron. Then the virgin said to him, "I adjure you, by the head of the Emperor, if you condemn me to this thing of your own self, to command them to put me into the cauldron little by little, without stripping my apparel from me, so that you may know the patient endurance which I have through Christ for the sake of my purity." As they were dipping her little by little into the cauldron, for a very short space of time, immediately the pitch reached her neck it became cold; thus she delivered her soul to God, and she was crowned with a good martyrdom. A great congregation of holy men and women were made perfect (i.e. they suffered martyrdom) at that time in the church of Alexandria, and they became worthy of that land which the meek inherit. Potamiaena was martyred, with her mother Marcella, in the reign of Septimius Severus. Here ends the triumphs of Isidore, and Dorotheos, and the virgin Potamiaena.

DAY 04

Didymus
(Born A.D. 309 or 314)

TOGETHER WITH THESE I ALSO SAW A CERTAIN BLESSED MAN who was in Alexandria, and whose name was Didymus, and who also, with us, wrote these things; now he was blind, and he could not see at all; he was a marvelous man, and I went several times to see him. He was eighty years of age, and he told me that he became blind when he was four years old and could not see at all, but according to what he himself related to me, "After forty years I perceived the faces (or external aspects) of things." Although this man had never learned the Testaments, and had never entered a school, the gift of excellent mind had been given to him by God. He became learned in the knowledge of books through an enlightened understanding. He was adorned with goodness and with the knowledge of the truth to such a degree, and was so ready and was so wholly wise that there was fulfilled in him that which was written, "The Lord opens the eyes of the blind." He could interpret the Old and New Testaments word by word in its proper place and had investigated carefully the commandments and could repeat all the words which were in them. He was so thoroughly well acquainted with the belief of the truth, and he comprehended so deeply all heresies that his knowledge was more excellent than that of many who were before him in the Church.

Once when he was urging me to make a prayer in his cell and I was unwilling to do so, he spoke to me and related to me concerning Abba Anthony who, he said, "Came three times and visited me in this cell. When I begged and entreated him to pray, straightaway he knelt down upon his knees, and prayed, and waited not for me to speak one word about it, but at the first word he corrected me by his obedience. He did not let me finish my speech, but by work he made manifest obedience." Didymus said to me, "You also, if you wish to walk in his footsteps and to imitate him in his life and deeds, and in hospitality, and if you would walk in the life of excellence and in the love of God, remove yourself from contention."

This blessed man Didymus himself told me the following story. Once upon a time I was suffering by reason of the wretched Emperor Julian. One day, when it was even tide, and I had eaten no food through my anxiety about this matter, whilst I was sitting on my seat I dropped into a light slumber, and there fell upon me a marvelous thing. I saw and behold, there were white horses galloping about, and they had on them riders who were dressed in white, and they were crying out and saying, "Tell Didymus that Julian died this day at the seventh hour. Rise up, eat, and make this news known to Bishop Athanasius, so that he also may know and rejoice." I wrote down the day, the hour, and the month in which this vision took place, and it was found that it had happened even as it had been told to me in the vision.

DAY 05

The Maiden Alexandra

THERE WAS A CERTAIN MAIDEN OF ALEXANDRIA whose name was Alexandra. She left the city and shut herself up in a tomb until the end of her life; she used to receive her food and whatever she needed through a window, and no man and no woman saw her face, neither did she see the face of any man, for twelve years. A few days afterwards she yielded up her soul. She lay down and went to her rest in peace. When her serving woman went to visit her according to her custom, she knocked at the window, but Alexandra gave her no answer, and straightaway she knew that she was dead, and she came and made known to us concerning her mistress. We took off the door of her cell and we found her body dried up.

The blessed woman Melania also related to us the story of Alexandra, saying, "I have never seen her face to face." I stood outside the cell, close to the window, and entreated her to tell me for what reason she had shut herself up in the grave. Alexandra answered saying, "Inasmuch as the thought of the love of God was present in my mind, I prayed before the Lord, and I entreated Him to permit me to offer to Him my virginity in the state in which it had been born with me. A certain young man regarded me in his thoughts, and looked upon me, and desired me, and sought to destroy me. But because I did not want to grieve him, or to say what was evil to him, or to be to him an occasion of sin, I chose rather to shut myself up alive in this grave than to cause a man who was made in the form of the image of God to stumble."

I said to her, "How can you bear to live here without seeing the face of any man and without being driven to despair?" Then she said to me, "I occupy myself with my prayers and with the work of my hands. I have no idle moments. From morning until the ninth hour I weave linen, recite the Psalms and pray. During the rest of the day I commemorate in my heart the holy fathers. I revolve in my thoughts the histories of all the Prophets, Apostles and Martyrs. During the remaining hours I work with my hands and eat my bread, and by means of these things I am comforted whilst I await the end of my life in good hope." These things we have heard from the blessed woman Melania who told the story of the maiden Alexandra. But in this history I must not underrate those who have toiled in the faith of Christ, to the glory of the perfect and to the admonition of those who hear.

Abba Macarius the Alexandrian and a Certain Virgin

THERE WAS IN ALEXANDRIA A CERTAIN VIRGIN who though meek in appearance was of a haughty disposition. She was exceedingly rich and had possessions without number, but she never relieved the poor, and the strangers, and those who were in misery, and she never gave a drachma to the Church. Notwithstanding the frequent rebuke with which the Fathers rebuked her, she never allowed any portion of riches to leave her. This woman had kinsfolk, and she adopted her sister's daughter, to whom she used to promise by day and by night to give her all that she had, for she had fallen from heavenly love. It is a customary thing which belongs to the deception of Satan that he produces avarice under guise of love of family, for that he has no genuine care for kinsmanship is well known from the fact that he taught murder in order that he might make war between brethren and is admitted by the Holy Book. If he imagined that he implants solicitude for kinsfolk in the hearts of men, it must be remembered that he is not moved to do this on their behalf because of his love for them, but only that he may minister to his own will, for manifestly he knows the sentence of judgment which has been passed, that the wicked shall not inherit the kingdom of God.

For if a man be moved by spiritual understanding and by divine desire, he will be able to care for his kinsfolk if they be in want without bringing himself into contempt; but if he devotes the whole of himself to the care for his kinsfolk, and he brings himself into contempt by making himself to labor under poverty, he will fall from the divine law. The divine man David sings in the Psalms concerning those who possess themselves of the solicitude of the fear of God, and he says, "Who shall go up into the mountain of the Lord?" Whenever he says, "Who," he makes known concerning the smallness of the number who shall go up. Again he says, "Who shall stand in His holy place? He whose hands are clean and whose heart is chosen, and does not give himself to poverty." For those who devote themselves to poverty are those who think that the soul is dissolved with this body.

This virgin, who was so in name only, became a stranger to the various kinds of spiritual excellence. And there was a certain priest whose name was Macarius (or Isidore) who wished to cut away as with iron and to lighten the weight of the possessions of those who loved money, and he had the care of, and was the governor of a house for the poor who were sick and infirm in their bodies.

This man thought out the following plan whereby he might entrap the virgin. From his youth he had been a skilful workman in the cutting of gems, and he went to her and said, "Certain very precious emeralds and gems have fallen into my hands, and whether they have been stolen or not I do not know; their value cannot be ascertained, because they are above price, but the man who has them will sell them for five hundred dinars. If you wish to take them you will be able to recover the price of five hundred dinars from the sale of one of the gems, and the rest you will be able to employ in the adornment of your sister's daughter." When the virgin heard this she was perturbed, and fell down at his feet making an entreaty to him, and said, "I beseech you to let no other person take them." Macarius says to her, "Come to my house and see them," but she would not consent to this; and she poured out for him five hundred dinars, and said to him, "According to what you do require even so take, but I do not wish to see the man who is selling them."

Having taken the five hundred dinars he spent them on food and on things for the use of those who were hungry, and on the poor. When much time had passed, inasmuch as he was a famous man in Alexandria, this blessed man was well known for his love of God, and for the merciful disposition which was in him, and he was almost one hundred years old, and we also knew him and had tarried in his house with him, the virgin was ashamed to call the matter of the five hundred dinars to his mind. But finally she found him in the church and said to him, "I beseech you to tell me how you have disposed of the gems for which we gave you the five hundred dinars." He answered and said to her, "When you gave me the money I gave it for the price of the gems; if you wish come and see them in my house, for there they are deposited. Come and see them, if it pleases you to do so, and if you will not then take your money." So she went with him joyfully.

The place to which she went was a house of the poor; in the upper parts of it were lying women whose bodies were destroyed, and in the lower parts were men. When they had come there Macarius brought her in through the door, and said to her, "Which would you see first, the emeralds or the gems?" She says to him, "Whichever you please." Then he took her up to the upper parts of the house and showed her the women whose faces and bodies were diseased and deformed, and said to her, "These are the gems;" and he brought her down to the lower parts, and showed her the men, saying, "These are the emeralds. If these please you good and well; but if not take your money." Then the virgin was ashamed, and went out and departed. By reason of her grief she fell into a sickness, because it was through God and of her own will that she had in this way performed the matter. Finally, however, she came to herself, and was exceedingly grateful to the priest, and as for the maiden for whose wedding feast she was laying up her riches, she died.

DAY 07

The Monks who Lived in Nitria

HAVING HELD CONVERSE WITH MANY OF THE SAINTS, and having gone round about among the monasteries which were near to Alexandria for three years, and having met about two thousands of the great and strenuous men who lived there, and who were adorned with the excellence of spiritual lives, I departed from there and came to Mount Nitria.

Between this mountain and Alexandria there lies a certain lake which is called "Mareotis," which embraces a space of seventy miles. Having seated myself in a boat I crossed this lake in a day and a half, and I came to the mountain to the south, which is joined to the desert which reaches to Cush (Ethiopia). In this mountain of the Mazaki and of the Mauritanians there live excellent men who are adorned with diverse kinds of ascetic virtues. Every monk leads the ascetic life as he wishes and as he is able, either by himself or in a community. In this mountain there are seven bakers who make bread and who minister to them, and to the chosen men of the inner desert, of whom there are six hundred, and also to the people of that mountain. When I had dwelt in this mountain for a year, and had profited by the fathers, the pious and blessed men, I mean Rabbi Brasses i.e. Arsisius, Busiris, Peta-Bast, Agios, Khronis, and Serapion, the elder, and had learned from them also concerning the ancient and first spiritual fathers who had lived there, I entered into the inner desert in which is Mount Nitria.

In this mountain is a great church, and in the courtyard of it are three palm trees, in each of which hangs a whip. One of these is for the correction of the monks who transgress through folly; the second is for the punishing of the thieves if they are found falling on the place; and the third is for the chastising of the strangers who flock there and who transgress in any matter whatsoever. It is the same with anyone who shall commit any offence, they bring him to the palm tree and punish him, and he receives upon his back the number of stripes which they have appointed to him. Adjoining the church is a house in which the strangers who arrive there may lodge, and if any man wishes to work there one year, or two, or until he departs of his own accord he may do so; and every week of days they permit him to rest, so that he may do nothing, but they give him work during the remaining days of the week, either among the bakers, or in the refectory. If there was among these anyone who was sufficiently educated they used to give him a book to read, but they did not allow him to converse with any man until the sixth hour. There were also in this mountain physicians for the use of the sick, and those who sold cakes; and they also used wine which was sold there. All these people worked at the weaving of flax with their hands, and there was no needy man there. Now when the evening comes you must rise up to hear the praises, and the Psalms, and the prayers which are sent up to Christ by the people from the monasteries which are there, and a man might imagine, his mind being exalted, that he was in the Paradise of Eden.

The monks only came to church on the Sabbath and on the First Day of the week.

Belonging to this church there were eight priests and governors, but as long as the first one lived none of the other ministers in the church; he neither judged nor spoke with any man, and lived with him a life of silent contemplation. This great man Arsisius and many of the ancient holy men whom we saw were followers of the rule of the blessed man Anthony, and Arsisius himself told me that the holy man Ammon, who was from Nitria, and whom he knew, and whose soul was taken up and carried by the angels into heaven, even saw Anthony. And Arsisius also spoke to me concerning the blessed man Pachomius, who came from Tabenna of Hekham, and who possessed the gift of prophecy and who became the governor and head of three thousands men, of this man I will relate the virtues at the end of this book.

DAY 08

Abba Ammon

CONCERNING THE BLESSED MAN AMMON, he used to say that he became a monk in this way: When he was a young man, about twenty-two years old, he was left an orphan by his parents. His father's brother wanted to give him a wife, and because he was unable to resist the counsel of his uncle he was compelled by force to marry one, and to fasten the crown of bridegroom upon his head, and to take his seat in the marriage chamber, and to fulfill everything according to the law of the marriage feast. Ammon submitted to everything outwardly, but after everyone had gone forth having put Ammon and his wife to bed in the marriage chamber, the blessed man rose up and shut the door and seated himself. He called to the true and blessed woman his spouse, and said to her, "Henceforth you shall be my lady and my sister; come therefore, and I will relate to you concerning a matter which is more excellent than marriage. The marriage which men contract is a perishable thing but let us choose for ourselves the marriage which does not perish, and the marriage feast which never ends. Let us each sleep alone, for in this wise we shall please Christ; and let us guard the glory of our virginity unspotted, so that we may take our rest at the marriage feast which is incorruptible."

Then he took out a book from his bosom and read to the maiden passages, which were uttered by the Apostles and by our Redeemer, and since she had no knowledge of the Scriptures, he added to their words from his own divine mind. He read many passages to her and talked much to her concerning virginity and purity, and at length, by the grace of Christ, she was persuaded. Then she answered and said to him, "Master, I know well that a rule of life of purity is very much more excellent than marriage; therefore whatever pleases you, that do. I also from this time forth will be persuaded to do whatever you wish to do."

Ammon said to her, "I beg and entreat you to let each of us from this time forth dwell alone." She would not agree to this, and said, "Let us live in the same house, and let each of us have a separate bed." So, they dwelt together in the same house for eighteen years. In the morning Ammon used to go out and spend the whole day cultivating the balsam trees which he had in his garden. The balsam tree is like the vine, and must be planted and pruned and cultivated, and it demands great attention and in the evening he entered into his house, and recited his prayers, and then ate with her. He also rose up to say the praises of the night, and as soon as the dawn had come he would depart to the garden. As they were doing these things, they both removed themselves from passions, and attained to impassibility, and the prayers of Abba Ammon helped his wife.

At length the blessed woman said to him, "Master, I have something to say to you, if you will hearken to me, and I am convinced that for God's sake you love me." The blessed man said to her, "Tell me what you wish to say?" And she said to him, "It is not right seeing that you are a God-fearing man, and one who lives a life of righteousness, and that you have also made me, outwardly, to yearn for this path of life, and by the help of divine grace I have gotten purity, to live with me. It is not good that, for my sake, you who dwell with me in purity for our Lord's sake, should hide the spiritual excellence of your philosophy; for it is not seemly that your fair deeds should be hidden, and should not be known. Let your dwelling be apart from me and thus you shall benefit many."

Then Ammon praised God, and said to her, "O lady, this mind is beautiful, and if it be acceptable to you do remain and abide in this house in peace, and I will go and make another for myself." Having left her, Ammon departed and entered Mount Nitria, whereas the monasteries were not numerous, indeed up to that time there were no monasteries at all there, and built himself a habitation there, and dwelt there for twenty-two years. Having attained the highest practice of the labours of the ascetic life, he ended his days, that is to say, the holy man Ammon went to his rest and slept when he was sixty-two years of age. Twice in these years he went to see his spouse. He died in his virginity, and his wife likewise, brought the years of her life to an end in purity.

The following wonderful thing is told concerning him by the blessed Athanasius, the Bishop of Alexandria, in the book, which he, Bishop Athanasius, composed about the life and deeds of the blessed Anthony. Once when he was about to cross the river which is called the "Wolf" with Theodore his disciple. He was ashamed to take off his clothes lest he might see the nakedness of his person. Being doubtful in his mind how he should cross over, wonder fell upon him, and through an angel he crossed the river without any boat whatsoever on his part. It was the same Ammon who saw the blessed man Anthony, who lived and died so wise that his soul was taken to heaven by angels, and it was he who passed over the waters by the might of the Holy Spirit. Concerning this river, which is called the "Wolf," I myself was once in great fear when I was crossing it in a boat, because it is filled with the overflow of the waters of the Nile.

The Blessed Man Hor

IN MOUNT NITRIA THERE WAS A CERTAIN MAN whose name was Hor, concerning whom men, especially all the brotherhood, testify to many of his triumphs, and also that marvelous and excellent woman Melha (i.e. Melania), the handmaid of Christ, who went into this mountain before I did. As for me, I never became acquainted with this man. In his history they say this one thing: "He never told a lie in his life, and he never used oaths; he never uttered a curse, and beyond what was absolutely necessary he never spoke at all."

The Blessed Man Pambo (d. A.D. 393)

IN THIS MOUNTAIN THERE ALSO LIVED THE BLESSED MAN Pambo (or Panbis), who was the teacher and master of the Bishops Dioscorus, Ammonius, Eusebius, Euthemis (Eutymius), and Origen the nephew of Dracontius, a marvellous man. This man

Pambo possessed the power to utter words of prophecy, and splendid triumphs, yet with all these, he despised gold and silver, even as the Word demands. The following things concerning him were related to me by the blessed woman Melha (i.e., Melania).

When I first came from Rome to Alexandria, I heard concerning the life and deeds of Pambo, since the blessed man Isidore, who also brought me to him in the desert, told me about him. I brought to him a basket, which was filled with stamped silver (i.e., coined money) three hundred pounds in weight, and I begged him to accept some of my possessions for his needs. He was sitting and plaiting the leaves of palm trees, and as he was doing this he merely blessed me, and said, "God gives you your reward!" Then he said to his steward, whose name was Origen, "Take and distribute this among all the brethren who are in the Island and Libya"; for these monasteries are exceedingly poor, and he commanded the steward not to give to any man who dwelt in Egypt, for those who dwell there have abundant means of subsistence. I stood there and I expected to be treated with honour or to be praised for the grace of the gift, but when I heard nothing from him, I said to him, "Master, do you know how much money it is, and that there are three hundred pounds in the basket?" Then Pambo, without lifting up his gaze, said to me, "My daughter, He to whom you have offered your money has no need to know the weight. For He who weighed the mountains in a balance knows how much is the weight of your silver. If you had given the money to me, you would have done well to have informed me concerning the weight of it; but since you have given it to God, who did not despise the two mites of the widow, what need have you to tell Him? Hold your peace."

Our Lord so directed that on the day on which I entered the mountain this blessed man died without having been ill, for he died whilst he was sewing together palm leaves for mats, without fever and without sickness. And he was seventy years old. He was sewing together palm leaves for a mat, and coming to the end of it he sent and called me.

When he had finished sewing it, he said to me, "Take this mat from my hands, so that you may keep me in remembrance, for I have nothing else whatever to leave you." Having given it to me he straightaway died. I wrapped his body in linen swathes, and buried him. Then I departed from the desert; and I shall treasure the mat as a sacred relic until the day of my death.

At the time of the death of this holy man Pambo there were standing before him certain famous men, Origen the priest and steward, and Ammonius, together with the remainder of the brethren, and they told me that at the time of his death, he said, "From the day in which I came into this desert and built this cell in which I have lived until this day I know not that I have ever eaten the bread of idleness which did not come from the labor of my own hands; and my soul repents not that I have ever spoken an empty word in my life; thus I go to God like one who has, as yet, not made a beginning in the fear of God."

Origen and Ammonius, the servants of Christ, in telling us the story of his life, bore witness concerning him that he was never asked a question by any man about a saying from the Book, or about the rules and labors of the ascetic life which he did not either answer immediately, or say, "I have not as yet understood the matter."

> Now there were times when he spoke these words only after three months' consideration of a matter; and he used to make answers with such understanding that every man received the things, which were said by him with as great reverence as if they had been said by God." This excellence was also attributed to Anthony the Great and to the rest of the holy men. Among

other things which are said concerning the holy man Pambo is the following. The blessed man once went to Pambo's cell and took with him some bread, and Pambo made a complaint, saying to him, "Why have you done this?" Then Abba Pior made an answer, saying, "Let this thing be not grievous to you." But Pambo was silent and sent him away. After some time Abba Pambo went to the cell of Abba Pior, and took with him bread which had been dipped in water; and being asked, "Why have you done this?" The blessed man Pambo said to him, "Let it not be grievous to you that I have also dipped the bread in water."

The Blessed Ammonius

THIS MAN AMMONIUS AND HIS THREE BROTHERS i.e. Dioscorus, Eusebius, and Euthinemius, who were called the "Tall Brothers" by Sozomen, and his two sisters, were disciples of Abba Pambo. When they had attained to the perfection of divine life and conversation they departed from the desert and founded two monasteries, I mean, one for men and one for women, but they placed the monastery of the women at a sufficient distance from that of the men, for Ammonius did not greatly love the intercourse of speech.

It was for this reason that a certain city, he should be its bishop, and the people of it drew near to the blessed man Timothy, Bishop of Alexandria, and entreated him to make the blessed Ammonius their bishop. And Timothy who from 381-385 was the Bishop of Alexandria told them to bring Ammonius to him and that he would make him their bishop. Then they took with them many people, and they went to Ammonius to bring him, and when he saw them he tried to find means to take to flight. But when he saw that he was unable to escape from them, he tried to persuade them, with many oaths that he would not accept it, but he was unable to make them give up their intention.

When they would not be persuaded by him, he seized a razor and cut off his left ear at the root, and said to them, "Now I am indeed persuaded that I cannot be that which you are urging me to be, for the Law also commands, the man whose ear has been cut off shall not draw near to the altar." So they left him and went and informed the Bishop, who said to them, "This law is observed among the Jews, but even if his nose was split and he had fine qualities I would make him Bishop." Then the people went to Ammonius again and entreated him to come, and when the pious man would not be persuaded by them, they wanted to take him and to make him come by force; but he said to them, "If you do not leave me, I will also slit my tongue." When they heard this they left him and departed.

Concerning this man Ammonius, so wonderful a thing as the following is said. Whenever a carnal thought entered his mind, he never spared his body, but he would make a piece of iron hot on the fire and lay it upon his members, so that they might always be in a state of wounds. From his youth up, his rule was as follows: whatsoever had been cooked by fire he would never eat. He could repeat the books of the Old and New Testaments by heart, and he used to read also the books which were composed by excellent men, by Origen, by Didymus, by Pierius, and by Stephen containing about ten thousands and six hundred sayings; concerning this the great fathers who lived in the desert bear witness. It is also said that this man possessed the power of foretelling events, and living in his cell he was so great a comforter to the brethren who lived in the desert that no other man could be compared with him. The blessed Evagrius, who was clothed with the spirit, and was skilled in examining thoughts, used to say, "I never saw any man who had attained more closely to impassibility than Ammonius."

Once a certain need of those who were dwelling in the desert called the blessed Ammonius, and Rufinus who was at that time the prefect also greatly persuaded him, and he went up to Constantinople. With him, there were also the holy bishops, and other monks who had come from various provinces to be present at the service of restoration of a certain martyrium which Rufinus had built. Rufinus wished him to receive him after holy baptism at the service of restoration of the temple which he had built, and so the blessed man received him from the bishops who had baptized him. Thus, as was right, Rufinus paid to the blessed man, Ammonius, the honour which is due to a life of asceticism, and he used to listen to him in everything, and after a short time he died and was buried in the martyrium which is called the "martyrium of Rufinus" and many helpful acts took place at his grave on behalf of those who were worthy of help.

DAY 11

The Blessed Benjamin

THERE WAS ALSO IN THE MOUNTAIN OF NITRIA a marvelous man whose name was Benjamin, who attained to a high state of perfection in the ascetic life, for he had fasted and toiled for eighty years. Now he was held to be worthy of the gift of the craft of the physician, and from every wound upon which he laid his hand, and which Christ blessed or gave him the power to heal, straightaway every pain departed. And this man, who was worthy of such a gift, collected water in his body for eight months before his death, and he was so much swollen that he might well have been called a second Job . Dioscurus took us, that is to say, the blessed Origen and myself, and said to us, "Come and see a new Job, who whilst suffering from such a severe disease of the body as this, heals others." Benjamin gave thanks concerning his affliction beyond measure, and glorified God continually. His soul rejoiced and was glad in the hope which was laid up for the saints.

When we had gone and seen the swelling of his body we found that it had become so large that a man could not with all his hand encircle one of his fingers; and being unable to look upon such a terrible affliction through disease, we turned away our eyes. Then the blessed man Benjamin said to us, "My sons, pray that the inner man may not collect water. Even when this body was in health, it in no wise helped me, and now that it is sick, it in no wise hinders me." During the last eight months of his illness they made a broad chair for him, and he used to sit on it always, because he was not able to lie down upon a bed because of the necessity of his belly and of the other members of his body.

Whilst he himself lived in such suffering through all his afflictions, he was healing others, and it is for this reason that I am compelled to narrate to you concerning the affliction of this righteous man, so that when such an affliction as this happens to the righteous, we may not hold the matter to be hard. When this blessed man died, the whole of the framework of the doorway had to be removed to enable them to bring out his body from his cell, for his body was very large indeed.

Apollonius the Merchant

AGAIN ANOTHER MAN, WHOSE NAME WAS APOLLONIUS, used to dwell in this Mount Nitria; and he was a merchant who had come there to learn to lead the life and conversation of an anchorite. This man found no handicraft at the exercise of which he could employ himself, and he could neither fast nor keep vigil like the other ascetics to any great extent. During the twenty years which he lived in this mountain, it was his rule of life and triumph that by his own labour and toil, he used to buy from Alexandria everything which was required by the brethren, and the things which were needed for the healing of the sick and carry them to the sick. And it was a marvellous thing to see him going about among the monasteries and cells of the brethren each day, from the earliest dawn, when he set out, until the ninth hour, and he used to stand by the door and say, "Is there, perhaps, anyone sick here?" He carried about pomegranates, and dried cakes, and raisins, eggs, and other things, which are necessary for the sick.

He found this rule of life easy to acquire, and to continue until his old age. He was able to attend to the affairs of the five thousand brethren who were dwelling in the mountain. When he died, he left whatever he had to another man like himself. He begged him to carry out this ministry, because the place where the monks lived was a desert and was destitute of the things of the world.

The Natural Brethren Paesius and Isaiah

THERE WERE ALSO THERE TWO BRETHREN, whose names were Paesius and Isaiah, who were the sons of a certain merchant who traded in Spain; and when their father died, they divided his inheritance between them, and there came to each of them money which amounted to five thousand dinars, and furniture, and raiment, and slaves, and property of all kinds. These blessed men took counsel together and meditated together and said to each other, "By what manner of trafficking shall we live in this world? If we continue to exercise the trade of our father, we shall only double our labours and toil for the benefit of others; and perhaps our wealth will fall into the hands of thieves by land or of pirates by sea." Whilst they were being troubled by such thoughts as these, they answered and said to each other, "Let us come to the way of truth, and let us acquire the life and conversation of the Christians, whereby we shall both keep the benefit of what our father has left us, and get possession of our soul."

This proposition concerning the labour of the dwellers in the monasteries was pleasing to them, and each of them found in his discipleship the power to judge as to what work he should embrace. Having divided their fathers' inheritance, they both possessed the eager care to please God by the various kinds of labours of life of the mourner. One of them divided everything which had come to him and gave it to the churches and monastic habitations, and distributed it among the poor and needy; and he learned a handicraft at which he could work and earn his daily bread, and he was constant in prayer and fasting. The other brother did not distribute his possessions, but he built himself a monastery and gathered together a few brethren. All strangers and poor folk, and all the aged men and sick folk who thronged to him, he used to receive and relieve their wants. Every first day of the week, and every Sabbath, he used to prepare three tables and relieve the wants of everyone who happened to be present there; and thus he spent all his possessions.

When the two brothers died, abundant blessing was ascribed to them by the whole brotherhood, but the one brother pleased some of them most, and the other the others; and although the brethren praised both brothers, a dispute arose among them concerning the superior merit of one or the other of the two brothers. Then the brethren went to the blessed Pambo and related the matter to him and wished to learn which rule of life and labour was the greater and more excellent. Pambo said to them, "They are both perfect. One man manifested the work of Abraham by his hospitality, and the other the self-denial of Elijah."

Again the brethren said to him, "How is it possible for the two to be equal in merit? We praise and magnify him who braced poverty, for we find that he did the work of the Gospel in selling everything that he had and giving it to the poor and that every day, and at every season, both by day and by night, he took up his cross and followed after his Lord by his fasting and his prayers." Again the other brethren contended with them, saying, "The other brother showed such supreme compassion on those who were strangers and on those who were afflicted that he would even sit in the highways and gather together the passers-by who were in trouble; and not only did he relieve his own soul, but he also brought a light to many souls that were heavily laden, and he would make ready the dead for the grave and bury them."

The blessed Pambo said to them, "Again I say to you that both are equal in merit, and I will tell you how each of them became so. Unless one had fasted, he would not have been worthy of the goodness and compassion of the other, and again, the other in relieving the wants of strangers also lightened his own load, for although a man may think that he has trouble in receiving them yet he also gains rest of body. But stay here a few days so that I may learn the answer from God, and come back and I will declare it to you." After a few days they came to him, and they asked him to tell them what had been revealed to him and he answered and said to them, "I have seen them both standing in the Paradise of Eden, in the presence of God."

Macarius, The Child of His Cross

THERE WAS ALSO A CERTAIN YOUTH WHOSE NAME WAS MACARIUS. When he became a young man about eighteen years old, he used to pasture flocks and herds, along with other young men of his own age and position, by the side of the lake which is called Mareotis. And without wishing to do so, he unwittingly committed a murder; and without saying a word to any man, he straightaway rose up and departed, and he went out and journeyed into the desert. Thus he attained to the fear of God, and to the love of men, in such ways that he esteemed himself lightly; and he passed three years in the desert, in the open air, and without a roof over his head. In that country there was no rainfall, and this everyone knows, either from hearsay or from actual experience.

After three years he built himself a cell and dwelt in it for twenty-five years and performed great labours. He was held worthy of the divine gift of being able to treat with contempt the devils, and he was completely happy in the ascetic life and in the noble labours of it. I dwelt by this man for no short time, and once I asked him, "What is your thought about the sinfulness of that murder which you did commit?" He said to me, "I am entirely untroubled by it, for I am bound to confess that the sin of this involuntary murder was the good cause of the redemption of my life.

The testimony of the Book confirms this view, saying not even Moses, the servant of the Lord, would have been held worthy of the divine vision unless, through fear for the murder which he had committed, he had forsaken Egypt, come to Mount Sinai, where he was held to be worthy of converse with God, and to compose the commandments of the spirit. We speak these things, not because we wish to help murder, but only so that we may particularly show that spiritual excellences spring from tribulations, when a man is not of his own will persuaded to draw near to goodness. Some spiritual excellences arise from the will, and some from tribulation; and in the works which I have found appended to this history, I have discovered that the murder which Macarius committed belonged to this latter class.

Macarius prayed always, and he prayed with his arms and hands extended in the form of a cross. And when he had drawn near to the end of his course, which was not caused by illness, at that time, I say he stood up in the corner of his cell, and extended his hands and arms in prayer, and thus praying, he yielded up his spirit. When he who used to bring him food came and saw him standing by the side of the wall with his hands stretched out, he remained standing outside thinking that Macarius was standing up in prayer, as was his custom. Having waited for about three hours, he opened the door, went in, and said to him, "Bless, master!" When he did not answer him he drew near and shook him. When he saw that he was dead, he came, and told us. Having come, we saw him standing in the form of a cross, and we marvelled. When we had laid him out upon the ground, we were unable to bring his hands near to his body, and so we dug his grave in the form of a cross and laid him in it. I was sorely grieved because of his departure, fell into a slumber and slept. A voice came to me, saying, "Inasmuch as during his lifetime he loved the cross, which he bore through his good works, in it also he shall have his rest; in the form of that which he desired longingly has he been buried, and in the same form shall he stand up at the right hand on the day of Christ." Having heard these things I awoke, and I glorified God and the power of the Cross.

DAY 14

The Blessed Nathaniel
(d. about 376 A.D.)

THERE WAS ALSO ANOTHER MAN AMONG THE AGED ONES whose name was Nathaniel. I never met him in his life, for he died fifteen years before I entered this mountain. But I have met those who dwelt with him for a long time. Having made inquiries of these, I learned concerning the triumphs of the man, and they showed me his cell in which at that time no man was living, because it was near to the world. Abba Nathaniel built it long ago when the monks were few in number.

They used to relate concerning this man that his patient endurance in his cell was such that he never moved from his place to go outside the door of his habitation for the disposition of his will. In the beginning, he was laughed at by the evil, who mocks at and leads astray every man. The evil made Nathaniel feel the weariness in his first cell, so he went and built himself another cell in the neighbourhood of the city. After he had built the other cell and had dwelt in it, some three or four months later, the devil waged war against him once more. The evil came by night holding in his hand a sling like a hunter and was dressed in the garb of the Romans, and he was slinging stones with the sling. Then the blessed man Nathaniel said to him, "Who are you? Who does these things in the place where I dwell?" The devil said to him, "I am he who made you flee from your first cell, and I have come that I may make you flee from this place." When he knew that the devil was laughing at him because he had departed from his first cell, straightaway he turned and went back to it, and he lived in his first cell for the space of thirty seven years in such strict abnegation that he never passed outside the door, and meanwhile he was warring with the devil.

The wicked devil made him experience so many afflictions and troubles in order to drive him out of his cell that it would be impossible for any man to recount them. The evil watched and obtained his opportunity in the arrival of the Bishops who came to Nathaniel (now they were all holy men), and whether the ordering of the matter was due to the will of God, or to the temptation of the evil, we do not know, but he made Nathaniel to fall away somewhat from his intention.

When the Bishops had prayed and had gone forth, Nathaniel did not escort them the distance of one step, and the servants who were with them said to him, "Do you possess the faculty of pride that you will not accompany the bishops?" Nathaniel said to them, "I died once and for all to my lords the Bishops, and to the whole world. I have a secret matter, God only who knows my heart, and why I did not go to escort the bishops." Then that devil took upon himself the form of a young man who was about twenty years old, and he was following after an ass which was carrying bread in the bed of the river.

When it was far into the evening the young man passed close to the cell, he pretended that the ass had fallen under its burden, and he began to cry out, saying, "Abba Nathaniel, help me, come and render me assistance." Nathaniel heard the voice of the young man who he thought was crying out, and opened the door. As he was standing inside, he spoke with him, and said, "Who are you? What do you want me to do for you?" The young man replied, "I am such and such, and I am carrying bread to such and such a brother because he wishes to make a love feast, and the day which dawns tomorrow will be the Sabbath, and bread for the Offering will be necessary. I beg you, not to tarry in assisting me, lest the hyenas come and devour both me and the ass." There were many hyenas in that place.

Then the blessed Nathaniel stood still in great astonishment and was much troubled in his mind by the mercy which had revealed itself to him. He meditated within himself, saying, "It is either through the command of God that I must fall, or through my will having reached its limit." Finally he meditated within himself and said, "It is better for him who has guarded for all these years the limit of his will, and has not passed over his door, to remain in the same condition which will put the evil to shame, than to go out." He prayed to God. Then he made an answer to him, whom he believed to be a young man crying out, and said to him, "Young man, hear me! I believe that God Whom I serve will send you help if you need it, and that neither the hyenas nor anything else will harm you. But if you are a temptation, may God discover your craftiness!" He shut the door and held his peace. That devil was put to shame, and by reason of his wickedness he took the form of a whirlwind and the forms of wild asses which dance about and skip and break wind. This is the story of the triumph of the blessed Nathaniel, and this is the story of his labour and of his ending.

DAY 15

Abba Macarii

CONCERNING THE HOLY AND IMMORTAL FATHERS, that is to say Macarius the Egyptian, and Macarius the Alexandrian, who were men to be feared and who were invincible athletes, and concerning the strife of their life and deeds, and conversation, it is exceedingly right and good that we should tell the story. Perhaps it will not be accepted by the unbelievers, and therefore I find it difficult to relate their history, and to set it down completely in writing, lest by doing so I should be accounted a liar; and that the Lord destroys those who speak falsehood. As I myself do not put to the lie the help of Christ, do not you, O Lausus, you believer in men, become an unbeliever in the triumphs of the holy fathers which are spoken of, but adorn yourself more and more with the deeds and conversation of these glorious men who were in very truth, even as they are called, blessed men.

The athlete of Christ, the first Macarius, was by race an Egyptian, and the second Macarius, although he was second to him in the matter of age, was nevertheless first in the opinion of the monks; and this man, whose name also was Macarius, which is interpreted blessed, was from the city of Alexandria, and he was one of those who sold dried fruit and wine.

In another manuscript I have found a different version of the history of the two Macarii which I have used in the preparation of this history, and I set this down here also; now it reads as follows:

As concerning the two blessed men whose names were the same, inasmuch as their rule of life and conversation were of an exceedingly exalted character, perhaps many will not believe what I write. I, however, am afraid lest I may understate and belittle their triumphs in any way whatsoever, and lie concerning them, for it is written, "You will destroy those who speak falsehood." The Holy Spirit has passed this sentence upon me, therefore, O beloved and faithful men, believe me. One of these two blessed men was an Egyptian by race, and the other was an Alexandrian who sold dried fruits. First of all I will tell the story of the ascetic excellences of Macarius the Egyptian, the whole of whose years were ninety. He was thirty years old when he went up to the desert, and he lived in it for sixty years. He was given the gift of performing mighty deeds in such a remarkable manner that he was called by the fathers, the aged youth, because quickly he ascended to the highest grade of ascetic excellence and gifts, and to the power of interpreting the Scriptures, and to spiritual foresight. The gift of possessing power over devils was also given to him, and he was esteemed worthy of the priesthood.

With this blessed man there lived in the inner desert, which is called "Scete", two disciples; one of these was his servant, for many folk were accustomed to come to him to be healed, and the other remained always in a cell which was near to Macarius. When much time had passed by, Macarius looked and said to him that ministered to him (now his name was John, and he afterwards became the elder in the place of the blessed man); He said to him, "Hear me, O John, and receive the rebuke with which I rebuke you. For you are suffering temptation, and behold the spirit of the love of money (i.e. avarice) tempts you, for even so have I seen. I know that if you will listen to me, your end in this place shall be praised, and no harm shall draw near to your habitation. But if you will not hearken to me, because of the love of money, which moves you, the leprosy of Gehazi shall come upon you at the end." It came to pass some fifteen or twenty years after the death of the blessed man, John forgot his commandment, and because he used to steal from the poor, his body became so covered with leprosy that there was not in the whole of it one sound spot large enough for a man to lay his finger upon. Thus the prophecy of the blessed Macarius concerning John came to pass.

If we were to attempt to describe the food and drink of the holy man, we should do what is superfluous, because among the thoughtless monks who lived in that place, there was not to be found any one thing which could lead to excess either in eating or drinking; first because of the poverty of the spot, and second because of the divine zeal which they display towards each other. But I may mention his sad and stern habits of self-denial in various other ways. And they relate concerning him that he was at all times in a state of wonder at some divine vision, and that he used to become like a drunken man because of the vision. His mind was more often exalted to God than it was concerned with the things which are in this world, and those which are under the heavens. And, concerning the wonderful things which God wrought by his hands, it is not seemly that we should keep silence, and of him the following marvellous things are told.

A certain Egyptian loved another man's wife, but since he was not able to entice her to love him and to make her yield to his will, he spoke to a certain magician, saying, "Make this woman love me, or employ your sorcery in some way so that her husband may hate her, and cast her out." When the magician had received money, he made use of his sorceries, and he made the woman appear in the form of a mare; and when her husband went into his house from outside, and saw her, he was astonished at the sight of a mare lying upon his bed. Then he lifted up his voice in a sorrowful cry, and he wept tears, and heaved sighs; and he spoke with her, but she made no reply to him, and she did not answer him a word. Having seen what had taken place, he went to the elder of the village (i.e. the Sheikh Al-Balad), and told him concerning this matter, and brought him and took him in and showed him what had happened. For a space of three days he did not know what the matter was, for the mare neither ate dried grass like an animal nor did she partake of bread like a daughter of man; and she did without food of either kind. Finally, however, in order that God might be glorified, and a miracle might be made manifest at the hands of the blessed Macarius, and his spiritual perfection be made known, it entered into the mind of the man who was the woman's husband to take her to the desert to the blessed Macarius. And having saddled her like a mare, and thrown over her a halter, like an animal, he led her away and departed to the desert.

When the man arrived at the cell of the blessed Macarius, the brethren who were standing by the side of the cell of the blessed Macarius saw him, and they wanted to keep back the husband of the woman, and strove with him, saying, "Why have you brought this mare into the desert?" The man said to them, "That she may receive mercy, and be healed." They said to him, "What ails her?" He answered and said to them, "She is a woman who has been suddenly transformed into a mare, and behold, she has eaten no food for three days." Then the brethren went and told the blessed Macarius what the matter was, and when they came to inform him, they found him standing inside his cell and praying for her, for God had already revealed this matter to him, and he was praying for the woman. The holy man Macarius answered and said to his disciples: "You are mares which have the eyes of horses; but that mare is a woman. She has not been changed from her nature as a woman except in the sight of those who have made a mistake; and that she appears as a mare is only an error in the sight of those who see her."

Then the blessed man took water and blessed it, and he threw it over the woman's head and it ran down all over her body; the blessed man prayed and straightaway he made her appear in the form of a woman to every man. Then he gave her some sacramental bread and made her eat it before every man, and then he sent her away, healed with her husband; and they departed from him rejoicing and praising God. The blessed man exhorted the woman, and said to her, "Be not at any time remote from the Church, and deprive not yourself of the Holy Mysteries, for all these things have happened to you because for five weeks you did not partake of the Offering."

Let us now speak about his other excellences, and of his stern habits of self-denial in other particulars. Because the large numbers of people who came to be blessed by him gave him much trouble, he thought out the following plan in his mind. He dug out a trench in his cell, which was about twenty measures in width, and he made from it a tunnel of considerable length, and it extended from his cell to the distance of half a mile; at the place where the passage came to an end; he made above the end of it a small cave.

When large numbers of people came to him and troubled him, he used to leave his cell secretly and pass along hidden by the tunnel and hide himself in the cave, where no one could find him. He used to do this whenever he wished to escape from the vain praise of the children of men. And one of his most strenuous disciples told us, saying, "As he was going from his cell to the cave, he used to recite twenty-four antiphons, and as he was coming back twenty-four also. Whenever he went from his cell to the church he used to pray twenty-four prayers during his passage, and twenty-four as he was coming back." Moreover, they say that he gave life to a dead man in order that he might convert a certain heathen who did not believe in the resurrection of the dead, and this was spoken of throughout the desert.

Once a certain unmarried man who was vexed by an evil devil was brought to Macarius, being carefully fettered by two other men, and his mother who bought him. The devil used to act upon him in the following manner. After he had eaten three baskets of bread and drank three bottles of water, he used to vomit, and scatter the bread and water in the air in the form of smoky vapour, and in this way, his food and drink were consumed in waste, even as anything which is cast into the fire is consumed.

Now there are certain kinds of devils, which are called "fiery," for there are varieties among devils even as there are among men. And insofar as his mother had not that with which to satisfy him, he used to eat his own offal and drink his own water; and his mother begged the blessed man with tears on behalf of her son. Macarius took him and prayed over him, and entreated God on his behalf. A day or two after he had healed him of his trial, the blessed man cried to the mother of the young man, and said to her, "How much food do you need for him everyday?" She said to him, "Ten pounds of bread." Then he rebuked her and said, "You have said too much." After seven days, Macarius made the young man eat three pounds only, which was sufficient for him to work upon and live. Now this miracle, God wrought by the hand of the blessed Macarius, whose soul now sojourns with the angels. I never saw this man, for he died one year before I entered the desert.

DAY 16

Macarius the Alexandrian

As for the other Macarius, the Alexandrian, I did see him, for he was an elder in the place which is called the "Cells" in which I myself lived for nine years, and he lived for three years after I entered it. Some of his wonderful acts I myself have seen, and some of them I have learned from others, and of others I have also heard rumours.

His stern life of self-denial was as follows: Whenever he heard of any beautiful deed being done by any man, he must straightaway carry it into practice in a fuller form. He once heard from a certain man that all the brethren of Tabenna never tasted any food whatsoever which had been cooked by fire during the whole of the Forty Days Fast, and he straightaway determined within himself that for seven years he would not eat any food which had been cooked by fire, and that he would not partake of anything except young wild herbs, and vegetables which had been made soft by soaking in water, or similar things. When he had completed this rule of life, he heard of a monk in a certain monastery who only ate one pound of bread each day, and he straightaway broke his bread into pieces and cast it into a vessel with a narrow mouth, and he determined within himself that he would eat nothing that his hand could not draw up out of the vessel the first time he put it in. Time after time, he used to tell the story with a smile, and say, "When I put my hand down I could fill it readily, but I could not draw it up full because the mouth of the vessel was too narrow, and it would not let me take it out full." He lived this hard life for three years, and ate daily only four or five ounces of bread; and of water he drank sufficient to enable him to eat his bread. Of oil he took only one flask each year, making use of it only on the great First Day of the Resurrection, and on the great day of Pentecost, and at the Nativity, and at the Epiphany, and when he received the Mysteries during the Forty Days Fast.

I will also tell you about the various other practices of his hard life. He was determined once to vanquish sleep. It is related that he never entered under a roof for twenty days; he was burnt up by the exceedingly great heat of the sun at noon and during the nights he was without rest. He himself told us, "Had I not quickly gone in under a roof and slept, the brains in my head would have dried up, and I would have become like a drunk man." But, he would say, "I have been conquered against my will, for although the nature of the body has been overcome, I have given it what it needs."

Again, once when he was sitting in his cell, a gnat bit him in the leg and he suffered pain, and he crushed the gnat in his hand and killed it. Then straight away he despised himself because he had avenged himself upon the gnat, and he passed upon himself the sentence that he should go to the place, which is called "Scete," that is to say, the inner desert, and sit there naked for six months. For there were many great gnats (i.e. mosquitoes), and they were so savage that they could pierce the skins of pigs, and they resembled wasps; and his whole body was so eaten and swollen that a man would have thought that he had the hide of an elephant, and when he came back to his cell six months later they could only recognize from his voice that he was Macarius. Again he desired greatly to go and see the garden of Jannes and Jambres, the magicians of Egypt, because, as he himself told us, they had obtained power, riches and dominion, and had built there a tomb, and had established their great works in marble. Now their tomb was ornamented with many things, and they had also placed there gold and things of a marvelous character, and trees and plants, for the place had been made into a garden, and they had also dug a well there. Because Macarius did not know the way, he observed the course of the stars, and travelled thereby; and thus he journeyed through the open desert as upon the sea. He took with him a bundle of thin reeds, and at the end of each mile, he used to drive a reed into the ground like a rock, so that he might be able to find the way when he had to come back. When he had journeyed for nine days, and had drawn near the place in which was the tomb, the evil, who always wages war against the athletes of the Lord, gathered together all the reeds which the blessed man Macarius had driven into the ground, and put them under his head for a pillow whilst he was asleep.

When Macarius was about one mile from the garden, and when the blessed man woke up, he found the reeds. It is probable that God permitted this thing to happen for His own glory and for the triumph of His servant, so that Macarius might not put his confidence in reeds, but upon God, Who by means of a pillar of cloud led the children of Israel in the desert for forty years. Macarius told us, saying, "Seventy devils came forth against me from that garden, and they flew about before my face like ravens, and they were crying out and groaning, and saying, "What do you seek here, O Macarius? What do you seek, O monk? Why have you come here? You cannot stay here." I said to them, "I only want to go in and see the garden, and then I will depart. I entered it, and I saw everything, and I found hanging over the well, an iron chain with a brass bucket, but they were rusted through age; and the pomegranates which were in it were dried up and burnt by the sun." Having seen the garden he turned and came back in twenty days.

When he was coming back, he lacked water, and the bread also which he had carried was finished, and he was about to perish, and was in great tribulation through thirst, when suddenly he saw a damsel who was arrayed in a spotless linen garment and who carried a pitcher of water from which water dripped, and she was distant about half a mile from him. Then he followed her for three days, thinking that he would overtake her and drink, but he did not do so, although she seemed to him to be standing still in one place and bearing a pitcher. Then he despaired of obtaining water to drink, and he was brought very low, when suddenly there appeared a herd of buffaloes. And among them there was one, which had with her a little sucking calf, and she stood still before him; and he drew near and sucked milk from her. She came with him through all the desert even to his cell and gave him milk to drink, and she would not let her calf suck from her in those days.

On another occasion the brethren were digging a well in a certain place, which was called Thronon, when a serpent, which belonged to the class of deadly serpents, bit him. Then Macarius took hold of the serpent with his two hands and, grasping him tightly, tore him in twain, from his head even to his tail, and said to him, "Since Christ did not send you, why did you dare to come here?" The blessed man had four cells in the desert: one in Scete, in the inner desert, one in Libya, one in the "Cells," and one in Mount Nitria.

Two of these were without windows, and in them he used to dwell in darkness during the Forty Days Fast. Another was so narrow that he could not stretch out his legs, but another, in which he used to receive the brethren who came to him, was wide and spacious. And he healed so many people who were possessed by devils that no man could count them. Once when I and the blessed Evagrius were there in his cell, they brought to him from Thessalonica a certain virgin who had been a paralytic for many years, but by means of prayers and by anointing her with oil with his hands, he cured her in twenty days and sent her away, whole, to her city and home; and when she had departed, she sent to him gold and goods of various kinds.

Again, he heard from a certain man that the monks of the Monastery of Tabenna lived stern lives of self-denial, and he took counsel with himself, and put on the garb of a young man and a husbandman, and in fifteen days he went up to the Monastery of the Broken Ones by the way of the desert, and came to the Monastery of Tabenna, seeking to see the head of that Monastery whose name was Pachomius. Now Pachomius was a man, elect and perfect, and he had the gift of prophecy, but the business of the blessed Macarius was hidden from him. And when Macarius saw him, he said to him, "Abba, I beseech you to receive me into your monastery that I may be a monk." Pachomius said to him, "You are an old man, and are not able to fast. The brethren are men who fast, and you cannot endure their labours, and because you are not able to do this, you will be offended, and you will go forth and will abuse them." He would receive him neither the first day nor the second day, nor any day until seven days were passed. But since he remained fasting throughout all these days, he said to the head of the monastery, "Abba, receive me. If I do not fast like you, and toil as you do, command them to cast me out." The head of the monastery persuaded the brethren to receive him. The number of the members of the brotherhood of that monastery was four hundred men, and they are thus even to this day; and they brought in Macarius.

When a few days had passed, the Forty Days Fast drew near, and Macarius saw that large numbers of brethren kept the fast and observed the rule of the house in various ways. There were some who ate daily at eventide, and some who fasted for some nights, and there were also some who ate once in five days; and some stood up the whole night through, and sat down in the daytime. The blessed man Macarius took a large quantity of leaves of date palms, and brought them to his cell, and he stood up in one corner of it, and he neither touched bread nor water, nor bent the knee, nor lay down, until the forty days had passed, and the days of unleavened bread had come; but each Sunday he used to eat a few moist cabbage leaves so that he might pretend to be taking food. Whenever he went outside his cell for a needful purpose, he returned straightaway and stood up in his place without speaking a word to any man; and he stood in his place and held his peace, and he used to do nothing else except pray within himself, and as he stood up, he wove rope of the palm leaves.

When all the brethren saw him, they made a tumult against the head of their monastery, and said to him, "Why have you brought upon us this man, who has no body and who is incapable of being tired out, to judge us and to take vengeance upon us? Either send him away and let him depart, or know that we all will go away." When the head of the monastery had heard from the brethren concerning the fasting of Macarius and his rule of life, he prayed to God and entreated Him to reveal to him who this man was. It was revealed to him by God. Then he went and took him by his hand, and he brought him to the house of prayer to the place where the altar was established, and he answered and said to him, "Come, O blessed old man, you are Macarius, and you have hidden yourself from me. For the past many years, I have earnestly desired to see you. Now I thank you that you have broken the heart of the brethren somewhat, so that they may not imagine any longer that they observe their fast with excessive rigour. Go then in peace to your place, for in no slight measure have you edified us, and do continue to pray for us." Pachomius, having persuaded him, Macarius departed from there.

Macarius used to say, "Every kind and variety of rule of the life of self-denial and fasting which I have desired to observe with all my heart, have I kept, but there came upon me the desire that my mind should be with God in heaven if only for five days, and that I should be exalted above the anxious cares and thoughts of material things." Having meditated upon this thing, I shut the door of the courtyard and of the cell, I constrained myself so that I might not give a word to any man. I continued thus, began to fulfill this thought on the second day of the week, and commanded my mind, and said to it, "You shall not descend from heaven, for behold, there you have angels, and the Archangels, and all the hosts which are in heaven, and especially the Good and Gracious God, the Lord of all. You shall not come down from heaven."

Continuing thus I was sufficient for this thing for two days and two nights, and I constrained the evil to such a degree that he became a flame of fire and burnt up everything which I had in my cell. At length the very mat upon which I stood, blazed with fire. I thought that I should be wholly consumed. When, finally, fear of the fire took hold upon me, my mind came down from heaven on the third day, because I was unable to keep my mind collected in the state in which it had been. I came down to the contemplation of the world and its things. This happened so that I might not boast.

On another occasion I went to his cell, and I found a priest lying there by the side of the door; his whole head was consumed and was eaten into holes by the disease which is called cancer, and the bone of his skull was showing through. This man had come to him to be healed, but Macarius did not wish to see him. I myself begged the blessed man and said to him, "I beseech you to have mercy upon him, and to give to him a word." Then he answered and said to me, "He is not worthy to be healed, for this punishment was sent upon him from God. But if you desire that he shall be healed, persuade him to forsake the ministry at the altar, for he used both to be minister at the altar and to commit fornication, and for this reason he was punished. Persuade him then to forsake his ministries, and God will heal him."

Having said these things to the sick man, he pledged himself and swore an oath, saying, "I will never minister at the altar again." Afterwards Macarius received him, and said to him, "Do you believe that God exists?" The priest replied, "Yes, master." Again Macarius said to him, "Perhaps you are able to scoff at God." The priest said to him, "No." Then the blessed man said to him, "If now you acknowledge your folly, and also that your punishment was from God and that it was a fitting punishment for your deeds, first of all confess your transgressions." The priest gave a promise that he would not sin again, and that he would not minister at the altar, but that he would lead a life which was suited to the capacity and grade of those who were in the world. Macarius laid his hand upon him, and in a few days he was made whole, and the hair grew upon his head again, and he went to his house healed whilst I was looking at him.

Again a certain young man who had an evil devil was brought to him and he laid one hand on the head of the young man and another on his heart, and he prayed until he made the devil to rise up in the air, upon which the young man breathed out his breath and became like a great empty skin bottle; and he suddenly uttered a cry, and water flowed out from all parts of his members, and he was made whole and became as he was before the devil entered into him. Then Macarius anointed him with the oil of the martyrs, and commanded his father that he was not to taste flesh or wine for forty days, until he was thoroughly healed.

Again on a certain occasion, certain thoughts of vainglory vexed him, and urged him to go forth from his cell and to depart and heal the multitudes in Rome and to give assistance to those who were lying there sick, for the grace and might of God were inciting him greatly to heal those who were possessed of devils and to make whole those who were diseased. Although he was much disturbed in his mind on this matter, yet he was not persuaded to go, for the Evil greatly pressed upon him in his thoughts. Finally, however, he lay down inside the door of his cell, and having set his legs on the threshold, he cried out and said, "Pull, unclean devils, pull hard, for I will never go thither on my legs, and if you are able to carry me you must do so thus." He took an oath to them, i.e. the brethren, saying, "I continued to lie thus until the evening, and if you had not lifted me up, I would never have moved from my place." When the night had come, he stood up.

Again, on another occasion, when these thoughts were mounting up in his mind, he filled with sand a basket which held two or three bushels, and lifting it on his shoulders, he began to wander about with it in the desert. His kinsman, Theosebius the

Antiochian, met him and he said to him, "What are you carrying on your shoulders, father? Tell me so that I may carry your load, and that you may not toil yourself." He said to him, "I am making to work that which has made me to work, for it wishes to go forth from its state of rest, and it fatigues me." Having walked about for a long time, he went into his cell, having exhausted his body.

One day, there laid hold upon me the chills of fever, and I went and sat down, and watched him from the window, in the feebleness of his old age. I was thinking about him that he was like one of the brothers of old, and I began to listen to him so that I might see what he was saying, or what he was doing. He was alone inside his cell, and he was one hundred years old, and moreover, his teeth had fallen out because of his old age. I listened to him and to what he was saying, and he was striving with his soul and with Satan, and he was saying to himself, "What do you wish for, O you wicked old man? Behold, you have eaten oil, and you have drunk wine, what more do you wish for? Would you eat Satan's white food?" He was reviling himself. Moreover he said to Satan, "I cannot conquer you in any way, and you are not able to do anything to me; go away from me." He said to himself, "How long shall I be with you?"

Paphnutius, the disciple of this man, related to myself and to the blessed Evagrius, saying, "One day a female hyena took her whelp, which was blind, and came and knocked with her head at the door of the court when he was sitting in, and she dropped the whelp at his feet. And he took up the whelp, and prayed, and spat in its eyes, and straightaway its eyes were opened and it saw; and its mother gave it suck, and then took it up and went forth. And one day later she brought to the blessed man a sheep-skin cloak, that is to say, a skin which has been stripped off a sheep; and the blessed woman Melania spoke to me concerning this sheep-skin cloak, saying, "I myself received this sheep-skin cloak from the hands of Macarius as a blessing." Paphnutius also spoke thus, "From the first day on which he received baptism, he never spat upon the ground, and he lived for sixty years after his baptism."

In his latter days, he was beardless, and he only had a small quantity of hair upon his upper lip and upon his chin, because of his excessive fasting and the abstinence of his solitary life, not even the hair of his beard would grow. I once went to him when weariness of the ascetic life had laid hold upon me, and I said to him, "Father, what shall I do? For my thoughts vex me, and say to me, you are doing no good, get you out from here." He said to me, "Say to your thoughts, For Christ's sake I will guard these walls." I have written for you these few things out of a very large number concerning the life and deeds of the holy man Macarius, and concerning the solitary monks who were his companions; and everything is indeed true.

I entreat all those brethren who read in this book, or who desire to take a copy, not to forget to write after this section the narrative which is found in certain of the codices at the end of the above history which relates to the matters of Macarius, as if these histories had been composed by Hieronymus, but they must know that of a certainty that they were composed by Palladius. For I have found the absolute ending of this book which belonged to the histories of the matters of Macarius, with an apology and a preface which were composed by Palladius and addressed to Lausus the Prefect, in which he makes known concerning all the various kinds of the diverse histories of men and of women which were composed by him; and I will prepare this apology and preface, and by the help of God I will write them down in the proper place.

DAY 17

Paul the Simple

NOW THERE WAS A CERTAIN HUSBANDMAN whose name was Paul, who was more simple and innocent in nature than are usually the children of men; and he had a wife who was beautiful in her appearance, and wicked in her deeds and actions, and she had wandered from him and had been committing adultery for a long time. And one day, suddenly Paul went into his house from the field, and he found her and another working impurity together; now this took place so that Divine Grace might incite Paul to follow that which was more excellent. And having gone in and seen them, he laughed chastely, and answered and said, "It is good, it is good, truly she is not accounted mine by me. By Jesus, henceforth I will not take her again. Get you going, and behold she is yours, she and her children: and as for me, I will go and become a monk." Saying nothing to any man, he went away on a journey of eight stages, and he arrived at the cell of Saint Anthony the Great. Having knocked at the door, the blessed man

St Anthony went out, and he said to Paul, "What do you seek?" Paul said to him, "I seek to become a monk." Saint Anthony answered and said to him, "You are an old man eighty years old, and it is impossible for you to become a monk here; but depart to the village, and work in the fields for your living, and give thanks to God at the same time that you are not able to endure the afflictions of the desert."

Again Paul answered and said to him, "Whatever you will teach me, that will I do." Anthony said to him, "I have told you that you are an old man, and you cannot do it; but if you wish to become a monk, get you gone to some monastic house, and abide where the brethren are many, and where they will be able to bear with your sickness. As for me, I live by myself here, and I only eat once in five days, and even then I do not eat a full meal." With these and suchlike words did Anthony frighten Paul. As he would not be persuaded to depart, Anthony went into his cell, and shut the door upon himself for three days, and because of him, he did not go outside his cell for three whole days, not even for his need's sake. Nevertheless Paul did not go away; and on the fourth day, when his need compelled him, Anthony opened the door and went forth. He said to Paul, "Get you gone, O old man, why you trouble me? It is impossible for you to stay here." Paul said to him, "It is impossible for me to die in any other place except this."

The blessed Anthony, having looked carefully and saw that he was carrying no food with him, and no bread and no water, and that he had fasted during the four days which he had remained, said within himself, "Perhaps he will escape and die, and will plunge my soul in tribulation." He accepted him and brought him into his cell. And because of Paul during those days, Anthony performed exceedingly severe ascetic labours, the likes of which he had never performed. He soaked palm leaves in water, and gave them to Paul, and said to him, "Take these palm leaves, and weave a mat even as I do myself."

The old man Paul took them, and wove them into a mat fifteen cubits long, until at the ninth hour he was exhausted. Anthony, seeing what he had woven, was angry with him, and said to him, "You have woven the leaves loosely, un-weave them, and weave them over again neatly and closely." Paul un-wove what he had woven, and wove the leaves over again, but still he wove too loosely, because the leaves had become twisted through the former weaving and unweaving. Meanwhile Paul was fasting all these days, and Anthony laid these hard labours upon him while his soul was vexed with hunger, so that he might become disgusted and depart from him.

When Anthony saw that Paul was neither angry nor wrathful, and that he made no complaint, his mercy made itself manifest; and behold when Paul had lived there another day, he said to him, "Do you wish to eat a piece of bread?" The old man Paul said to him, "As it pleases you, father." This also especially shamed Saint Anthony that he did not hasten in his desire to the promise of food, but that he cast all his desire upon him. Thus Anthony said to him, "Set the table and bring bread." Anthony placed on the table four loaves, each of which was of the weight of about six ounces, and he dipped them in water because they were dry, and he placed one before himself and three before Paul.

Having placed them there, he sang a psalm which he knew twelve times, and he recited twelve prayers that he might try Paul, but Paul prayed with him in gladness; and after the twelve prayers, they sat down to eat in the late evening. Having eaten one loaf, Anthony did not touch another, but the old man Paul ate slowly, and when Anthony had finished, Paul had still some of his loaf to eat, and Anthony was waiting for him to finish it. And having finished it, he answered and said to him, "O my little father, will you eat another loaf?" Paul said to him, "If you will eat another I will also; but if you will not, I will not." Anthony said to him, "I have had enough, for I am a monk." Paul said to him, "I also have had enough, for I also seek to become a monk." After these things Anthony again stood up, and made twelve prayers, and when they had said together the psalms twelve times, they slept for a little during the night, and then they sang and prayed until the morning.

When Anthony saw that the old man was carrying out, with gladness, a rule of life similar to his own in every respect, he said to him, "If you are able to bear every day passed in this way, then stay with me." Paul said to him, "Although I know nothing else, yet the things which I do know I can perform easily." On another day, Anthony said to him, "Behold, you have become a monk." A few months afterward when Anthony saw that his soul was perfect before God, and that he was simple beyond measure, and that Divine Grace was helping him, he built him a cell at a distance of about three or four miles away, and said to him, "Behold, you are a monk, and henceforth you must live by yourself so that you may receive the temptation of devils." When Paul had lived by himself for a year, the gift of healing and of casting out devils was given to him.

In those times they brought to Anthony a certain man who was vexed by a fierce devil, and that devil was one of the princes of the devils, and he was so fierce that he would even revile and blaspheme the heavens. When Anthony saw the man he said, "I cannot heal this man, for over this race of princes neither the gift nor the power of healing has been given to me; to Paul it belongs to heal this man." Anthony therefore took them with him and went to him, and said to him, "O Abba Paul, cast out this devil from this man, so that, being made whole, he may depart to his house." Paul said to him, "And what will you do?" Anthony said to him, "I am not able to do it, for I have other work to do."

He left the man with Paul and went back to his cell. Then the old man, Paul, arose up, prayed a prayer with great feeling, and began to speak to that devil, saying, "Father Anthony says, Go forth from this man." The devil answered with blasphemies, saying, "I will not go out, O you who eat white bread." The old man took his shoulder garment (or skull cap), and began to smite the devil on his back and sides, saying, "I tell you that Abba Anthony says, Get out from him." The devil began to curse and revile Abba Anthony and the old man Paul. Finally Paul said to him, "Will you go out, or must I go and tell Christ, yes Jesus? For if you will not go forth I will go and tell Christ, and great woe shall come upon you." Again he blasphemed and said, "I will not go forth."

Then the blessed man, Paul, was angry with him, and he went out of his cell. It was the season of noon, and the heat at this time is so fierce that it is akin to the heat of the fiery furnace of the Babylonians. He stood upon a stone and prayed, and spoke thus, "Behold, O Jesus Christ, Who was crucified in the days of Pontius Pilate, I will not come down from this stone, and I will neither eat nor drink until I die, unless You do cast out that devil from this man, and do set him free from him." Whilst these words were still in his mouth the devil cried out in tribulation, and said, "By Hercules, by whom am I ruled, by Hercules, I am being persecuted with violence, for the simplicity of Paul pursues me; whither shall I go?" Paul says to him, "To the uttermost depths of the abyss."

Straightaway the devil went forth from the man, and he transformed himself and became like to a mighty dragon, seventy cubits long, and he wriggled along the ground and in this way, went down to the Red Sea, that might be fulfilled that which is written, "Perfect faith removes mountains." This is the triumph of Paul, who was called the "Simple" by the whole brotherhood.

DAY 18

Pachomius

THERE WAS ALSO ANOTHER MAN WHOSE NAME WAS PACHOMIUS, who was seventy years old who dwelt in that mountain called "Scete." I went to him once when lustful thoughts concerning women were afflicting me, my mind was dark and obscured by the thoughts of lust, and by the visions and heaviness of the nights. I was well near departing from the desert, for lust laid upon me many things hard to bear. I did not reveal to my neighbours and to the brethren who were living with me, my tribulations, and not even to my master Evagrius, but I went forth and I began to wander about in the desert, and I saw one of the old men who had grown old in the place.

They were all perfect fathers and after this, I saw this blessed old man Pachomius, and I found that he was superior to them all in his life, deeds, and in his understanding. I took courage to reveal to him the strife of my mind, and he spoke to me thus, "Do not imagine that this is a strange matter in any way. This thing has not happened to you through your own negligence, and the place itself in which you live is a witness for you, for it is restricted in the matter of things of every kind, and there is no woman in it; this lust has fallen upon you through your strenuousness. For this warfare of lust and also of fornication is threefold; sometimes it sets our body against us when it is healthy and well-fed, and at others, lust itself, with the natural passion which is implanted in us, attacks us, and at others the Evil himself, because of his envy. I have watched it many times, and I have found that it is even as I have said to you." He said to me, "I, the old man whom you see have lived in this cell for forty years, and I have taken the utmost care for my life for the redemption of my soul, and even in this period of great old age, in which you see that I am, I am greatly tormented by lust."

He assured me with an oath, saying, "When I was fifty years old, lust placed itself upon me for twelve years, never going away from me either by day or by night, and I thought in my mind that God had forsaken me. Therefore, (for to such an extent had lust gained dominion over me) I determined in my heart that I would either suffer death through dumb beasts, or that I should become laughing stock or a man condemned through the lust of the body. I went forth and wandered in the desert, and I found a den of hyenas, and I laid myself down naked at the entrance of it, that they might come out and devour me. When it was evening as it is written, 'He has made the darkness, and it becomes night, in which all the beasts of the forest do move.'

The lions roar to break their prey, the hyenas, both male, and female, came out, and they all sniffed at me and licked my body from my head to my feet, and while I was thinking that they would eat me, they went away from me; and there I remained the whole of that night, and they ate me not. Again I thought that God had had compassion upon me, and straightaway I returned and came to my cell. That devil of lust, having borne with me a little, returned once again, and moreover, he attacked me more fiercely than before, and he did so with such vigour that because of my affliction I nearly cursed myself. This devil of lust used to take the form of an Ethiopian damsel whom I saw in my early manhood gathering canes in the summer, and he came in her form and sat upon my knees, and he used to set me on fire with lust to such an extent that I imagined I was having intercourse with her, and when through the burning of my heart and the madness of it, I gave her the cheek, straightaway she would lift herself up from me and take flight. From the time when I touched her, my hand was so polluted that for the space of two hours afterward whenever I brought my hand near me, I was unable to free it from her foulness. But again, I went forth because of my affliction, and I began to wander about in the desert, and I found a small wasp, and I took it and placed its head upon the members of my body, and I squeezed the head of the wasp so that it might bite me and I might die, and so find relief, but it bit me not.

After this, I heard a voice which came to my ears and said to me, 'Depart, Pachomius, and be strong; I have allowed you to be overcome in order that you might not imagine that you are a mighty man and a man of perfection, and that you had triumphed through your own life and deeds, but that you might know your infirmity, and the feebleness of your nature, and that you might not rely upon your asceticism but might confess the help of God and cry out to Him always.' Having heard these words I returned to my cell, and I dwelt in it with great boldness of heart, and I never again had anxious care concerning this warfare of lust, but I continued in peace for the rest of my days after this warfare. The devil of lust, seeing that I no longer meditated about the matter, never again approached me.

With these words about the striving against Satan, the holy man Pachomius confirmed me, and he made me strong to play the man more and more, and to be mighty in the warfare against the devil of fornication, and he dismissed me and said to me, "Be strong and mighty in our Lord."

DAY 19

Stephen

STEPHEN WAS A MAN WHO WAS BY RACE, OF THE LIBYANS, who dwell by the side of Marmarica and Mareotis, and he lived there for sixty years. Now in another codex, the text reads differently, thus: There was also in the desert a certain blessed man whose name was Stephen, and he was by race a Libyan from the border (or side) of Marmarica; and he dwelt there in the desert for sixty years. Having attained to the heights of a perfect rule of life, he was esteemed by Divine Grace, worthy of the gift of discerning prudence and of the faculty of giving consolation to such an extent that whosoever drew near to him, being afflicted in any way whatsoever, departed from him with joy. The blessed Anthony was acquainted with this man. This Stephen continued in this life even to our own days, but I never lived with him and I never met him, because the mountain in which he dwelt was a long way off from me.

The holy men Ammonius and Evagrius, however, who went to visit him related to me stories concerning him, and they said, "Having gone to him, we found him grievously sick of a certain sore sickness which had come upon him, for a cancerous sore had broken out in the lower parts of his body. Now this sore is called gangrene, and we found him being cut by a certain physician. Nevertheless the holy man was working with his hands and was plaiting palm leaves, and he held conversation with us whilst portions of his body were being cut off. And he possessed the faculty of patient endurance to such a degree that it seemed as if the body of someone else was being cut instead of his own.

Now when his members had been shorn off like hair, he continued, through the grace of God, to be without perception of it. Whilst the physician was binding him up, he sat still and plaited baskets with his hands, and he conversed with us, rejoicing and giving thanks to God. Moreover, he displayed such patient endurance whilst his member was being cut off that one might have thought that it had not been cut off at all, and he resembled altogether a man from whose body threads of hair are being plucked. We stood there and marveled at this affliction, for we could not bear to see the man who had led a life of such ascetic and spiritual excellences fall into such a state of suffering, that at length, amputation of his members was necessary.

The blessed man, having perceived our thoughts and seen that it grieved us, answered and said to us, "O my sons, do not be afflicted concerning this matter, and do not lessen your faith because of this thing, for God never performs anything whatsoever that is evil, on the contrary, He looks for a happy conclusion to His work. Oh, how many times were these members condemned to punishment! For they merited being cut off, and it is better that they should receive their reward here than after their departure out of this world."

These were the things which he spoke to us, and he comforted us and sent us away, saying, "Do not be scandalized when you see trials of this kind coming upon holy men, for by such, God has built us up and comforted us, and has made us to be confirmed in the laws which are against tribulations." I have related these things in order that we may not wonder when we see the saints falling into tribulations.

It prefaces concerning those who have fallen into the Errors of Satan. It is necessary, O my brethren, that we should also keep in memory the histories which concern the life and deeds of those who have tripped up and fallen as an excellent admonition of those who come across this book (just as among the trees that were in Paradise the Tree of Good and Evil was also found). Thus, if it happens that certain men lead good lives through the Grace and help of God, Who is accustomed to help those whose motive of soul is directed straight to the mark, they may not be exalted overmuch and have pride in their works of ascetic excellence. For on many occasions this very excellence itself has been the cause of a fall when it has not been made perfect by means of a correct motive, for it is written, "I have seen the righteous man who has perished in his righteousness, which also is vanity."

Valens the Palestinian

THERE WAS A CERTAIN MAN WHOSE NAME WAS VALENS, who was by race a Palestinian and by education a Corinthian. The blessed Paul ascribed to the Corinthians, as a special attribute, the passion of pride and inflatedness. Having come to the desert and dwelt with us for many years, at length he arrived at such a degree of vaunting that he was laughed at by the devils; and from this state he went astray, little by little, until he was ridiculed by them, and they became able to make him think that angels were appearing to him. Therefore, one day, according to what they relate concerning him, as he was working in the dark at the labour of his hands, the needle with which he was sewing together the palm leaves fell down on the ground, and although he searched for it, he could not find it; and a devil lit a fire for him until he found it, and because of this thing he became prouder. And at length he became so proud, and allowed such arrogant thoughts to rise up in his mind that he despised and thought scorn of the

Holy Mysteries of the Body and Blood of Christ. And moreover, it came to pass that certain men of discernment came and brought to the church some dried fruits as a means of obtaining a blessing, and the blessed Macarius, our elder, received them and sent them to the brethren, that is, some to every man in his cell, and among the brethren he also sent some to Valens. Valens took the man who had been sent to bring the fruit to him, and heaped insults upon him and struck him, saying, "Go and say to Macarius, I am neither inferior to you nor am I more of a servant than are you, that you should send me a blessing."

Macarius knew that he had been laid hold upon by error, and he rose up and went to him at the turn of the day that he might persuade him, and he said to him, "Valens, Valens, you have made yourself a laughing stock, and have fallen into error; receive then correction"; but seeing that he was unwilling to hearken to his admonition and reproof, he left him and departed. Having become more confirmed in his pride, and having reached the summit of it, that devil, who had completely led him astray, went and made to himself a form in which he resembled our Redeemer; and he came to him by night, together with phantoms of angels in great numbers who marched along bearing lamps and wax candles, and they advanced with chariots and carriages of fire, as if that devil were Christ Himself. Then one of the angels came forward to him, and said to him, "Christ loves greatly your life and deeds, and your boldness of speech, and He has come to see you. Get out of your cell and do nothing except such things as I shall tell you. When you see Him afar, fall down and worship Him, and go back to your cell."

Therefore when Valens had gone forth and seen the ranks of phantoms bearing lamps of fire, and Antichrist himself sitting upon a chariot of fire, now he was distant from him about a mile, he fell down and worshipped him. And Valens was so much injured in his mind that at the turn of the day he was sufficiently mad to come into the church and to say before all the brotherhood who were assembled, "I have no need to become a partaker in the offering, for this day I have seen Christ Himself." Then the fathers tied him up and put iron fetters upon him for about the space of one year, and in this way they made him whole. He was praying continually, and they humbled him and brought him down from the exalted conception which he held concerning himself by means of sundry and diverse works of a lovely and humble character, and thus they rooted out from him pride, even as it is written, "Each opposing sickness must be healed by medicines which are contrary and opposite to it."

DAY 21

Hero the Alexandrian (Bishop of Diospolis about A.D. 365)

THERE WAS ALSO MY NEIGHBOUR, a man whose name was Ahron (Hero), who was by race an Alexandrian. Now his early manhood was exceedingly glorious, and he was enlightened in his mind, and his intellect was keen, and the habits of his life were pure. This man, I say, after performing many labours was also seized by the passion of boasting and pride, and he wavered and fell. He evolved in his mind and imagined great things against the fathers, and he also reviled the blessed Evagrius, saying, "Those who allow themselves to be persuaded into accepting your doctrine certainly go astray and err, for men require no other teacher than Christ."

He put forward and urged in witness to his words, with foolish intent, the speech from the Gospel (which our Redeemer also spoke), "You shall call no man master on the earth." His understanding became so greatly blinded that iron fetters fell, and he was fast bound, because he would neither be persuaded nor would he receive or be a partaker of the Holy Mysteries, although he loved the truth greatly. Now, the food upon which he lived was too little and the habits of his life were immeasurably strict, for according to what those who were continually with him used to relate. On several occasions he only partook of a meal once in three months, the participation in the Mysteries only being sufficient for him; but if it happened that he came across some wild herbs, by chance, he would eat them.

I myself, with the blessed man Albinus, received an experience of him when we were going to Scete. Scete was forty miles distant from us, and we partook of two meals and drank water three times on the way, whilst he tasted nothing at all during his journey with us. He travelled on foot, and he was repeating passages from the Scriptures by heart. During the time that he went with us; He repeated passages from the Scriptures and sang fifteen Psalms, and he repeated the Beatitudes and the Epistle to the Hebrews, and the book of Isaiah the Prophet, and a portion of Jeremiah, and after that the Gospel of Saint Luke, and after that the Proverbs; and in spite of all this we were unable to overtake him as he trudged along. Now therefore this man was at length persecuted by lust as by a fire, and he was never again able to dwell in his cell, but he went to Alexandria, and by reason of his pride it happened to him, through Divine Providence, even as it is said, "One good is rooted up by another."

Nevertheless, having fallen willingly into a state of indifference, he finally found redemption. He was present continually at the shows of the theatres and circuses, and he was never absent from the public drinking rooms of the taverns; and thus whilst he was leading this life of prodigality and drunkenness, he fell and was brought to a standstill in the miry ditch of the lust of women. At length he went to one of those women who are at the head of the grade of harlots, and because of his passion with all boldness, he held a conversation with her. These things having thus been done by him there, broke out in the place of his nature, a carbuncle which grew with great vigour, and his sickness waxed sore upon him for a space of six months, and his members rotted away and they had to be cut off. By these means he became finally cured, but he remained without members; and afterwards he went back again to the integrity of his nature, and to divine thoughts. He came to the desert and confessed all these things to the fathers, and though he remained not a long time there, he did not flee from leading the ascetic life, nor from weeping because of what had happened to him, nor from offering up the repentance which was right. After a few days, he died and departed from this world.

Ptolemy the Egyptian, Who Was in Scete

THERE WAS ALSO ANOTHER MAN WHOSE NAME WAS PTOLEMY, and he was by race from Egypt, and he observed a rule of life which no man is able to describe, or rather it is very difficult to relate the story of his life. He dwelt away, beyond Scete, in that district which is called "Klimax." It is impossible for a man to dwell in this place for its ruggedness. It was distant from the stream of water from which the brethren used to draw twelve miles. This man Ptolemy used to take many vessels for water, and carry them to a certain spot where much dew fell, and in December and January he used to collect it, for in those countries the dewfall is abundant.

Having gathered together for himself water in sponges from time to time they were squeezed out by him, and the water which he had collected from the dew ran out, and this he was in the habit of doing during the fifteen years which he dwelt there. This man, having for much time been deprived of teaching, and of the meetings with the holy fathers, and of the intercourse of edifying speech, and especially of participation in the Mysteries, went as wholly astray from the straight path as if he had said, "The matters of service, that is to say, the Holy Mysteries, are nothing at all." From this state he senselessly departed and went on until at length he went into Egypt and delivered himself over to prodigal and riotous living, and he never more spoke a word of excellence to any man. And his madness came upon Ptolemy also because of the senseless and exalted opinion which he held of himself, even as it is written, "Those who are not under the law of the governors shall fall like leaves."

Abraham the Egyptian

THERE WAS ALSO A CERTAIN MAN WHOSE NAME WAS ABRAHAM, and he kept a rule of life of the sternest hardness in the desert; and he was hurt in his understanding by reason of the vain opinion which he held concerning himself. One day he came to the church and strove with the elders, saying, "I have been made an elder by Christ during the past night, and you must associate me in the ministries of the priesthood." When the fathers had come to a decision concerning him, and had brought him out of the desert, they laid a light rule of life upon him, and in this manner they cured him of his arrogance, and brought him to the state of being sensible of his feebleness, and of having knowledge of his infirmity, through which the devils made a mock of him.

A Certain Virgin Who Was in Jerusalem

MOREOVER, I SAW A CERTAIN VIRGIN IN JERUSALEM who had been

clothed in sackcloth for three years, and she had secluded herself in a solitary cell, and had never permitted herself to enjoy any of the desirable things in which there is pleasure. Now this woman, having been forsaken by the Divine Providence, because of her immeasurable pride and arrogance, fell into the ditches of fornication. She opened the window of the habitation in which she had secluded herself, and received the man who ministered to her, and she had intercourse with him. She did not continue to persevere in faith and in the ascetic life with a perfect will, and with a mind which possessed Divine love, but departed from there for the sake of men, that is to say, for the sake of vainglory. Moreover, with an evil intent and with a corrupt and lascivious mind for her own thoughts having been cut off, since they had been robbed of the Divine understanding, she came to the condition of casting blame upon others. The guardian of chastity did not remain with her.

The Virgin Who Was in Caesarea of Palestine

AGAIN THERE WAS A CERTAIN VIRGIN who was the daughter of an elder in Caesarea, and having been beguiled and led astray by a man, he who led her astray taught her to bring an accusation against a certain reader of the church of the city. The time having arrived when it was known to all that she was with child, and being called upon by her father to confess her matter, she made an accusation against that reader. Her father, the elder, because he believed her implicitly, made known the matter to the Bishop. The Bishop was a holy man, and a fearer of God, and one who did not hastily pass a sentence of death or punishment upon any man. So, the Bishop went and shut himself up until the matter was made plain to him; and because God informed him that the reader had never been near to the woman, he held him to be innocent, and condemned the virgin.

DAY 24

A Certain Woman Who Fell and Repented

THERE WAS A CERTAIN VIRGIN WHO WAS A NUN, and who dwelt with two other nuns, and she had led a life of abstinence and voluntary self-denial for nine or ten years. Having been beguiled and led astray by a certain singer of Psalms, she tripped, and fell, and conceived, and gave birth to a child; now she hated with the fullest hatred him that had beguiled her. And she repented within herself with a perfect repentance, and she followed after repentance with such vigour that she went beyond the bounds of what was seemingly, and she continued to observe fasts with such self-denial and strictness that she nearly died of hunger. In her prayers she used to make supplication, saying, "O God, who supports and sustains all creation, and who does not desire the death and destruction of those who err and commit sin. If you wish me to live before you, show me a marvellous thing in this matter, and gather in this fruit of sin which I have brought forth, lest, because I cannot again attain to chastity, I kill myself through reproach and disgrace." Having made supplication for this thing, she was hearkened to, and he who had been born to her did not remain very long alive.

From the day in which she fell and onwards she neither saw him that had beguiled her and led her captive, nor held converse with him, but she gave herself to frequent fasting and to ministering to the women who were sick and smitten with disease for the whole of a period of thirty years. Thus, her repentance was accepted by God, and He at length revealed to a certain holy old man concerning her, saying, "Such and such a woman is very much more pleasing to me by her penitence than by her virginity."

I write down these things in order that, if any man be observing a correct rule of life of any kind whatever which is pleasing to God, he may take heed lest he fall, and that even if he be tripped up in a snare and fall, he may not come to despair, and remain in his fallen condition. However, by leaning upon the staff of the hope of the Divine Mercy, and by arraying himself through repentance in the apparel of simplicity and humility he may again become strong enough to stand up, for we should not despise those who truly repent.

DAY 25

Another Virgin who Fell and Repented

A CERTAIN VIRGIN, THE DAUGHTER OF AN ELDER in Caesarea of Palestine, having been beguiled and led astray by a man, fell, and he who had beguiled her instructed her to make an accusation against a certain reader of the church of the city. And the time having arrived when her conception became known, and being called upon to confess her matter by her father, she made the accusation against that reader, and the elder. Her father, , like one who believed her implicitly, made the affair known to the Bishop. Then the Bishop laid his hand upon the shrine, and commanded that the reader should be called, and his affair having been enquired into. Like one who was confident in his own integrity, he was unwilling to confess that he had done the wrong; for how was it possible for him to accuse himself of that which he had not done?

The Bishop, becoming angry, said to him, "Will you not confess, O wretched and polluted man, you guilty one who is full of uncleanness?" The reader answered him, saying, "Master, I have neither knowledge nor feeling about this matter, for my thoughts and mind are clean in respect of it, and no thought concerning this woman has ever entered my mind. But if you wish to hear that which has never taken place, I will say that I myself committed the offence." Having spoken thus, the Bishop immediately removed the reader from his position. Then the reader drew near and entreated the Bishop, saying, "Master, since I have tripped up and fallen, give the command that the woman be given to me as a wife, for I am no longer a cleric, and she is not a virgin." The Bishop gave the woman to the reader to wife, because he thought that he was held by love of her, and that he could not cut the affair concerning her out of his thoughts.

When the reader had received the woman from the Bishop, he placed her in a religious house for women, and he begged the woman who ministered, to take great care of her immediately. A short time afterwards, the day arrived in which she must give birth to her child. The poor creature was not able to give birth as she could hardly bear the cruel and violent pains. Her child did not come forth. Three days passed by until the seventh day arrived, and by reason of her great and frequent sufferings, the woman was near to come to Sheol; and she neither ate, nor drank, nor slept, but she was crying out and saying, "Woe to me, for I am dying, and I made an accusation of fatherhood against such and such a reader." The women who were standing before her having heard these words made them known to her father, who, however, fearing lest he should be blamed severely because he had made an accusation of fatherhood against the reader, held his peace concerning the matter for another two days.

Meanwhile, the young woman neither gained relief from her sufferings nor died. Therefore when the nuns could no longer bear the pain of her violent shrieks, they ran and told the Bishop, saying, "Such and such a woman has for some days past been crying out and confessing that she made an accusation of fatherhood against the reader." Then the Bishop sent deacons to him with the message, "Pray you, that the woman who made an accusation against you may have relief"; but the reader answered them without a word. Now he had not opened his door since the day on which the accusation had been made against him, but he entreated God and made supplication to him that the matter might become known and the truth revealed.

Thereupon the father of the woman went to the Bishop, and prayer was offered up in the church, but even by these proceedings the woman did not obtain relief. Then the Bishop rose up and went to the reader, and knocked at the door and the reader opened it to him, and he went in to him and said, "Eustathius, rise up and unloose that which you have fastened." At once the reader knelt down with the Bishop, and they prayed to God, and immediately the woman gave birth to her child. Thus were the supplication of this man and his constant persistence in prayer, was he able to clear away oppression and to chastise and rebuke the woman who made the false accusation. For from that day onwards, she fulfilled the days of her life with good works; and we should learn to be constant in prayer and to recognize the power of it when it is offered to God with the deep feeling of the whole heart.

DAY 26

The Blessed Woman Thais or Thaisis

AND NOW I DESIRE TO NARRATE TO YOU the excellent history and the great repentance of the blessed woman, Thais or Thaisis. For speech concerning her is most excellent, and it is full of encouragement and penitence of soul to those who love God. This woman had a mother who, because her daughter was beautiful, made her take up a position in the market. The rumour of her beauty travelled to every place, and those who were living far off desired greatly to see her. No man who looked upon her was satisfied with the sight of her face, because she burned like a flame of fire into the hearts of those who saw her, and many by reason of their mad love for her, sold whatever property they had to her parents that they might have commerce with her. When Bessarion, the servant of God, heard these things concerning this woman and that through her beauty she was dragging many to destruction, he arrayed himself in the apparel of a man who was in the world, and took with him one dinar and went to her.

When he saw her, he brought forth the dinar and gave it to her; and having taken the dinar she said to him, "Let us go into a room," and he said to her, "Yes, let us go in." Having gone in, the blessed man Bessarion saw the couch, which was laid out, now it was a very high one, and the woman said to the old man, "Come, get up on this bed"; and he said to her, "Have you not inside this chamber, another room?" and she said to him, "Yes." Then he said to her, "Let us then: go in there." Thais answered and said to him, "If it is that you are ashamed of men seeing you, know that no man can see us in this chamber; but if it be God of Whom you are afraid, He can see us in whatever place we enter." The blessed man Bessarion hearing these words, said to her, "My daughter, do you know that God exists?" She said to him, "Yes, I know that God exists, and that there will be kingdom, and judgement."

Then the old man said to her, "If you know that God exists, and that there will be kingdom and judgement, why do you destroy men in this manner?" Immediately the woman cast herself at his feet, and said to him, "I know that there is repentance for those who sin. But I beseech you, master, to tarry with me for three hours, and whatsoever you wish to do to me, that do, because of all the evil things which have been done by me." Having told her in what place he would await her, he left her and went away.

Then in that same hour, the woman took everything which she had gained by fornication and burnt it with fire in the midst of the city, and she said, "Come, all you who have had commerce with me, and see that I am burning before your eyes every possession which I have gathered together by means of sin." The things which were burned were worth three hundred pounds of gold, and there were also goods and apparel of all kinds. After she had burned up everything, she went to the blessed man Bessarion. When Bessarion saw her, he took her by her hand and led her to a religious house of sisters, and he shut her in a little cell, leaving her only one small window in the wall through which a woman can pass in food to her.

The blessed Bessarion said to the head of the house, "Give her a pound of dry bread each day, and water according to her need." Then the blessed woman Thais said to the venerable Bessarion, "With what petition do you command me to pray to God, that He should forgive me my sins?" The blessed Bessarion said to her, "You are neither worthy to pray to God, nor to make mention of His Name with your lips, nor to stretch out your hands to Him; for your lips are unclean and polluted, and your hands are contaminated with impurity. You shall only sit down and gaze towards the East, and you shall say nothing except, 'O You who did create me, have mercy upon me.'" Having dwelt in that cell for a space of about three years, the blessed Bessarion had mercy upon her, and the blessed man went to Abba Anthony that he might learn from him whether God had forgiven her sins or not. Then having spoken concerning her to Anthony, that blessed man called to his disciples, and said to them, "Let each one of you shut himself in his cell all night and pray to God that we may see the matter regarding the blessed Bessarion."

When they all had done as they had been commanded and when a long time had elapsed, the blessed Paul, the chief of the disciples of Saint Anthony, looked into the heavens and saw a couch which had been spread with great splendour, and three angels who were carrying three lamps, were standing before that couch, and a crown of glory was laid upon it. Having seen all this glorious sight, he said, "This couch can only be for my father Anthony." Then a voice came to him from heaven, saying, "This couch is not for Anthony, your father, but for Thais the harlot." The blessed Paul rose up early in the morning and related the vision, which he had seen.

The blessed Saint Bessarion came back from Abby Anthony in great joy, and he went to the religious house of the sisterhood, and he opened the door that he might bring the woman out from the cell in which she was secluded. However, she made an entreaty to him, saying, "Leave me here until my death, for my sins are many." Then the blessed man said to her, "Behold the merciful God has had compassion upon you, and He has accepted your repentance." Then she wished to go forth from her cell. She answered and said to him, "Believe me, O Father, from the day in which I entered this cell, I have made all my sins a mighty burden and I have set it before my eyes, in such a way that as the breath of my nostrils have not separated itself from me, so my sins have not separated themselves from me until this hour."

The blessed Bessarion answered and said to her, "God has not forgiven your sins because of your repentance, but because of the thought which you had that you would deliver yourself over to Christ." This blessed woman, Thais, lived after her repentance fifteen days, and departed to our Lord in peace. Thus, was the crowning of the blessed Thais, who was lost and found, and was dead and came to life by the grace of Christ, to whom belong mercy, and compassion, and glory, and honour, forever and ever. Amen.

Abba Elijah

THERE WAS A CERTAIN MAN WHOSE NAME WAS ELIJAH. He loved the virgins exceedingly, for there are souls which are thus inclined. Having compassion upon the order of virgins and women who lived celibate lives in Thebes, and in the cities which were round about, and in the city of Atrepe, near Akhmim, and possessing many flocks and herds, he built a large nunnery, and he gathered together there every woman who chose to adopt the garb of the nun, and placed them there. With a ready will, he took care to provide them with everything which was necessary for them, and he supplied everything required for their well-being, and he also made a garden for them.

He filled their every want with great zeal and care, for our Lord's sake. Inasmuch as these women were gathered together from various places, they used to quarrel with each other continually, and because it was right to keep them in order (now he had gathered together about three hundred), he was obliged to take means to pacify them; and he listened to their affairs and arranged the disputes which broke out among them for the space of two years.

This man being young, that is to say, being about thirty or forty years old, more or less, was vexed by the passion of lust, and for this reason, he departed from that nunnery, and wandered about for two days in the desert. He made entreaty and supplication to God, saying, "O Lord, either kill me so that I may not see those who are in trouble and may not become afflicted thereby, or remove from me this passion, so that I may be able to provide for the women in everything." When the evening had come, he lay down and slept in the desert and, according to what he related, three angels came to him and took hold of him, saying, "Why did you leave the nunnery?" He related the matter to them and said to them, "I was afraid lest I should do harm, not only to them, but also to my own soul." The angels said to him, "If now we make you free from this passion, will you go and take care of the women in the nunnery?"

Having promised that he would do this, they required an oath from him. The oath, which he uttered was as follows; the angels said, "Swear an oath to us," and he said, "I swear by Him who takes care of me, that I will take care of them." Then having laid hold of him by his hands and his feet, one of them took a razor and mutilated him, not indeed in very truth but only apparently and in a phantom like manner, and he imagined in the vision that, as one might say, he had been cured of his malady. Then, they asked him, "Do you feel that you have been helped?" He said to them, "I am greatly relieved, and I feel sure that I have been set free from the pain and suffering, and that I have already been delivered there from." The angels said to him, "Depart and return."

After five days, whilst the women who were in the nunnery were weeping because of what had taken place, because he had forsaken them, and because the care he had taken for their needs had ended, he entered into the monastery in which they were; and he dwelt there from that time onward in the cells, in a place which was near to them, and according to his power he ordered their lives for them. He lived another forty years, and said to the fathers, "This passion of lust has never since roused itself up in my mind." This act of grace happened to that holy man because of care, which he exhibited in respect of that nunnery.

Dorotheos

THERE WAS THERE BESIDES THIS MAN ELIJAH, the chosen man Dorotheos, who had grown old there, leading a life of excellent and sublime ascetic rule; and as he did not wish to dwell in the nunnery by the side of the women, as Elijah had done, he shut himself up in a certain upper chamber, but left there a window which faced and looked into the interior of the nunnery; and when he knew that it was proper to do so, he used to open it or shut it. He always sat by the window, and he showed the women that he knew everything, which they were doing, and by these means they were rebuked and prevented from quarrelling. Thus he grew old in that upper chamber, and no women ever went up to him, and he was unable to go down to them, for there was no ladder. Thus, in this manner of life he brought his days to an end according to the will of God by the help of His grace.

DAY 28

Pachomius, The Great

IN THE REGION OF THE THEBAID, and in the district called Tabenna, within the Thebaid, there was a certain blessed man whose name was Pachomius. This man led a beautiful life of ascetic excellence, and was crowned with the love of God and of man. Therefore as this man was sitting in his cell, there appeared to him an angel who said to him, "Since you have completed your discipleship, it is unnecessary for you to dwell here. But come, and gather those who are wandering. You will be dwelling with them, and lay down for them such laws as I shall tell to you." The angel gave him a book in which the following was written:

I. Let every man eat and drink whenever he wishes. According to the strength of those who eat and drink, impose work. You shall restrain them neither from eating nor fasting. Furthermore, on those who are strong, you shall impose severe labors; and upon those who are of inferior strength, and upon those who fast, you shall impose light labors.

II. You shall make for them a cell, and they shall dwell together three by three.

III. They shall partake of food together in one chamber.

IV. They shall not take their sleep lying down, but you shall make for them seats so that when they are sitting down, they shall be able to support their heads.

V. At night time, they shall put on garments without sleeves, and their loins shall be girded up. They shall be provided with skullcaps. They shall partake of the Offering on the Sabbath and on the First Day of the Week, wearing skull caps without any nap upon them. Each skullcap shall have in the front of it a cross worked in purple.

VI. You shall establish the monks in twenty-four grades, and to each grade give a letter of the Greek alphabet from Alfa to Taw (i.e. from A to Z); every grade a letter.

The blessed Pachomius performed and fulfilled these things according to the command of the angel. When the head of the monastery asked him concerning the affairs of the brethren, the man said to him, "The voice of Alpha and the voice of Bita salute the head of the monastery." Thus the whole of that assembly of brethren had letters of the alphabet assigned to them, according to the designation of the twenty-four letters. To those who were upright and simple, he assigned the letter yodh, and to those who were difficult and perverse, he assigned the letter ksi (i.e. E), and thus according to the dispositions and according to the habits and rules of life of the orders of monks, did he assign letters to them.

The angel commanded that a monk who was a stranger and who had a different garb from theirs, should not enter with them to the table. The man who sought to be accepted as a monk in that monastery was obliged to labor for three years, after which time, he was permitted to receive the tonsure. When the monks were eating together, they were to cover up their faces with their head coverings so that they might not see each other eating. They might not hold conversation together over the table, or gaze about from one side to the other. The angel commanded that during each day they should repeat twelve sections of the Psalter, and during each evening, twelve sections of the Psalter, and during each night, twelve sections of the Psalter, and that when they came to eat they should repeat the Great Psalm.

The blessed Pachomius said to the angel, "The sections of the Psalter which you have appointed to us for repetition are far too few." The angel said to him, "The sections of the Psalter which I have appointed are indeed few, so that even the monks who are small (i.e. weak) may be able to fulfill the canons, and may not be distressed thereby. For to the perfect no law is laid down, because their mind is always occupied with God. But this law which I have laid down is for those who do not have a perfect mind so that although they fulfill only such things as are prescribed by the canons, they can acquire openness of face." Numerous nuns adhered to this law and canon.

There were living in that mountain about seven thousand brethren, and in the monastery in which the blessed Pachomius himself lived there were one thousand three hundred brethren living there. Besides these, there were also other monasteries, each containing about three hundred, or two hundred, or one hundred monks, who lived together; and they all toiled with their hands and lived thereby, and with whatsoever they possessed which was superfluous for them, they provided and fed the nunneries which were there. Each day those whose week of service it was, rose up and attended to their work; and others attended to the cooking, and others set out the tables and laid upon them bread, and cheese, and vessels of vinegar and water.

There were some monks who went in to partake of food at the third hour of the day, others at the sixth hour, others at the ninth hour, others in the evening, and others ate once a day only. There were some who ate only once a week; and accordingly as each one of them knew the letter, which had been laid upon him, so was his work. Some worked in the Paradise (i.e. the orchard), some in the gardens, some in the blacksmith's shop, some in the bakers shop, some in the carpenters shop, some in the fullers shop, some wove baskets and mats of palm leaves, one was a maker of nets, one was a maker of sandals, and one was a scribe. All these men, as they were performing their work, were repeating the Psalms and the Scriptures in order.

There were large numbers of women who were nuns, who closely followed this rule of life. They came from the other side of the river and beyond it. There were also married women who came from the other side of the river close by. Whenever any of them died, the other women would bring her and lay her down on the bank of the river and go away. Then certain brethren would cross over in a boat and bring her over with the singing of psalms, with lighted candles, with great ceremony and honor. When they had brought her over, they would lay her in their cemetery; without an elder or deacon. It happened that a certain tailor, who was a stranger, came to that nunnery looking for work, and one of the sisters went out to talk with him, and said to him, "We have our own tailor." One of the sisters saw her speaking with him.

She held her peace and informed no one with this matter. After a short time, the two women had a dispute about a certain matter, and the sister who had seen the other talking to the tailor, went and brought an accusation against the other before all the sisters, talking about her in an evil manner, saying, "This is the Satan who has sown the strife among us." Many of the women having heard these things believed them. The sister, not being able to endure the accusation with which she had been accused without cause, by reason of her distress, went and cast herself into the river and drowned. When the sister who had made the accusation against the other perceived this, seeing that she had calumniated her evilly, that she had caused the sisters pain in a most serious manner, she also secretly drowned herself. The elder who had been made guardian of them, knowing this matter, commanded them that none of the sisters who had believed that sister who had made the accusation against her companion should receive the Offering. He was not reconciled to them and prevented them from participating in the

Offering for seven years.

In that same nunnery there was a certain sister who was a virgin. She made herself an object of contempt, and had had a devil in her. The other sisters used to treat her so contemptuously that they would not even allow her to eat with them. The woman herself was well content at this treatment. She would go into the refectory, serve the food and wait upon the whole company there. She became the broom of the whole nunnery; and indeed she made manifest that which is written in the Book of the blessed Apostle.

This woman used to throw over her head a roughly cut piece of cloth, whilst the other women wore veils, well cut and well made, according to the rule, which they had. In this garb, she used to minister in the refectory, and they would not allow her to sit down with them at the table. Whilst she was eating they never looked at her, and she never touched a whole loaf of bread, but used to eat the broken bits and crusts that fell from the tables. She drank the rinsing of the basins and of the hands, and they sufficed her. She neither reviled any of them, nor murmured, nor spoke superfluous words, though they constantly reviled her, struck her, and thrust her away with harsh words and blows.

At that time the blessed Piterius, that man of wonder, appeared. He dwelt in the region, which was called "Porphyry Mountain." An angel appeared to him and said, "Why do you hold in your mind the proud opinion that you are more excellent in ascetic practices than many? If you wish to see a woman who is more excellent than you, go to the nunnery, which is in Tabenna, and behold, you shall find there a woman with a roughly cut piece of cloth thrown over her head who is far superior to you in ascetic practices. This woman is far more excellent than you are, for although she ministers as a servant to a great congregation, her whole heart is set upon God. As for you, though you dwell here, your mind wanders about in many countries." When the man who had never gone forth from his monastery heard those things, he went quickly to the nunnery, and begged their visitor (or inspector) that he might be allowed to see the nuns.

When he had gone inside the house, they all came that they might be blessed by the blessed man, Piterius, except the woman who had made herself a creature of contempt, did not show herself at all. The blessed man Piterius said to them, "Have all the sisters come, for there is one lacking?" They said to him, "Master, we have one more, but she is a woman of no account, and she is in the refectory." Piterius said to them, "Bring her that I may see her also." They went to bring her, but she did not wish to come, for she felt that the matter of herself would be certainly revealed to him. Since she did not wish to go to the blessed man, they dragged her along and brought her to him by force, saying to her, "Saint Piterius wishes to see you." When she had come, the blessed man looked and saw the roughly cut piece of cloth which was thrown over her head, according to the sign which the angel had given concerning her. Then he bowed down before her, and said to her, "Bless me, Mother." She fell down at his feet, saying to him, "Bless me, O Master." When the sisters saw this they were all struck with wonder, and said to him, "Let there be no disgrace to you, master, for she is a creature of no account."

Then the blessed man Piterius answered and said, "You yourselves are creatures of contempt, but this woman is your Mother and mine. I entreat God that He will give to me a portion with her on the day of judgment." When all the sisters heard this from the blessed man Piterius, they fell down at her feet, and offered to her regrets for everything, which they had done to her; for some of them used to throw the rinsing of the vessels over her, others used to buffet her, and she endured many insults from them all. So the blessed Piterius prayed over them and left that place. A few days afterwards, because the blessed woman could not endure the honour and the praises of all the sisters, and the penitence which they showed to her, she went away from that house altogether. No man knows where she went to and where she died.

An Apology, Preface and Admonition

THEREFORE, O MY BROTHER, IT SUFFICES FOR ME that I have called to mind all these things, and that I have handed them on in writing; for this thing did not happen without the Will of God, because you were moved in your mind to command me to make this compilation and also to hand down in writing an account of the lives and acts of the holy fathers. According to the command of the love of God which is in you, I will write down also the upright lives of holy women who have prospered in the good works of patient endurance; and afterwards I will also write down the account of the stumbling of those who have fallen away from a straight rule of life through the pride which seized upon them, and through the wicked and vain opinion that came upon their souls, and who were tripped up, and stumbled, and fell through their weakness and the war of the Adversary, although not of their own will, for after their fall they triumphed still more gloriously, and acquired rectitude.

I will do this for the benefit of those who are about to meet with this compilation, so that they may set the edifice of their building upon the firm ground of humility with zeal and care, and may fly from pride, and may take refuge in humility; and it shall be my object to write with extreme care concerning the humility of the holy men, and concerning their long-suffering, and concerning their patient endurance, and the questions which they asked each other, together with their answers, and the sundry and diverse things which I shall be able to call to mind concerning the lives of the holy fathers.

O you faithful servant of Christ, having lighted upon this book with pleasure, having derived from it sufficiently a demonstration of the Resurrection, of the lives and labors of the holy fathers, of their patient endurance, being able to grow up in a good hope, and to advance easily in virtues, turn yourself round for once, so that you may see that which is behind you, and seeing my feebleness do you pray for me. Take good heed to guard your soul, even as I know you have been able to do from the time when you held the consular power of Titianus to this day; and again as I found you when you were the prefect and officer of the bed-chamber of the God-fearing king. For the man who has such power, and is able to enjoy himself with wealth in abundance, must not forget the fear of God, and must take the greatest care possible to emulate Christ. Who heard from the Calumniator these words; "All these things will I give to you if you will fall down and worship me." Therefore take good heed to yourself, and be vigilant, so that you may at all times be exalted over the necks of your secret invisible enemies. Amen.

The Virgin of Alexandria who Hid Athanasius

THEREFORE IT IS NECESSARY FOR US TO REMEMBER also the chosen and mighty women to whom God also gave an equal measure of strength of will as to men, so that they might have no cause for being feeble in the performance of the labour of ascetic excellence. I have seen large numbers of widows who were exceedingly glorious and excellent in the performance of ascetic virtues, and among the chaste virgins whom I saw in Alexandria, there was one whom I estimated to be seventy years old, and all the clergy testified concerning her that when a young woman, about twenty years old, she possessed exceeding beauty, and she was more looked at than many women, and because of her beauty she fled lest she should become the cause of stumbling to men.

Once when the Arians were plotting against the blessed Athanasius, Archbishop of Alexandria, and were acting craftily in respect of him that they might do him harm through the prefect Eusebius, and through the wicked men who were his partisans in the days of the Emperor Constantine the Less (i.e. Constantius), and were spreading abroad infamous reports about him, and were accusing him of many things which were unseemly for Christians to do, Athanasius fled that he might not be condemned in their wicked and corrupt hall of judgment. He told no man, neither kinsmen, nor friends, nor ecclesiastics, nor any other men where he was going. As soon as certain men from among the magistrates had entered into the Episcopal palace suddenly, and began to search for him and to enquire for him, he rose up at midnight, and took his tunic, and fled to this virgin who, being greatly astonished and struck with wonder at the matter, was moved exceedingly.

The blessed Athanasius said to her, "Because I am sought for by the Arians, who are making unseemly accusations against me, and because I do not want to spread about an unseemly opinion of myself, and I do not wish to prepare a great punishment for those who would be condemned for my sake, and be made guilty for me, I determined to take myself to flight. God gave me a revelation this night, saying, 'There is no other person with whom you can find deliverance except this virgin.'"

Therefore because of her exceedingly great joy, she removed herself, and set aside all thoughts of shame, and she became wholly the servant of our Lord. She hid that holy man for the whole period of thirty years, that is to say, until the death of Constantine. She used to wash his feet, prepared everything he had needed, and attended to his bodily wants. Whatever he needed she provided, and she borrowed books and brought them to him. No man in Alexandria knew during that whole period of thirty years where the blessed Athanasius was. When the death of Constantine (i.e. Constantius) was announced, and Athanasius also heard of it, he rose up and came by night. He was suddenly found in the church, and all those who saw him marvelled as they gazed carefully at him, for he looked like a man who had risen from the grave. He made an apology to those who truly loved him, and spoke to them, saying, "I did not flee to you, for the reason that there might not be to you an occasion for swearing false oaths. Moreover, because of the search and enquiry, which they were sure to have made for me, I fled to that woman concerning whom no man could suspect of harm, for she is young and beautiful. I have gained two things, my own life and hers; I have helped her in many things, and I have taken care and preserved myself."

DAY 31

Piamon the Virgin

PIAMON WAS A VIRGIN WHO LIVED ALL HER DAYS with her mother, and she spent her nights in constant vigil, and she ate food at the time of evening, and she laboured at the weaving of linen; and she was held to be worthy of the gift of knowing what was going to happen before it happened. It happened on a time that there was in Upper Egypt a certain village which was fighting with another village, for the villages quarrelled with each other concerning the division of the waters of the Nile, and they fought so violently that frequently murders were committed, and men were beaten to death.

The village which was stronger than the village of this virgin rose up against it in fierce wrath, and there came against the inhabitants of her village a crowd of boastful and violent men carrying staves and spears to kill them; and the angel of the Lord appeared to her, and revealed to her the craft of those who were ready to fall upon them secretly. Then she sent and called the elders of the church of her village, and said to them, "Go out to meet the inhabitants of that village, for behold they are coming against you, lest perhaps you and the village perish; and make entreaty to them that perhaps they may be turned aside from their daring attack, and they may spare the village."

The elders of the village were afraid. They fell down at her feet and made supplication to her, saying, "We do not dare to go out to meet them, for we are well acquainted with their miserable nature and their arrogance. If you wish to spare the village and your own house, you yourself go out to meet them." The virgin would not undertake to go out, but went up upon the roof, and stood up there in prayer the whole night long, without once kneeling down. She made bowings and entreaties to God, saying, "O Lord, you judge of the earth, who has no pleasure in whatever is iniquitous. O my Lord, when the prayer and supplication of Your handmaiden reaches You, let Your power transfix the enemy in the spot in which they are."

Immediately, on that very day, at a distance of three miles from the village they became fettered and stood still, being unable to move from the spot. It was revealed to them also that they were hindered from moving by the supplication of that woman, and thereupon they sent to the inhabitants of the village, and made peace with them, and became reconciled to them, and they also sent a message to them, saying, "Give grateful thanks to God, for it was the prayers of Piamon which prevented us from coming to you."

Our Blessed Mother Talida

IN THE CITY OF ANTINOE, THERE WERE TWELVE NUNNERIES. The women there conducted themselves according to a rule of beautiful spiritual excellence. Here I saw the aged handmaiden of Christ whose name was 'Mother Talida,' who had dwelt in the holy house, according to what she herself and those who were her associates told me, for eighty years. Sixty virgins lived there; they followed the path and rule of the ascetic life in purity, and led a life of happiness under the teaching of this good old woman. They loved that woman and depended on her. Because of the great affection which they poured out on her, the key was never taken away from any one of them, as is customary in other religious houses for women. Through her divine doctrine she changed them into a state of incorruptibility. This old woman arrived at a state of impassibility. When I entered in her presence and sat down by her side, she stretched out her hands and laid them on my shoulders, in the boldness and freedom, which she had acquired in Christ.

Virgin Taor

IN THIS NUNNERY, THERE WAS A CERTAIN VIRGIN whose name was Taor, who was the disciple of a certain old woman of ascetic excellence, and who had lived there for thirty years. She would not consent to receive neither beautiful apparel, a veil, nor sandals, saying, "I do not require them, for I am not compelled to go down into the market." Every First Day of the Week, the other women used to go down to the church to partake of the Offering, but this virgin used to remain by herself in the nunnery dressed in rags, and she would sit at her work at all hours. By these means, she acquired such a sagacious, wise, and ready appearance that every man who was accustomed to abhor the sight of women would have been near to being snared and falling at the sight of her, had it not been that shamefacedness, which is the guardian of chastity, was ever with her, and that she ordered her gaze in a chaste manner by means of shame and fear.

Virgin and Martyr Colluthus

THERE WAS ANOTHER VIRGIN there who was a neighbor of mine, and who dwelt near me, but whose face I had never seen, for, according to what they said about her, she had never gone down to the market from the day upon which she had become a nun, but had completed sixty years with the head of her nunnery. And finally, when she was about to depart from the world, the martyr, whose name was Colluthus, who had lived by the side of the nunnery, appeared to her, and said to her, "This day you are about to depart from this world to your Lord, and you shall see all the saints. But come and eat a meal with us in the martyrium." Thereupon she rose up early in the morning and arrayed herself in her apparel, taking bread, olives, and garden herbs in her basket;

she went forth as she had done for many years. Having gone to the martyrium, she prayed. Having watched for the space of the whole day for an opportunity when no man would be found there, she drew near and cried out to that martyr, and said to him, "Ask a blessing on my food, O Saint Colluthus, and accompany me on this journey by your prayers."

Having eaten her food and prayed, she came back at sunset to her nunnery, and gave to the Head of the nunnery the Book of Clement which is called "Stromata." It contains a commentary of Amos the prophet, saying, "Give this book to the Bishop who is in Alexandria in exile, and say to him, 'Pray for me, for I am about to depart.'" She died in the night without suffering either sickness or from pain in her head. But she rolled herself up in her garments and died.

The Virgin and Magistrianus

IN THE ANCIENT BOOK ASCRIBED TO HIPPOLYTUS, who knew the Apostles, I have found the following history written. There was a certain woman who was of noble birth and beautiful in her face. She came from the city of the Corinthians, and continued to live in a state of virginity. Certain people laid an accusation against her before the governor, who was a heathen, at the time of the persecution of the Christians, and calumniated her, saying, "She has abused the Government and the Emperors, she has uttered blasphemies against the gods (i.e. the idols), she has treated the sacrifices with contempt." Such were the lying words, which the wicked men concocted about her, because they had been led captive by her beauty. Because the governor was more addicted than they all to lasciviousness, he accepted such calumnies as those, and became mad with desire like lustful stallions, even as

it is written, "He was inflamed by lust."
The Governor tried to seduce her by means of cunning schemes of every kind, but was unable to do so. He became furious with her and handed her over to be punished, not by means of stripes and scourging, but wanted to make her earn her living by fornication. He commanded the man to whom he had delivered her, to collect daily from the money which should be paid to her for hiring three darics, and to bring them to him. This man, in order that he might not make use of the command in any sluggish manner, and that he might not lose money and also make the governor exceedingly angry, set her up as a gift before all those who wished to have her.

Therefore, when those who were as keen in their lust for the maiden, as are hawks for a snared sparrow, perceived those things, they went into the tavern of destruction (i.e. brothel), and having given money to the man to whom the virgin had been delivered, they drew near to her and spoke to her such things as they thought would be helpful to their intentions. But the virgin, who was wise among women, urged them on with blandishments in a gladsome manner, and strengthened her mind in the hope of Him for whom she had guarded her virginity, and she made petitions to them, saying, "I have a hidden sore in a certain place, and the smell of its running is exceedingly strong; and I am afraid that after you have embraced me it will bring you to hate me and that your souls will loathe me. I therefore beseech you to wait a few days until I am well again, and then you shall have the power to do whatever you like with me for nothing."

Having dismissed them with these words, she offered up to God during those days with her whole heart prayers, and supplications, and bowings to the ground that He would help her, and that she might be saved and delivered from such hateful destruction as this, and that she might be kept in a state of unsullied virginity. Then God, seeing her chastity, sent a fervent longing for her into a certain young man called Magistrianus, who was wholly excellent, both in mind and in body, and it burned like fire even to death. And he went as it were in a lustful passion, and at the time of evening he entered the house of the man who had been commanded to receive the money, and he gave him five darics, and said to him, "Let me be with the virgin this night"; and he permitted him to be with her. Then having gone into the place, which was her sleeping room, he said to her, "Rise up and save yourself."

Having stripped off her apparel, and dressed her in his own clothes, and covered her with his cloak, and completed her attire after the manner of that of a man, he said to her, "Muffle up your head in the hood of the cloak and go out. Having done this, she signed herself with the sign of the Cross, and went out. At the turn of the day, the fraud became known, and Magistrianus was delivered up and was cast to the beasts. Thus was the evil put to shame because that martyr, who is worthy of admiration, was able to crown himself with the two crowns of a double martyrdom, one on behalf of himself, and one on behalf of that blessed woman.

DAY 34

Melania, The Great

MELANIA, THE HOLY WOMAN IS WORTHY OF ALL BLESSINGS. She was of Spanish origin, and grew up in Rome, for she was the daughter of Marcellinus, a man who had held consular rank. Her husband was a man who performed a large number of duties under the Government, and she became a widow when she was twenty-two years old. Now this woman, having been held worthy to be seized upon by divine love, revealed the matter to no man, for she would not have been permitted to perform her own will, because she lived in the time of the rule of Valens (A.D. 364-378); and having arranged that he should be named the procurator of her sons affairs, she took everything which she possessed which could be easily moved and carried off, and placed it in a ship with tried servants, both men and women, and sailed hastily to Alexandria, where she sold her property and changed it into gold.

She went into the mount of Nitria, and saw the fathers, that is to say, Pambo, Arsenius, Serapion the Great, Paphnutius of Scete, Isidore the Confessor and Bishop of Hermopolis, and Dioscurus. She remained with them for half a year, and going around through the entire desert, saw all the holy men and was blessed by them. When Augustus, who was in Alexandria, sent into exile to Palestine and Caesarea, Isidore, Pissimius, Adelphius, Fisanis, Paphnutius, and Pambo (now with these also was Ammonius, that is to say, twelve holy bishops), this blessed woman clave to them, and ministered them from her own possessions. When the servants whom she used to send to them were stopped, this brave woman (according to what the holy men Pisanis, Paphnutius, Isidore, and Ammonius related to me, for I used to hold converse with them) used to clothe herself in the garment of one of her servants, and carry to them late in the evening, the food which they needed.

When the Governor of Palestine learned this thing, wishing to fill his purse, and hoping and expecting to make profit by her, he seized her and cast her into prison. The Governor was unaware that she was a noble rank woman. Then she sent to him a message, saying, "I am the daughter of such and such a man, and the wife of such and such a man, and I am the handmaiden of Christ. Do not treat lightly my poor garb and estate, for I have the power to exalt myself if it pleases me to do so, and you have no authority either to hamper me in this fashion or to carry off any of my property. In order that you may not dare to do anything in ignorance, and fall under condemnation, behold, I send you this message; for it is right that towards senseless and foolish men we should act in a masterful manner, and with pride, even as our noble rank enables us to do, and should treat them as fools and men of no understanding." When the Governor learned this thing he apologized to Melania, entreated her to forgive him, fell down and did homage to her, and gave orders that she should have the power to visit holy men without hindrance.

After the return of these blessed men from exile, this holy woman built a house in Jerusalem, in which she dwelt for twenty-seven years, and in which she had a congregation of sisters, who were in number about fifty; and moreover, the honorable nobleman Rufinus, who came from Italy and belonged to the city of Aquileia, clave to her whole life long, and he led a life of glorious works, and finally he was held to be worthy of the office of elder. Now among men one would not quickly find one who was more understanding, and gracious, and pleasant than he. Rufinus and Melania during the whole of that period, of twenty-seven years, received and relieved at their own expense all those people who came to Jerusalem to pray, bishops, dwellers in monasteries, and virgins. They edified and benefited all those who thronged to them. They healed the schism of the Paulinists, who were in number about four hundred monks, and they all were heretics who fought against the Holy Spirit; and having made entreaty to them, they turned them back to union with the Church. They loaded with their gifts all the clergy who were in the cities. They provided food to all strangers and the needy. In this manner, they ended their lives, and never became a stumbling block to any man.

As concerning the possessions of which she stripped herself, and the things (i.e. money) which she distributed, being hot as fire with divine zeal, and blazing like a flame with the love of Christ, I alone am not able to recount, for it belongs also to those who dwell in the country of the Persians to declare it. There was no man who was deprived of her alms and gifts whether he came from the east, the west, the north, or the south. She lived in exile for thirty-seven years, and her possessions sufficed for her to give alms to churches, to religious houses, to strangers, and to those who were in prison. Meanwhile her relatives and her kinsfolk were sending money to her continually, to her own son, and those who had charge of her property also sent some of their own money to her; and she never lacked anything, and during the whole of the time in which she was in exile, she never consented to the acquisition of a span of land. She was never drawn to long for her son, and the love for her only child neither parted her nor divided her from the love of Christ, but through her prayers, her son attained to perfect discipline and to the ways and habits of excellence. He became the son-in-law of honorable and noble people, and there also came upon him much power and diverse positions of great honor; now he had two children, one boy and one girl.

After a long period of time had elapsed, when she heard that the daughter of her son and her husband wished to be sanctified, and fearing lest they should fall into the hands of the heretics who would sow in them evil doctrines, and lest they should grow up in a life of dissolute luxury, that old woman, who was then sixty years old, embarked once again in a ship, and sailed from Caesarea, and after twenty days, arrived in Rome. Whilst she was there, she converted and made to become a Christian, a man called Apronianus, who was of exceedingly high rank and was also a pagan; and she moreover persuaded him by means of most perfect admonition and exhortation to become sanctified, and also his wife, who was her own sister and whose name was Avita, to receive the garb of the followers of the ascetic life, and to become prosperous in all patience, in the labors of the life of abstinence and self-denial. She also strengthened by means of her excellent counsels the daughter of her son, whose name was Melania, and her husband, whose name was Pinianus, and she also converted her daughter-in-law, whose name was Albina; and she persuaded all these to sell everything which they possessed and to give the money to the poor; and she brought them out from Rome, and led them into the quiet and peaceful haven of the life and labors of asceticism.

She contended with all the women of senatorial rank and with the women of high degree, and strove with them as with savage wild beasts, for the men tried to restrain her from making the women do, even as she had done, that is to say, to prevent her from converting them and making them to forsake their worldly rank and position. She spoke to them saying, "My children, four hundred years ago it was written that that time was the last time. Why do you hold fast thus strenuously to the vain love of the world? Take heed lest the day of Antichrist overtakes you, and keep not fast hold upon your own riches and the possessions of your fathers"; and having set free all these, she brought them to the life of the ascetic and recluse. As for her grand son Publicola, who was a child, she converted him and brought him to Sicily; and she sold the whole of the residue of her possessions and taking the price of it, came to Jerusalem, and, having distributed it in a wise fashion and arranged all her other affairs, after forty days she died at a good old age, being crowned with an abundance of gratification and happiness; and she left in Jerusalem a house for religious folk and money for the maintenance of it.

When all those who clave to her had gone forth from Rome, the great barbarian whirlwind, which had also been mentioned in ancient prophecies, came upon the city, and it did not leave behind it even the statues of brass which were in the market-places, for it destroyed by its barbaric insolence everything whatsoever; and it so thoroughly committed everything to destruction that the city of Rome, which had been crowned and adorned for twelve hundred years with edifices and buildings of beauty, became a waste place. Then those who without contention had been converted by means of her admonition, ascribed glory to God Who, by means of a change in temporal affairs, had persuaded those who did not believe her; for whilst the houses of all the latter were plundered, the houses of those only who had been persuaded by her were delivered, and they became perfect burnt-offerings to the Lord, through the care and solicitude of the blessed woman Melania.

It happened by chance that I and they once travelled together from Aelia to Egypt, and we were accompanied on our journey by the gentle virgin Sylvania, the sister of Rufinus, a man of consular rank, and Jovinianus was also with us. Now he was at that time a deacon, but subsequently he became bishop in the Church of God of the city of Ashkelon, and he was a God-fearing man and was exceedingly well versed in doctrine. And it came to pass that a fierce and fiery heat overtook us on the way, and we came into Pelusium that we might rest therein; and Jovinianus, who is worthy of admiration, came by chance upon a trough for washing, and he began to wash his hands and his feet in a little water that by means of the coolness of it, he might refresh himself after the intensity of the blazing heat. Then having washed himself, he threw on the ground a sheepskin upon which he might rest from the labor of the journey. And behold, the mighty one among women stood up over him like a wise mother, and in her simplicity rebuked him by her words, saying, "Seeing that you are still in the heat of youth how can you have confidence that by means of carefulness on your part you will be able to resist the natural heat of the constitution of the body which still burn in your members? Do you not perceive the injurious effects which will be produced in you by this washing? Believe me, O my son, for I am this day a woman sixty years old; from the time when I first took upon myself this garb water has never touched more of my body than the tips of the fingers of my hands, and I have never washed my feet, or my face, or any one of my members. Although I have fallen into many sicknesses, and have been urged by the physicians, I have never consented nor submitted myself to the habit of applying water to any part of my body; and I have never lain upon a bed, and I have never gone on a journey to any place reclining on a cushioned litter."

This wise and blessed woman loved learning, and turned her nights into days in reading all the books of the famous Fathers, I mean to say the works of the blessed Gregory, of the holy man Stephen, of Pierius, of Basil also, and of other writers, more than two hundred and fifty thousand sayings; and she did not read them in an ordinary fashion or just as she came to them, and she did not hurry over them in an easy and pleasant manner, but with great labor and with understanding, she used to read each book seven, or eight times. Because of this, she was enabled, being set free from lying doctrine, to fly by means of the gift of learning, to have great opinions, and she made herself a spiritual bird, and in this way was taken up to Christ her Lord. May He, in His mercy, grant to us through her prayers, the power to the Almighty, even as she did, and may we see her with all the saints who love Him, and with them may we lift up praise to the Father, and to the Son, and to the Holy Spirit forever and ever.

DAY 35

Melania, the Younger

INASMUCH AS I HAVE ALREADY PROMISED ABOVE, to relate the history of Melania the Younger, it is right that I should pay my obligation, for it is not just that I should consign to oblivion a young woman who, though so very young in her years, by reason of her indefatigable zeal and knowledge was very much wiser than the old women, or that I should omit to make manifest by words, the history of one who, though a girl in stature, was old in the mind of the fear of God.

Therefore the parents of this maiden drew her by force into marriage, and they united her to one of the nobles of Rome, but she kept in mind continually the words which had been spoken to her by her aged relative, and kept herself as was fitting, and became strengthened especially in the fear of God. And she had two sons, and as both of them died, she came to be possessed of such a hatred of marriage that she said to her husband, whose name was Pinianus, the son of Severus, a man of consular rank, "If you wish to live with me a life of purity, I will regard you as the husband and lord of my life; but if, inasmuch as you are a young man, this is too hard for you, take everything which I have and leave only free to me my own body, for in this way I shall be able to fulfill my desire which is in God, and I shall become the heir of the excellences of that woman after whose name I have been called. For if God desired me to lead the life of this world He would never have taken away the children to whom I gave birth."

When they had been for a long time debating the matter, at length God had mercy upon that young man, and He placed in him the zeal of the fear of God to such a degree that he also sought to be excused from all the material things of this world, and thus was to fulfill the word which had been spoken by the Apostle, saying, "How do know you, O woman, whether you shall give life to your husband or not? Or how do you know, O man, whether you shall give life to your wife or not?" When she was married to her husband, she was about twelve or thirteen years old, and she lived with him for seven years, for she was twenty years of age when she withdrew from the world.

First of all, she bestowed all her raiment of silk upon the holy altars, which also did Olympias, the handmaiden of Christ, and the remainder of her apparel of silk, she cut up, and made it suitable for the service of the church in other ways. Her silver and gold, she entrusted to an elder whose name was Paul, who was a monk from Dalmatia, and she sent it by sea to the countries of the East, I mean to Egypt and to the Thebaid, to the amount of ten thousand darics; and she sent in this manner ten thousand darics to Antioch, and to the countries which were near there, but to Palestine she sent fifteen thousand darics. To the churches which were in the islands, and to the people who were in exile, she sent ten thousand darics, and to those who were in the West, I mean in the churches, and in the monasteries there, and the houses for the reception of strangers, and to all those who were in want, she distributed her gifts with her own hands.

I speak as before God when I say that she must have given away four times these amounts, besides, and that she snatched away her money from Alaricus, her confidential servant, as from the mouth of a lion. Of those who wished to be free among her servants, she gave freedom to about eight thousand in number, and of the remainder who had no wish to have their freedom, and who preferred rather to remain in the service of her brother, she bestowed three thousand darics. All the villages which she had in Spain, and in Aquitania, and in the island of Tarragon, and Gaul, she sold, as well as those which she had in Sicily, and in Campania, and in Africa, and received the proceeds of it in her own hands, so that she might give them to the monasteries, and churches, and all those who were in want. Such was the wisdom of Melania, this lover of Christ, and such was the mature and divine opinion which she adopted in respect of the weighty burden of these riches.

Her manner of life was thus. She herself ate once a day, though at the beginning she ate once in five days, and the young women whom she had converted and who lived with her, she commanded to partake of food every day. And there lived with her also the mother of Albins, who observed the same rule of life, and who distributed her possessions among the needy, after the manner of Melania; and sometimes they dwelt in the plains of Sicily, and sometimes in the plains of Campania, and they had with them fifteen men who were eunuchs, and a proportionate number of virgins who ministered as servants.

And Pinianus, who had once been her husband, was now one who helped in the work of ascetic excellence, and was her associate, and he dwelt with three hundred men who were monks and read the Holy Scriptures, and he enjoyed himself in the garden, and conversed with the people. Now these men who were with him, helped and relieved us in no slight degree, and we were very many in number, when we were going on our way to Rome on behalf of the blessed man, John the Bishop, for they received us with the greatest good will and they supplied us with provisions for the way in great abundance, and they sent us on our way in joy and gladness.

Their kinsman, whose name was Pammachius, a man of consular rank, withdrew from the world as did they, and he lived a life which was pleasing to God, and during his lifetime he distributed his possessions among the needy, and left them to them after his death; and thus he departed to our Lord. In like manner the man Macarius, and Constantinus, who was the assessor to the prefects in Italy (now they were well known men and men who merit mention), arrived at the highest pitch of ascetic excellence which I describe even as it is; and they abide in the body at this present and lead a life of glorious and divine deeds, and are awaiting the perfect life, which is full of happiness.

DAY 36

Olympias

THE HOLY AND CHASTE WOMAN OLYMPIAS, whilst journeying in the footsteps of this woman Melania, was emulating her in the excellence of her divine life and labours, and she was seized with a fervent desire of travelling in the path which leads to heaven, and in every respect, she made herself cling close to the Divine Books. This woman, was in the flesh, the daughter of Count Seleucus, but, if we say what is true, in the spirit she was the daughter of God. She was the daughter of the son of Ablavius, a man who had held consular rank in Constantinople, and she was for a few days, the daughter-in-law of Nebridius, the sub-prefect of Constantinople, but in truth she was not the wife of the man, for they say concerning her that she died in purity and in her virginity, and that she only lived according to the Divine Word in chastity, in which was mingled true humility, and that she made herself a friend of and ministered to all those who were needy.

Her abundant riches sufficed for this work, and it is impossible to reckon up that which she used to distribute to everyone with a sincere intent; for there is not a city, or a district, or a desert place, or an island, or a shore which did not enjoy the gifts of this glorious woman. She gave gifts also to the churches for their maintenance and to the houses in which strangers were received, and also to the prisons and, moreover, to those who were in exile, and, so to speak, on the whole world, this blessed woman scattered her alms broadcast. And she leaped upon and ascended the uppermost part of the lofty mountain of humility, in which nothing whatsoever was to be seen of the acts and deeds of vainglory or of deceitful action; but the life of simplicity, and the common garb, and the emaciated body, and the submissive mind, and the understanding which is without arrogance, and the lowly heart, and the watching of vigil, and the spirit which is without anxious care, and the love which has no limit, and friendship without end and the holding in contempt the operation of the feelings, and the restraint from everything harmful, and the mind which is simple towards God, and the hope which never fail, and the loving kindness which is unspeakable, and the thoughtful care of all poor folk.

This woman suffered many temptations through the agency of that evil devil, who loves hateful things and who has never had experience of things which are good, and she endured great contending for the sake of the name of Christ. And she gave herself to tears which were without measure, both by day and by night, and she submitted herself to all sorts and conditions of the children of men for the sake of God, and she bowed down reverently before the holy Bishops, and she paid homage to the elders, and she entreated in an honourable manner the clergy, as well as the orders of monks who dwelt in the monastic houses.

She welcomed the virgins, and she visited the widows, and she reared the orphans, and she strengthened those who were in a state of old age, and she had care for the sick and she mourned with the sinners, and she led the erring into the right path, and she tended every one, and she converted many women among those who did not believe, and prepared them for life. She left behind her to the world a beautiful remembrance, and she changed slavery into freedom for all members of her household, who were about a myriad in number, and she showed to them honour in the same degree as to her noble family; and if, as is right, we must tell the truth, she made them to become of more account than herself.

It was impossible for any man to see apparel worse than hers on anyone, for the garments of this brave woman were not as good as those of the people who cover themselves with the oldest rags; and the food which she offered to her body was of such an inferior class that on account of its poorness, it was rejected even by her servants. By this woman, who was clothed in Christ, no blame was ever found in anyone, not even in her neighbours. Her life was full of vehement tears; one may perhaps see a fountain which, owing to the violence of the heat, has dried up, but no man ever saw the eyes of this woman, which were fixed upon Christ, lacking tears. But of what use is it for us to tell and to devote myself so strenuously to narrate things concerning her?

For the contendings of this woman, who was perfect in excellence, were so exceedingly numerous, that they were more in number than those which were declared concerning her, and men would only imagine concerning me that I was narrating from hearsay great things which were not true about this woman, Olympias. She became a vessel of honour of the Divine Spirit, raised above all passions. Nevertheless I was a spectator of her excellence and of her angelic acts and deeds, and I was, as it were, a member of her household, and her kinsman in the Spirit, and she made, by my counsel, gifts to many from her possessions. And this woman who never thought about the things which were in the flesh, suffered many vain calumnies for the sake of the truth, and those who were living in Divine fear in Constantinople rightly deemed that she should be numbered with the confessors, because even to death, she persisted in striving for righteousness sake, and in performing her works, she received perfection. She waited hopefully for the never-withering crown, which was full of all blessings in the everlasting mansions on high, with all the saints who were like to her, and she sought after the reward of her good deeds with freedom of speech.

DAY 37

Candida

AFTER THE MANNER OF THE BLESSED WOMAN CANDIDA, the daughter of the blessed man Trajan, the general, also laboured, and she arrived at the perfection of ascetic excellence; and she offered to the Bishops, who were the ministers of the Mysteries of Christ, the homage which was right for them. She provided suitably for the performance of all the service of the church, and supplied the clergy with gifts, to each man according to his grade. She converted her daughter and placed her in the ranks of the virgins, and she offered to God this gift of the fruit of her womb, and sent her before her, and finally she herself also became like her daughter, in the chastity of her purity, distributing her wealth among the poor and needy. I know every night this brave woman used to rise up from her bed and grind corn, and heat the oven, and make bread for the Offering, and bake it with her own hands, and she was accustomed to say that she did this in order to reduce the strength of her body, for, she added, "Because I am unable to receive any benefit from fasting, I have taken upon myself this labour for watching, so that I may do away with the greedy appetite of Esau."

She separated herself from every kind of meat where there is blood. Fish alone is exempted. She made use of oil and vegetables, but these only on festival days; and on all other days she used to live on dry bread dipped in vinegar, and it sufficed her. She awaited with hope, the Resurrection which was to be full of happiness, in return for these stern labours, and she hoped to enjoy the everlasting delights which God has prepared for those who love Him.

Gelasia

GELASIA, THE DAUGHTER OF A MAN OF THE RANK OF TRIBUNE, desired earnestly to follow in the fear of God after this woman whose life and deeds were glorious, and her excellence consisted in never allowing the sun to go down upon her wrath against man, neither against her servants nor against any other man; and this blessed woman fled from the path of men of wrath which leads to everlasting death.

DAY 38

Juliana

AGAIN, THERE WAS A CERTAIN VIRGIN, whose name was Juliana, in Caesarea of Cappadocia, and it was said concerning her that she was a believing woman, and a woman of understanding, and that in the time of the persecution when the writer Origen was fleeing from the heathen, she received him and hid him in her house for two years; and she fed and kept him at her own expense, and made him to be satisfied and content with her ministration. Now I have found these things set down in a certain book which was in the handwriting of Origen himself, and I found this book in the possession of the excellent virgin Juliana in Caesarea who had hidden it, and who used to say that she received it from Symmachus, the expositor of the Jews. And I have not set down in writing the story of the excellences of these glorious women for any ordinary purpose, but that we may learn that by every means whatsoever we may, if we wish, find sundry and diverse occasions for obtaining spiritual advantage.

Heronion and His Wife Bosphoria

IN ANCYRA, A CITY OF GALATIA, I met a man whose name was Heronion, an "Apakomots," and an enlightened man, and his wife whose name was Bosphoria (or Dosphoria), and of their mode of living and acts I experienced an example. Now these folk had such a firm hope in the happiness which were to come, that they neglected even their children, for they awaited with hope the actual fulfillment of the things to come, and they distributed among the poor and needy the income which they derived from their villages, notwithstanding the fact that they had four male and two female children. To these children they never gave anything whatsoever, except to the daughters who had married husbands. Finally, they used to say, "After we are dead, everything will be yours, but during our lifetime, the income which we derive from our villages, we shall take for ourselves." They used to divide their money among the churches and monasteries, and houses for the receiving of strangers and among the poor and needy. Besides these things they performed the following act of excellence.

There was a great famine, and every man restrained his mercy, but these folk opened the storehouses which they had in their villages, and gave food to eat to those who were famished, and through this act, the heretics who were living in that country were changed and were turned to the true knowledge when they saw their unspeakable loving kindness; and they gave praise to God for the simplicity of their faith. Other examples of their excellence were the following: the modest garb, common and simple apparel, food eaten but rarely, and then only in such quantities as were sufficient to maintain life; and they lived meanwhile in a state of chastity which was acceptable to God.

They dwelt in the fields several days at a time, loving a life of silent contemplation, and they fled from the tumult of cities and from the evils which are begotten of them, lest when they were living among a crowd of people something might come upon them to disturb them, and they might fall from their divine state of mind. For this reason these blessed men were doing all these excellent things, because with eyes of understanding, they had already looked upon the good things which had been forever prepared for them.

Magna

IN THIS CITY OF ANCYRA THERE WERE ALSO MANY OTHER VIRGINS who led lives of ascetic excellence, and they were two thousand, or more, in number; and they kept themselves in restraint and served God with great humility. And among them were also famous women who triumphed with glorious strenuousness in the contending of the fear of God, and of those was Magna, the chaste and proved wife. Now I know not whether I ought to describe her as a virgin or as a widow, for this woman, owing to the pressure which was put upon her by her mother, was yoked to a husband. But she used to make pretences to her husband in diverse ways, and she avoided his embraces by urging the bodily sickness which she had on her as an excuse, and thus she was, according to what the members of her household said, preserved spotless from him.

Now, after a short time, the man died, and he left everything to her. She offered herself wholly to God and devoted herself to the things which belonged to the life which is to come; and thus, she lived a life in the great chastity of the fear of God, and even the Bishops were put to shame by the sight of her. The rest of the building (i.e. the edifice of her spiritual excellences,) she made perfect in the furnace of the love of voluntary poverty, and whatsoever there remained to her, she gave gladly to the churches, and monasteries and houses for receiving poor strangers, and to the orphans and widows; and she abode continually in the church and served God, and awaited the hope which was to come.

Monk Misericors who Lived in Ancyra

MOREOVER, WE FOUND IN THIS CITY A CERTAIN MONK, and we met him at the time when he had just received the laying on of hands as an elder; formerly he had been a husbandman, but he had laboured in the life of a solitary recluse for twenty years, and he had lived in close intercourse with the Bishop of the city, who was a holy man. He was such a benevolent man that even in the night-time, he would go roundabout and visit those who were poor and needy, and he was so indefatigable in his work that he neglected neither the prison-house, nor the house of the sick (i.e., hospital), nor the houses of the rich and poor, but helped everyone. He urged the rich with words which were full of mercy, and exhorted them to fair deeds, and he toiled with anxious care on behalf of the poor and needy, in respect of those things which were right for them. Those who were struggling in contention, he brought near to peace, and those who were naked, he clothed with raiment, and he laboured for the sick and brought them the bindings which conducted their healing.

Now there existed in this city of Ancyra that which exists rightly in large cities, that is to say, in the porch of the church, there lay a great number of poor folk, who were in the habit of going about, begging for their daily bread. Among them were certain men who had wives, and it fell out on the night of a certain day that one of these women was about to give birth to a child. Because the pain was darting through her, and the severe anguish of the birth pangs, she cried out loudly. The blessed man heard her outcries from the church as he was praying. He ceased praying, and went out to see what was happening, although it was winter. Seeing that there was no man near her, he himself filled the place of midwife, and did not consider the shame which attaches to those who give birth to children; for the great act of loving kindness which he was about to perform did not grant to him the perception of such things.

Of this blessed man, his garments were so utterly poor that they were worth nothing at all, for by reason of the great and loving kindness, which dwelt in him, he took no pains at all to acquire any possession whatsoever. For if anyone gave him a book, he immediately went and sold it. To those who enquired of him concerning it, saying, "Why did you sell the book?" He said, "How am I to persuade the Master that I have in truth learned His handicraft, unless I make use of His testimony as to the true meaning of His handicraft?" This holy man persists in this course of action until this day, and has left behind him a never fading remembrance. He is happy in the expectation of the good things, which are eternal. He waits to receive the reward of the labours of his triumphs in the kingdom from Him Who said, "I was hungry, and you gave Me to eat. I was naked and you clothed Me."

John of Lycus, a City on the Thebaid

JOHN, WHO LIVED IN THE CITY OF LYCUS, and who had learned in his youth the craft of the carpenter, and whose brother was a dyer, afterwards, when he was about twenty five years old, took upon himself the garb of monkhood; and having lived in diverse monasteries for five years, he finally departed by himself to the mountain which is in Lycus, to the lofty eminence which is on the top of the mountain, and made three cells for himself there. Now he built and prepared these for himself in the first year after he went to the mountain and went up into it. The first cell was for the needs of the body, in the second he laboured at the work of his hands and took his food, and in the third he said his prayers. And during the thirty years in which he was in seclusion, there he was accustomed to receiving whatsoever was necessary for him through the window from him that ministered to him.

This blessed man was worthy to receive from God the gift of being able to declare things before they came to pass, and on several occasions, he made known things before they happened to the blessed Emperor Theodosius. He foretold that he would conquer Maximus, the rebel, and would return from Gallia, and he also announced to him beforehand concerning the defeat of Eugenius, the rebel, and thus the fame of this holy man went forth greatly, and he was held to be a man of spiritual excellence. Therefore, when we were in the desert of Nitria, I and the members of the following of the blessed Origen, wished to gain exact information concerning the state of spiritual excellence to which the man had attained. Thereupon the blessed Evagrius said, "I am very desirous of learning from someone who is skilled in the investigation of the mind and understanding, what manner of man, John of Lycus is; for although I myself am unable to see him, still I can learn from another man concerning his qualities of excellence if he be able to narrate them, but I cannot go so far as his mountain."

When I had heard these things I said nothing whatsoever to any man, and I held my peace for a day, but on the next day I shut up my cell, and having confided myself to the hands of God, I set out on my journey to go to Thebaid, where I arrived after eighteen days; on some of which I walked on my feet, and on others I sailed on the river. For it was the period of the year when the river rises, and when many folk fall sick, which also happened to me. And when I had gone to John of Lycus, I found that he had shut himself up in the place in which he lived in seclusion. I took up my abode with the brethren in a great house which contained about one hundred men, and which the brethren had built a long time; for though they shut in John during the other days of the week, on Saturday and Sunday, they used to open his window.

When I had learned the rule concerning his seclusion, I waited until Saturday, and at the second hour, I drew near and found him sitting in the opening in the wall, in which he waited to administer comfort and consolation to those who thronged to him. And having saluted me, he said to me through an interpreter, "Where are you from, my son? Why have you come? You appear to belong to the congregation of Evagrius." And I said to him, "I am a stranger from the country of the Galatians." I confessed that I also belonged to those who were followers of Evagrius. Now whilst we were conversing together, behold, Alipius, the governor of the country, came to him. As the governor turned to him, John ceased to talk to me and I left them for a little space and gave them an opportunity to talk, and I rose up and departed from the mountain. When they had passed much time in their converse, I became impatient and angry, and I murmured against that excellent old man because it seemed as if he had treated me lightly and had paid honour to the governor. Being offended in my mind at this treatment, I made up my mind to go away because of his disregard for me. Then John called to his interpreter, whose name was Theodore, and said to him, "Go and say to that brother, be not angry and impatient, for I will dismiss the governor immediately, and then I will speak with you." Thus it appeared to me that, like a spiritual being, he had knowledge of secret things, and I made up my mind to remain.

When the governor had departed, John called to me and said to me, "My son, why were you vexed with me? What have you found which is worthy of being considered an offence? You have imagined things which are not to be found in me, and which are not creditable to yourself. Do you not know that it is written, 'Those that are whole have no need of a physician.' Only those who are in a very evil case have need of him. You, I can find whenever I wish, and if I myself do not comfort you, the brethren and the other fathers will do so. But this governor who has come to us is tightly bound to the Calumniator by means of the affairs of this world, and, having obtained respite for a brief space from the vain labour of his abominable servitude, he flees like a slave from his master and comes to be helped. Therefore it would not seem likely to leave him, and to be constant in attention to you, for you are at all seasons occupied with the cultivation of your life."

Having said these things I entreated him to forgive me, and I became certain in my mind that he was a spiritual man. Then with a smile, he patted my left cheek with his right hand, and said to me, "Many temptations will rise up for you to endure, and moreover, for many years past you have struggled to go forth from the desert, and you struggle even to this day, but you have been afraid; and the causes of it, which were thought by you to arise from the fear of God, has the evil himself sowed in your mind; and although you drove away your thought from you, you have kept him with you. For he sowed in you the thought of desire, which was also pleasant to you, that is to say, you did care greatly to bring out of the world your father and also your sister that they might take upon themselves the garb of the monastic life. There still remain to your father, seven other years of life, therefore continue to abide in the desert, and do not on account of these thoughts desire to go to your kinsfolk, for it is written, 'No man who has put his hand on the ploughshare and looks back is useful to the kingdom of heaven.'"

Therefore, being helped by these words whereby I triumphed, I gave thanks and praise to God Who had quieted and laid to rest in me the cause which was urging me to go forth from the desert. Then afterwards he said to me with a smile, "Do you wish to become a bishop?" I said to him, "I have already been made one"; and he said to me, "Where?" Then I answered and said to him, "I am the bishop of the public eating-houses, and of the taverns, and of tables, and of wine-pots, for I am a visitor of them. If the wine has gone sour, I know enough to observe it, and that which is fit to drink, I drink. Similarly I visit the cooking pot and if it needs salt, or any seasoning whatsoever, I season it with sauces and then I eat of it. For this, that is to say, my visiting, is my episcopate, and it is the love of the belly and gluttony which has made me the visitor of these." And with a smile, he said to me further, "Quit these words of jesting, bishop hood must call you, and then you have to labour and to be troubled greatly. If you wish to flee from tribulations and temptations, do not go away from the desert, for in the desert no man will make you a bishop."

When I had departed from him, I came to the desert, that is, to my place in which I dwelt, and having related these things to the blessed fathers, who after two months went and held intercourse with him, I forgot his words. Three years afterwards I fell sick with a sore sickness which was caused by my kidneys and stomach. I was sent to Alexandria by the brethren who believed that I was collecting water (i.e., becoming dropsical), and the physicians counselled me to leave Alexandria, and for the sake of the climate, to go to Palestine, where the climate was temperate and light and would be beneficial to my body. From Palestine, I went to Bithynia, where, for what reason I do not know, whether by the care and solicitude of men, or whether by the Will of God, Who is exalted above all things, I was held to be worthy of the laying on of hands for the episcopacy, which was far above my deserts, and I became an associate in the temptation which rose up against the blessed John Chrysostom, Bishop of Constantinople.

Having been secluded for a period of about eleven months in a dark cell I remembered that blessed man who had told me of the things which had happened to me before they came to pass. Now the blessed man John related the things to me, according to my opinion, that by means of the narrative he might incite my mind and bring me to continue to dwell in the desert; and he said to me, "Behold, I have passed forty eight years in this cell, and I have never seen the face of a woman during the whole time, and no man has either seen me eat or drink."

The handmaiden of Christ, Poemenia, came to the blessed man and begged that she might see him, but the blessed man would not allow her to do so. He sent her more spiritual words to give her consolation. He commanded her that when she was going down from Thebaid, she should not turn aside to Alexandria, saying that if she did so, she would certainly fall into temptations. But Poemenia, forgetting this advice and never letting it enter her mind again, turned aside to Alexandria that she might see the city. On the way, by the side of the city Nicius, she stopped her ship so that she might rest herself. When her servants had disembarked, through some untoward circumstance, strife broke out between them and the people of the country were hostile men. They cut off a finger of one believing man, and killed another. Without knowing it, they drowned the holy Bishop Dionysius in the river. They made the venerable woman endure many reviling and threatened to do much violence to her. They beat all her servants with many severe stripes, and they would hardly allow them to proceed on their way.

DAY 41

Possidonius

THE THINGS WHICH ARE NARRATED concerning the holy man Possidonius the Theban are so many that it is impossible to describe them all. He was so gentle, gracious, patient, enduring, and his soul had so much goodness in it that I do not know that I ever met another man who was like him. For, I lived with him in Bethlehem for a year. At the time, he was living beyond the Monastery of the Shepherds, which was close to the town. I observed in him many qualities of excellence, of which I will relate an example of one or two. He told me one day when I was living by the side of Porphyrites, "I have not spoken to a man for a whole year, and I have not heard the speech of one. I have not eaten bread, but the insides of palm leaves soaked in water and, whenever I could find it, wild honey. Once, however, the time came when these things failed me, and I was in sore tribulation because of it. I went forth from the cave that I might go to the habitations of men, and having journeyed the whole day, I was scarcely two miles distant from the cave. I turned and looked behind me, and I saw, as it were, a horseman whose appearance resembled that of a knight, and he had upon his head the similitude of a helmet, and thinking that he was a Roman, I turned back to the cave, and I found outside it a basket of grapes and new, ripe figs, and I took them and went with them into the cave rejoicing; and that food sufficed to be a consolation to me for a period of two months."

The blessed man wrought in Bethlehem the following miracle. A certain woman had conceived, and was possessed by an unclean spirit. Being near to the bringing forth of her child, she was greatly afflicted by birth pangs and was violently tortured by that spirit. As she was writhing because of the workings of that devil, her husband came and entreated the holy man to go and pray over her. We went into her house so that we might pray together. Having stood up and prayed, after he had knelt down twice, he cast out that unclean spirit. When he stood up, he said to us, "Pray, for immediately the devil shall go away." But there was a certain sign, the fulfillment of which he wished to show us, and therefore when that happened, the devil had gone forth. He overturned the whole of the courtyard wall to its very foundations. That woman had not spoken a word for a period of about six years. After that devil had gone forth, she brought forth her child and spoke.

Moreover, I also saw an example of the prophecy of this blessed man. There was a certain elder, whose name was Hieronymus, who dwelt in these parts. He was exceedingly well versed in the art and practice of grammar and eloquence. He was greatly skilled in the Latin language. But he possessed the vices of envy and evil-eyedness to such a degree that the excellence of his very great skill and ability was entirely hidden. The blessed man Possidonius had dwelt with him for many days, and he told me that the free woman Paula, who had taken care of him, departed from this world before her time in order that she might escape from his envy. According to my opinion, it was on account of this man that none of the holy men would live in these districts. The envy of this man continued to such a degree that it overtook his own brother, which took place even as he had foretold. He also persecuted the blessed man Oxyperentius, who came from Italy, the wonderful men, Peter the Egyptian and Simeon, who were seen by me. Possidonius the Great himself told me that for the whole period of forty years, he had not tasted food made of bread, and that wrath against any man did not abide with him as long as half of the day.

Chronius of the Village of Phoenix

THERE WAS A CERTAIN MAN WHOSE NAME WAS CHRONIUS, who came from the village which was called Tomarta (i.e. Phoenix) which was near the desert. When he had gone away a little distance from human habitations, and had departed from his village, having measured out along the road with his right foot about fifteen thousand paces, he prayed and dug in that spot a pit, and he found there good and sweet water. The well was about seven fathoms in depth; and he built there a little habitation in which to dwell, and from the day in which he shut himself up in that place, he prayed to God that he might never return to a region inhabited by men. When he had dwelt there some few years, he was esteemed worthy to become a priest to the brotherhood, for there were gathered together to him about two hundred brethren. These excellent things are said concerning him: during the whole period of sixty years, in which he was performing the ministrations of the altar, he never once went out of the desert, and that he never ate bread which he had not earned by the labour of his hands.

DAY 42

James the Lame (and Paphuntius Cephala)

BY THE SIDE OF THIS CHRONIUS, who is mentioned above, there used to dwell a certain man who was called James the Lame, and he was an exceedingly learned man; now both of these men knew the blessed Anthony. It came to pass one day that there happened to be there also Paphnutius, who is described as a man who watered gardens by machines, and who possessed the gift of knowledge to such a degree that he knew how to expound the Books of the Old and New Testaments without reading from them. He was such a gentle man that his meekness overcame the gift of prophecy which was found with him. The former was voluntary, and the latter was an act of Divine grace. Of this man it was said that he possessed spiritual excellence to such a degree that for a period of eighty years, he did not own two tunics. When I and the blessed man Evagrius came to these men, we desired to learn the reasons for the stumbling of the brethren and for their transgressions against the strict rules of ascetic life. It came to pass in those same days that Chaeremon, the anchorite, departed from the world whilst he was sitting on his seat, holding his work in his hand.

It came to pass that another brother was buried by a fall of earth when he was digging a well. Another died of thirst and need of water as he was coming from Scete. In addition to these we wished to learn concerning the matter of Stephen, which ought not to be spoken about, for he fell into foul lasciviousness. We asked concerning Eucarpius, and those which concerned Hero the Alexandrian, the Palestinian, Ptolemy the Egyptian, who were in Scete. We were asking among ourselves the question, "What is the reason why men live lives of this kind in the desert, whereby some receive injury mentally, and some are ensnared by lasciviousness?" Paphnutius, the man of great learning, made an answer to us in the following words, saying, "All the various things which take place in the world must be divided into two categories, for some happen through the direct Will of God, and others by His permission only. The things which are wrought to the praise of God, especially happen by the direct desire of God, but all those which appertain to loss, and danger, and to matters which produce tribulation take place by the permission of God. Permission arises from a fault on the part of the mind.

For it is impossible for the man who thinks rightly to fall into foul sins, or into the error which arises from the devils, for all of these, to take place through a corrupt intent, or disposition, and through the love of the approval of the children of men, and by the daring of the thoughts, which hope to make perfect spiritual excellence. Such men fall into reprehensible wickedness, and God permits them so to do, that they may be a help to others, that when they feel the difference which has come upon them through this permission, they may remember themselves and may turn again to spiritual excellence, either that which exists in the mind, or that which exists in deeds. Sometimes it is the mind which sins, that is to say, when that sin which takes place is committed with evil intent; and sometimes it is the deeds themselves which must be rejected, as, for example, when they are performed in a manner which is quite beyond everything which is right and seemly, and this latter case happens frequently.

Thus a man of lust will, with corrupt design, give alms to young women in order that he may fulfill his foul desire, even though at the beginning he may say, 'It is a beautiful act for us to offer help to the maiden who is an orphan, and alone in the world and in misery.' Again it may happen that a man may begin to do alms with a good and acceptable intent to those who are sick, or to those who have lost their riches and become poor, and that though he gives his gift in a niggardly manner, and may murmur at the expense and become angry, his motive in giving will be found to be a right one. The deed is not to be thought equal to the motive. For, it is right for the man who would show mercy to make his gift 'gladly and with a good eye.'"

They also spoke the following story: "There is a difference between the gifts, which exist in various souls. Some of them possess keenness of mind, and some of them find it exceedingly easy and simple to acquire the habits of ascetic self-denial, or to do that which is difficult for other souls to do; but when a man makes use of his gift of keenness of mind, without a good object for so doing, or when he exerts his faculty of performing things because it is easy for him to do so, or when men exercise the gifts which they have received, they do not ascribe, as would be right, the correctness of their spiritual excellences to God, but to their own desire, and to their own keenness of mind. Those to whom it is sufficient to perform fair works, are permitted by Divine Providence to be caught in a snare, either by filthy deeds or filthy passions, or by the contempt or by the disgrace which comes to them from the children of men, so that through the shame and the contempt which they receive from the multitude, they may little by little and by degrees, cast away their boasting of the spiritual excellence which they imagine they possess.

For he who is inflated and unduly exalted at the keenness of speech which he possesses, does not ascribe to God, as is right, such keenness, or the discovery of the knowledge which is from Him, but to his own training, amusingly, or to his own naturally keen disposition. Therefore does God remove from him the Angel of His Divine Providence, and the Angel being separated from him, this man is immediately vanquished by his Adversary, and he who was unduly lifted up in his keenness of mind and speech falls into lasciviousness, or into some kind of filthy passion, because he was unduly exalted. Because he was lifted up, and because the witness of chastity has separated himself from him, the things which are said by him become unworthy of credence, and those who fear God flee from the teaching of the mouth of the man who is in this condition. Even as they would flee from a fountain which is full of leeches, so that there may be fulfilled that which is written, 'To the sinner God says, "What have you to do with the Books of My Commandments? For, you have taken My Covenant, your mouth."'

For in very truth the souls of those who are moved by passions are like fountains of diverse kinds. The souls of gluttons and of those who live in impurity and drunkenness are like muddy springs. The souls of those who love money and are greedy are like wells which are full of frogs. And the souls of those who live in envy and pride, even though there be found in their nature a facility for receiving doctrine, are like wells which breed snakes, and which, even though their flow be continual, no man is able to drink because of the bitterness of their manners and habits. Because of this, the blessed man, David, asked and entreated God to give him three things: graciousness, knowledge, and instruction. For without graciousness, knowledge has no use, and if a man whose manner of life is thus, correct shall himself lift from off himself the cause of the permission from God, which is boasting, and shall take upon himself humility, and shall recognize his true capacity, and shall not, at the same time, exalt himself over any man, and shall confess and give thanks to God, the witness of knowledge will return to him again.

This is the behavior of spiritual excellence. For the spiritual words of a chaste mode of life do not permit to grow up together with them the parched spear grasses, and ears of corn which have been smitten by the drought, and which by reason of their appearance make men think they are full, whilst there is no flour of bread in them. Every lapse which takes place, either through the tongue, or through some feeling, or through some action, or through the whole body, takes place in proportion to the measure of a man's pride, and by the permission of God, Who shows compassion upon those who commit themselves to His Divine Providence. For if, in addition to their skill in ordering their speech and their keenness of nature, the Lord was also to testify to the beauty of their words by never permitting them to fall, the arrogance with which they would exalt themselves in impurity would probably surpass that of the devils.

The following also did these men of the house of Abba Paphnutius say to us: "When you see evil deeds and acts, that is to say, the conversation of him who leads an evil life and know that they are fair and exceedingly plausible, remember the Devil who, as we learn from the Holy Scriptures, spoke with Christ. Also the testimony which says, 'Now the serpent was the most subtle of all the serpents which were on the earth.' That it was by reason of his subtlety that destruction came upon him, because he possessed no quality of excellence, which attached itself closely to his cunningness. For it is necessary that the believing man, who fears God, should ponder upon that which God gives to him. Let him speak that which he meditates, and let him do that which he speaks. For if to the asseveration of words there be not attached a brotherhood in acts and deeds, it is bread without salt, which cannot be eaten, lest digestion be disturbed, even as the blessed man Job said, 'Can the thing which is insipid be eaten without salt? Or, is there any taste in the juice of the ox tongue plant?'

Even these polished words possess no savor at all unless they are made complete by works. Therefore there is one kind of permission which hides spiritual excellence in order that it may be revealed, as, for example, that of Job concerning which God made known when He said to him, 'Do not blame My judgment, and do not think that I have done these things to you for any other reason than that it might be known that you are righteous. You were known to me because I see secret things, but you were not revealed to the children of men, because they thought that you did care exceedingly for riches that you might make perfect my pleasure. It was for this reason that I brought upon you the trial of stripping you of your riches so that I might show them your gratitude towards me, and your patient endurance.'

There is another kind of permission which God gives in order to drive out pride, as in the case of Paul, for the blessed Paul was permitted by means of distractions and a goad. He fell into diverse tribulations, and said, 'There has been given to me a goad in my flesh, a messenger of Satan,' to buffet me so that I may not be unduly exalted, lest through the superfluity of the revelations, and signs, and gratifications of the spirit, and prosperity and honors which were found with him, he might become lax and fall into arrogance. The paralytic was permitted because of sin, even according to what our Redeemer said to him, 'Behold, you are whole; sin no more.'

Judas was permitted because he held money in greater esteem than life. Because of this he hanged himself. Esau was permitted, and he fell into filthy desire because he honored the dung of the bowels more than the divine birthright. Therefore, because the blessed Paul understood these things, he did say concerning men, 'Because they have not decided within themselves that they will know God, He has delivered them over to an empty understanding so that they may work that which is unseemly.' Concerning other men who think that the knowledge of God is in them, together with the corrupt mind which they possess, he said, 'Because they have known God, and have not praised Him as God, and given thanks to Him, He has delivered them over to the passions of disgrace.' Here from these things it is necessary that we should know that it is impossible for a man to stumble and fall into filthy desire without the permission of the Providence of God.

DAY 43

Solomon

I WENT ABOUT IN ARITINOE, OF THE THEBAID for a period of four years, and I learned the system of religious houses which were there; for about twelve hundred men dwelt by the side of the city, worked with their hands, and lived the life of spiritual excellence. Among these, there were a number of solitary monks who shut themselves up in caves, and among them was one who was called Solomon; a chaste and humble man, and to him was given the gift of patient endurance. He used to say that he had passed fifty years in the cave, during which time he had fed himself by means of his labour, and he could repeat the Scriptures by heart.

Dorotheos the Priest

THERE WAS DOROTHEOS, A PRIEST, who used to live in a cave, and he possessed more goodness than many men, and led a spiritual life of high excellence. He had been held worthy of consecration to the priesthood. He performed the offices of it for the brethren who dwelt in the caves. To this blessed man, Melania the Less, the kinswoman of Melania the Great, concerning whom we are about to speak later, sent five hundred darics and begged him to spend them on behalf of the brethren who were there. He only took three of them, and sent the remainder to the wandering monk Diocles, a man of knowledge and understanding, saying, "O our brother Diocles, you are wiser than I am; I am not equal to spending these." Having taken them, Diocles was able to spend them wisely on those whom he knew of a certainty to be in want.

Diocles

DIOCLES WAS ORIGINALLY ONE OF THOSE who were greatly skilled in grammar, but afterwards he became learned in philosophy. When he was twenty eight years old, he was called by the Grace of God, and he departed and removed himself from the house of instruction, and delivered himself over to the promise of Christ. Having dwelt in caves for thirty five years, he said to us, "The mind which removes itself from the meditation of God falls into lust." He used to say that lust was that of a savage, animal, and bestial character, for he said to us, "The mind which falls away from the meditation of God, becomes either a devil or a beast." We asked him to explain this saying to us, and he said, "The mind which makes itself to be remote from the contemplation of God must be delivered over either to the devil of lust, who leads it into lasciviousness, or to the evil devil of wrath, from which are produced animal passions." He said, "The feeling of lasciviousness is a bestial thing, but the feeling of wrath appertains to the devil." Making an answer, we said to him, "How is it possible for the human mind to be with God continually and uninterruptedly?" He said, "The mind of that soul which lives in the thought or deed of the fear of God, no matter what it may be, is with God."

Kapiton

BY THE SIDE OF THIS MAN THERE USED TO DWELL KAPITON, a man who had been formerly a thief, and he had lived in holes in the rocks for fifty years, at a place which was about four miles from Antinoe. He never went down from his cave, not even to the river Nile, for he used to say that he was unable to meet in the congregation of the children of men that still fought with him, namely, his Adversary.

The Monk who Fell

BY THE SIDE OF THESE BLESSED MEN, I SAW A MAN who also had made himself remote from the world, and he dwelt in holes in the rocks even as they did. This man was mocked by the devil of vainglory, and by the visions which he saw, and was deluded by things which appeared to approach him and then wandered away. He was lacking in mind, even as it is written, "Being exalted in his dreams, he pastures spirits and pursues after a shadow." He was chaste in his body, perhaps owing to the length of his years, or through vainglory, yet through the matters of spiritual excellence, he destroyed his understanding, and he was corrupted by empty and polluted glory, and because of this, he departed from the straight road of the ascetic life.

DAY 44

Ephraim

A CERTAIN MAN AMONG THE HOLY FATHERS saw in a dream the company of the holy angels who came down from heaven by the commandment of God, and one of them held in his hand a roll which was written on the inside yet oil on the outside; and the angels said to each other, "Who is fit to be entrusted with this thing?" Then some of them mentioned one man and others another, and others answered and said, "Assuredly those whom you mention are holy, and righteous, but they are not sufficient to be entrusted with this thing." Having reckoned up many names of Saints, they finally said, "No man is fit to be entrusted with this thing; except Ephraim." Then they gave the roll to him. When he had stood up in the morning, he heard that they were saying; "Behold, Ephraim teaches, and his words flow from his mouth like water from a fountain." Then the old man who had seen the vision knew within himself that the things which were proceeding from his lips were of the Holy Spirit.

Therefore, this Ephraim, who was one of those who had been held worthy of mention by the saints, travelled along the spiritual road, nobly and straight, turning neither to one side nor the other; and he was held to be worthy of the gift of knowledge which he possessed naturally, and subsequently he received the knowledge which enabled him to utter divine things, and perfect blessedness. Thus, he lived throughout the period of a certain number of years, a life of chastity, and stern asceticism, and contemplation, and edified all those who thronged to visit him, each according to his peculiar needs.

Finally he compelled himself to go forth from his cell for the following reason, namely, a mighty famine lay over the city of Edessa. For having compassion on the creatures of the human race which were perishing and being destroyed, he spoke to those who were heaping up grain in the store houses, for he saw that they were wholly without compassion, saying, "How long will you refuse to bring into your memories the loving kindness of God? How long will you allow your corruptible wealth to be the means of the accusation and condemnation of your souls?" Then they took counsel, and said to him, "There is no man whom we can trust to relieve the wants of those who are dying of hunger; for all the people are crafty and they act in a lying fashion concerning affairs of this kind."

Then Ephraim said to them, "What manner of man do you imagine I am?" His character was held in the highest esteem by every man in the city, and every man knew that he acted according to the truth and not falsehood. The people said to him, "O man, we know that you are God." He said to them, "Put your trust in me, then, and give me the means of relieving this distress, for behold, for your sake, I will set myself apart to become the keeper of a house for receiving strangers."

He took money, and he began to fence off places which were

suitable for his purpose, and he provided with great care three hundred beds, some of which were intended for use in the burial of those who were dying, and others were intended for those who, it was thought, would live; and, in short, he brought in from the villages which were outside the city all those whom famine had stricken, and put them to bed, and every day he performed for them with the greatest possible solicitude the constant service of which they were in need, paying for the same with the money which came to him, and he rejoiced by means of those who supported him in the matter.

It came to pass that, when that year of famine had been fulfilled, and there arrived after it a year of abundance, and every man departed to his house, inasmuch as he had nothing else to do he went into his cell; and after a period of one month he brought his life to a close, God having given him the opportunity whereby he might be crowned at the end of his life. He left behind him many books, and writings of various kinds, which were worthy of being preserved with the greatest care. It is said concerning him that when he was a youth he saw a dream, that is to say a vision, in which a vine grew up out of his tongue, and it increased in size, and filled the whole of the space which was beneath the heavens, and was laden with grape clusters in rich abundance; and all the feathered fowl of the heavens came and ate of the food of it, and all the time they were eating the grape clusters which were increasing both in number and size.

DAY 45

Innocent the Priest

CONCERNING THE MATTERS OF THE BLESSED PRIEST INNOCENT, who lived in the Mount of Olives, I think that you must have heard from many people, but you may also learn from us, not a few things, for we lived with him for a period of three years. Now therefore this man was exceedingly simple, and he was one of the nobles of the palace in the kingdom of the Emperor Constantine. He withdrew himself from the partnership of marriage, but he had a son whose name was Paule, who served in the household of the Emperor. This son was caught in a transgression with the daughter of a certain priest, and Innocent was exceedingly angry with him.

Then Innocent made an entreaty to God, saying, "O Lord, give him a spirit that will not find time to sin in lust of the body," for he thought that it would be better for his son to be delivered to a devil rather than to fornication. This actually came to pass, and the youth lives to this day, in the Mount of Olives, loaded with irons, and admonished by a devil. This man Innocent, the father of Paule, because he was of a most merciful disposition, though if I were to tell the whole truth I should say that he appeared to me to be lacking in sense; on very many occasions he stole things and hid them from the brethren, and gave them to those who were in want. But he was a simple man and had no wickedness in him; and he was held to be worthy of the gift of the possession of power over devils.

For a certain maiden, in whom was a devil, came to him, and whilst we were looking at her, the devil struck her, and threw her down upon the ground and made her body writhe and twist about. When I saw this, I wished to dismiss that maiden in order that she might go to her mother, because, on account of the cruelty of that devil, I thought she could never be healed. Whilst I was pondering those things, the old man, Innocent, came, and he saw her mother standing, and weeping, and tearing her face with her nails, and plucking out her hair, because of the contortions of her daughter. When, therefore, that blessed old man saw her, his mercy revealed itself because he was grieved on account of her tribulation, and he took the maiden, and went into his martyrium, which he himself had built, and in which was preserved a blessed relic of Saint John the Baptist. Having prayed there and made supplication to God from the third to the ninth hour, he gave the maiden back to her mother, and she was healed on that day, and he drove away from her the devil and his struggles with her.

A certain old woman lost a sheep and came to him weeping about it. He took her and said, "Show me the place where you lost it." They came, therefore, to a place, which was near the grave of Lazarus, where he stood up and prayed. Certain boys had stolen the sheep and had already killed it. Innocent, having prayed, and the boys being unwilling to confess that the flesh of the sheep was buried in a vineyard, a raven suddenly appeared, which had taken a piece of flesh from the carcass, and stood over the place where it was. When the old man saw this, he perceived that the sheep was buried there. Then those boys fell down and did homage to him. They confessed that they had taken the sheep, and paid the price of it to its mistress.

DAY 46

Elpidius

IN THOSE CAVES WHICH, IN ANCIENT TIMES, certain men had hewn out of the rock in the valley of the river near Jericho, in which those who had fled from before Joshua, the son of Nun, had gone up and hidden themselves, there dwelt Elpidius. He was a Cappadocian, who had been converted in the monastery of Timothy the Chorepiskopos. He was a wonderful man and was also held to be worthy of consecration to the priesthood. He came and dwelt in one of these caves, and he showed such patient persistence in his self-abnegation, that he surpassed and eclipsed many thereby. He followed for twenty five years his rule of life, and during that time he only ate food on the Sabbath day, and on the First Day of the week, and he dwelt like the chief and the king of the bees among the cells of the whole brotherhood. He used to rise up continually during the night and pray; and I myself also dwelt with him. He made that mountain to be so peaceful and to contain so many inhabitants that it resembled a city. During the night season, a man might see the various works, and the labours of all kinds which appeal to the ascetic life, being performed there.

One night, when this man Elpidius was reciting the service, now we were with him, a scorpion stung him, and he crushed the insect, without either leaving the place where he was or being in any way moved as a man usually is when he is suffering from the sting of a scorpion. One day as he was holding in his hand a vine branch, a certain brother took it from him; and as he was sitting by the side of the mountain, he dug a hole and pushed the vine branch into it, like a man who is planting vine. Although it was not the time for planting, the vine branch sprouted, and grew very large, and spread its branches abroad until it covered the whole church. The name of that brother was Enesius, a wonderful man.

Eustathius

EUSTATHIUS WAS A BROTHER OF ELPIDIUS whom we have mentioned above, and this man followed so strenuously after the acquisition of impassibility, and made his body so dry (i.e. emaciated) by the labours of vigilant prayer, that the light of the sun could be seen between his ribs. Of him the following story is told by the brethren who were continually with him, that is to say by his disciples: "He never turned himself towards the west, because close by the side of the door of his cave was a mountain which, because of its mighty bulk, was very hard to ascend; and he never looked at the sun after the sixth hour of the day, because the door of his cell was hidden by the shadow of the mountain, so long as the sun was declining towards its place of setting. Moreover he could never see those stars which appear in the western part of the sky, and for twenty five years, from the time when he entered the cave in which he dwelt, he never went down from the mountain."

DAY 17

Sisinnius

THIS HOLY MAN ELPIDIUS HAD A CERTAIN DISCIPLE whose name was Sisinnius, who was a slave by birth, though a free man in the faith. By race he was a Cappadocian, and it is necessary that we should make known the fact that he was so, for the sake of the glorifying of Christ, Who has made us worthy to be accounted His kinsmen, and to be exalted to that true family, which is full of happiness, of the kingdom of heaven. When this man, Sisinnius, had passed some time with Elpidius, and had struggled to lead the ascetic life strenuously for a period of seven years, he at length, shut himself in a grave for three years. He endured such privations therein that neither by day nor by night did he sit or lie down, and he never went out here from. This man was held to be worthy of possessing the gift of authority over devils, and now that he has come into his own country, he has been held worthy of the gift of the priesthood. He has made congregations of men and women, which, according to a sure testimony, lead lives of purity and chastity. He has trampled upon the lust, which is in men, and he has bridled the voluptuousness of women, so that there has been fulfilled that which is written, "In Christ Jesus, there is neither male nor female." He was also a great lover of strangers and of voluntary poverty, which was a reproach to those who were rich and miserly.

Gaddai

I SAW A CERTAIN OLD MAN WHOSE NAME WAS GADDAI, who lived without shelter all his days in the places, which were by the side of the Jordan. On one occasion the Jews rose up against him in fierce hatred by the side of the Dead Sea, and they drew the sword against him, and one of them took up a weapon to smite him. The man who dared to lift up a sword against the blessed man, had his hand wither immediately, and the sword itself fell upon the ground.

Elijah

THERE WAS IN THIS PLACE A SOLITARY MONK CALLED ELIJAH who used to dwell in a cave, and he passed his life in performing the works of spiritual excellence, and was worthy of praise. One day, a great many of the brethren thronged to him; now his dwelling place was a cave. He lacked bread, and he apologized to us because he was troubled on account of the insufficiency of the bread. Therefore, when the brethren went into his cell, they found three loaves of bread, and when twenty men had eaten and were satisfied, there still remained one loaf which, one said, satisfied him for twenty five days.

Sabas, the Layman of Jericho

THERE WAS A CERTAIN LAYMAN FROM JERICHO whose name was Sabas, and he had a wife. This man loved the monks so much that during the night season, he used to go round about in the desert, and pass by the cells of the solitary monks there, and outside the cell and habitation of each one of them, he would set down a bushel of dates and vegetables. One day, as he was carrying along a load of food for the usual needs of the monks, through the operation of the evil, who is the adversary of the monks, a lion met him, which terrified him, and wished to make him to cease from his ministrations to those holy men. And the lion having overtaken him about a mile from the place where the monks were, and having seized him by his hand, in order to turn him aside from his business, He Who by the hand of Daniel shut the mouths of the lions, shut the mouth of this lion also. The beast did not harm this lover of alms. Although the lion was exceedingly hungry, he only took a very little of the things which Sabas was carrying for the old men, and then departed. It is manifest that He Who gave this man his life, also satisfied the hunger of the lion.

Serapion of the Girdle

AGAIN THERE WAS A CERTAIN BLESSED MAN whose name was Serapion, who was called "Serapion of the girdle," because during his whole life, he neither put on nor was clothed with anything except the girdle with which he was girt about. He led a life of the strictest self-denial and poverty. Though he was a wholly unlearned man, he could repeat all the Scriptures by heart. And because of the greatness of his self-denial and the repetition of the Scriptures, he was unable to live in a cell, because he could not make use of anything which belonged to this world. But he went roundabout at all seasons and taught the multitudes, and he sold himself voluntarily. He preached, and taught, and turned many people to God. And this form of self-denial was of his own choosing, and it was by such means as this that he made his preparation for heaven.

There are many ways of leading a stern life of self-denial. Many of the venerable fathers relate concerning him that on one occasion, he took a fellow monk, who sold him to some comic actors for twenty dinars in a city of the heathen. And having received these dinars, he tied them up in a bag and sealed them, and kept them carefully. Then he became subject to and ministered in all humility to those actors who had bought him until he had taught them and made them Christians. He freed them from following the business of the theatre. And he never ate anything except dry bread and water, and his mouth never once ceased from uttering the words of the Scriptures.

The man who was the master of the actors was the first to become converted and enlightened by the word of God. Next was his wife, and finally their whole house was converted. During the first years after the actors had bought him, and when they did not know who he was, he used to wash their feet with his hands, and having taught them and baptized them, he made them remote from their occupation in the theatre, and they led a God fearing life in all righteousness. They held him in reverence, honoured him, and marvelled at his radiant life. Finally they said to him, "Come, O our brother, we will set you free from this servitude, even as you have set us free from the slavery of heathenism." Then he answered and said to them, "Since God has helped me, and your souls have been set free and they have life, I will tell you my story.

I undertook this kind of work in order that your souls might have life. By race, I am an Egyptian, and a free man but I am a monk vowed to self-denial and poverty, and for the sake of our Lord, I sold myself to you in order that your souls might be set free from the impurity of this world. Since now, our Lord has worked through my meekness, and your souls live. Take your gold, and I will go to another place, so that I may be able to benefit others also." They begged and entreated him, saying, "Remain with us, you shall be to us a father, a master, and a director." But he would not hearken to their entreaty. Again they answered him saying, "Give the gold to the poor, and let it be a pledge of life for us; and we entreat you to see us if it be only once a year."

This man, having gone roundabout, came to Hellas, and stayed in Athens three days, and no man gave him a morsel of bread. Now he carried nothing with him, neither purse, nor wallet, nor head-cloak, nor anything whatsoever. When the fourth day had come, he became exceedingly hungry. He went and stood up upon a certain high place where all the freemen of the city were gathered together, and he began to clap his hands, and to cry out with a loud voice, saying, "O men of Athens, send help." At the sound of his voice, they all marvelled, and the freemen and the soldiers ran to him, saying to him, "What ails you? Where did you come from? What has happened to these?" Then he said to them, "By race I am an Egyptian, and being a long way from my true country, I have fallen into the hands of three creditors; now two of these have departed from me, having taken that which was theirs, and now they have no debt against me about which to chide me, but the third will not leave me."

The philosophers made enquiries of him who these creditors were, and they said to him, "Show us who your creditors are, who is afflicting you, and we will entreat them to desist; show us who they are, so that we may help you." He answered and said to them, "From my youth up, the love of money, and fornication, and the appetite of the belly have oppressed me; from the first two of these, that is, the love of money and fornication, I have been freed, and they no longer oppress me, but I am wholly unable to set myself free from the appetite of the belly. Behold, it is now the fourth day since I have eaten anything and the belly constrains me, for it demands that which is its usual debt, and unless this debt be paid, I shall not be able to live."

Then certain philosophers thought that he had schemed this crafty device in order that he might gain some benefit, and one of them took a dinars and gave it to him, and having taken it, he spent part of it in buying bread in their presence; and he took one loaf of bread, and straightaway departed from the city, and did not come back to it again. Thus the philosophers knew that he was indeed a wonderful man, and they paid the price of the loaf of bread which he had taken, and received back the dinars.

Having departed to another city, he heard there concerning a certain other man, who was the chief of the whole city, and who was a Manichaean, with all his house, and who had several associates in the city. Then the monk, according to his former plan, sold himself to this Manichaean, and in two years, he was able to turn this man and his wife from their error, and to bring them into the Catholic Church. After they had learned what he did, they never again regarded him a slave, but they honoured him as a father, and as a master, and they ascribed praise to God.

Once he was determined to go to Rome. He embarked in a ship which was going there, so that he might go with them (i.e., with the sailors). When the sailors of the ship saw that he boldly embarked in the ship carrying nothing with him, neither bread, nor anything else, nor provisions for the journey, they thought that one of their number must have taken his baggage and placed it in the ship. Because of this thought, they received him unquestioningly. Having embarked, when the sailors had sailed from Alexandria, a distance of about five hundred stadia, each one of those who were sitting in the ship began at the time of sunset to eat, and the sailors also ate in their presence.

They observed that the monk did not eat on the first day and thought that he did not do so because of seasickness, and thus also was it on the second day, on the third day, and on the fourth day. On the fifth day, whilst all those who were on the ship were eating their meal, he sat in his place and was silent. They were looking at him and said, "Why do you not eat?" He replied, "I have nothing to eat." They began to make enquiries and to cry out among themselves, "Who among you has taken his things, or his provisions for the way?" When they saw that no man had taken anything from him, they began to argue with him, and said to him, "O man, how is it that you have embarked on the ship without provisions and money? Where will you obtain the money to give us for your passage?" He said to them, "I have not thought about it altogether, for an Egyptian has no anxious care about anything. Carry me back where you took me and cast me out if you wish."

Even if he had given them one hundred dinars they would not have been able to take him back to Alexandria. He therefore remained on the ship. They fed him until he arrived in Rome. Having come to Rome, he made enquiries and learned what monk or nun was there, and he found Rumnin (or Domnin), the disciple of Evagrius, whose bed, after his death, cured every kind of sickness. Having seen him and spoken with him, he was greatly edified by him, for he was a man who was greatly skilled in the labours of the ascetic life, and in speech, and in knowledge, and he learned from him what monk and nuns were in Rome, in order that he might see them.

The venerable fathers relate concerning him, that he once heard that there was in the city of Rome a certain nun who led a life of the strictest seclusion. She had never seen a man, and used to think that she was perfect. This blessed man threw himself into a ship and came to Rome. Having learned where she lived, he went and spoke with the old woman who ministered to her, and said to her, "Get in and say to the virgin, I desire to see you most eagerly, because God has sent me to you." And he waited two days and then saw her. When he saw her he said, "Sit down." She said to him, "I will not sit down, but will depart." He said to her, "Where are you going?" She said to him, "To God." He said to her, "Are you living or dead?" She said to him, "I believe, by God, that I am dead, for whoever lives in the body is not able to depart from it?" He said to her, "If you are dead, as you say, do that which I do." She said to him, "Tell me what can happen, and I will do it." Again he said to her, "To one who is dead to the world it is easy to do everything except commit sin." He further said to her, "Come down, and get out of your house." She said to him, "I have not gone out of it for twenty five years, why should I go out of it now?" He said to her, "If you are indeed dead to the world, and the world is dead to you, it is the same thing to you whether you go forth or do not go away; come, get out." She went out.

After she had gone out, she followed him to a certain church, and he said to her in the church, "If you wish me to believe that you are dead to the world and are not alive, in order that you may be pleasing to the children of men, do what I do, and then I will believe you, and I shall know that you are a dead woman, even as you say." She said to him, "Tell me what it is necessary for me to do, and I will do it." Then he said to her, "Cast off your garments and put them on your head, and walk through the midst of the city, and I will do likewise, and will go in front of you in this guise." The nun said to him, "I should offend many folks by such a remarkable act as this, and then they would say, 'This woman has gone mad, and has a devil.'" He said to her, "What need do you have to consider their words even if they should say, 'She has gone mad, and has a devil?' For, according to what you yourself say, you are a dead woman to them."

The nun said to him, "If there be anything else except this, tell me, for I cannot come to such a measure of disgrace as this." Then he said to her, "Do not imagine in your mind that you are more perfect than anyone else, or that you are dead to the world; for I am far more dead to the world than you are, and I can show you that I am indeed so, and that I can boldly do this thing without feeling shame or disgrace." Having broken her spirit and humbled her pride, he departed from her. There were many things of the same kind, which this same Serapion did in the world, for he despised both worldly shame and the glory, which passes away. He died at the age of sixty years, and was buried at a good old age, adorned with all virtues.

DAY 49

Eulogius

THE FOLLOWING STORY WAS RELATED TO ME BY CHRONIUS, the priest of Nitria, who said, "When I was a young man, I abhorred the monastery, and I fled from it, and from the head of the monastery who was my instructor, and having lost my way and gone roundabout, I came to the Monastery of Saint Anthony. He used to dwell between the mountains of Babylon and Herakleia, in a parched desert which led to the Red Sea, about thirty miles from the river Nile. I was there in that monastery in which dwelt those disciples of his, who buried him when he died, now their names were Macarius and Amatus, in a place which was called Espir.

I remained there for five days, so that I might be able to see the blessed Anthony, for they used to say that he was in the habit of coming to this monastery from the inner desert, once every five, or ten, or twenty days, as God directed and brought him, to give help to the souls who thronged into his monastery, and who awaited him there, in order that they might be relieved by him. The brethren also were assembled there and waited for him also, each one of them having his own individual matter to lay before him.

Among them was a certain man from Alexandria, whose name was Eulogius, and with him was another man, an Arian, whose body was destroyed (i.e. he was a leper), and they had come because of this matter. This man Eulogius was a scholar, and he was the most educated of all the learned men of this time, but the love of the living God had suddenly come into his mind. He made himself to be remote from the world and distributed all the money which he had among the poor. He left himself only a small sum which was just sufficient for his bodily needs, for he was unable to work or to enter into a monastery with many monks in it, and besides this lassitude was contending with him, and he sought a little companionship.

He went forth seeking to buy something which he wanted in the city, and he found in the market a certain man who was an Arian, whose whole body was destroyed. He had neither hands nor feet, but his tongue was sharp, and he employed it unsparingly upon every man whom he met. When Eulogius had seen him, and looked at him, he lifted up his eyes and his mind towards God, and he prayed and made this covenant between himself and God, saying, "O our Lord Jesus Christ, in Your Name, O my Lord, I will take this man, who is sick in his body, and I will relieve his wants all the days of my life, so that through him, my soul may live before You. I beseech You to give me power to endure in my ministering to him." After he prayed, he drew near to the man, and said, "I beseech you, O man, to let me take you to my house and to relieve your wants." The sick man said to him, "Why not?" Then Eulogius said to him, "I will therefore bring an ass, and carry you." He promised him saying, "I and he went and brought an ass and carried him to the place where he lived, and he took care of him with the greatest diligence." For a period of fifteen years, Eulogius relieved his wants with the greatest and most careful attention, and even washed him with his own hands. He did everything he could to alleviate the affliction of his sickness.

After fifteen years, a devil began to stir Arian, and Arian began to revile Eulogius, and to offer resistance to him. He cursed him and hurled after him insults and abuse, saying, "O you runaway slave, who has eaten your lord, you have stolen the riches of other folk and are spending them upon me, and you think to have life through me! Cast me out into the street, for I wish to eat flesh." Eulogius brought him flesh, and again he cried out, and said, "You will not persuade me to remain here by these means; I wish to go out into the street, and I desire to see the world. By Jupiter, carry me out and cast me where you did find me. If only I had hands, I would strangle myself." He spoke thus through the madness of the devil, which was with him.

Then Eulogius rose up and went to the neighbouring monks and said to them, "What shall I do? For this deformed man has brought me to despair. I would set him free, only I have given my right hand in covenant to God, and I am afraid to do so; but on the other hand, if I do not cast him out, he will bring upon me bad nights and bitter days. What to do with him?" They said to him, "Anthony the Great is still alive, go to him; take the man with you in a ship, go up to him, carry the man to his monastery, and wait there until he comes from the desert. Then tell him your business. Whatever word he shall say to you, you shall perform, for God shall speak to you through him." Then Eulogius was persuaded by them, placed the man in a small boat, and carried him to the monastery in which were the disciples of Anthony.

It came to pass that on the very day, after Eulogius had arrived there, that great man came from the inner desert to his disciples in the late evening, and he was clothed in his skin cloak. Whenever he came to his monastery, he was in the habit of calling out to his disciple Macarius, and saying to him, "O brother Macarius, have any brethren come this day from anywhere?" Macarius would say, "Yes." Then Anthony would say, "Are they Egyptians or Jerusalemites?" He had given Macarius this sign. When you see brethren who are simple and innocent, say they are Egyptians; but when you see brethren who are venerable and are skilled in speaking, say they are Jerusalemites. Therefore, according to his custom, Anthony asked Macarius, "Are they Egyptian brethren or Jerusalemites?" Macarius said, "They are neither Egyptians nor Jerusalemites." When Macarius would answer, "They are Egyptians," Anthony would say to him, "Cook them a mess of lentils that they may eat, and then dismiss them, and let them go in peace." He would say a prayer on their behalf, and would straightaway send them away. When Macarius would answer, "They are Jerusalemites," Anthony would sit down the whole night, and would converse with them to the benefit of their lives.

On that night he sat down, and called to them all, and he discoursed without any man having told him the name of one of them, and it was dark, and the night had come; and suddenly he cried out three times, thus, "Eulogius, Eulogius, Eulogius." And Eulogius the scholar did not answer a word, because he thought that Anthony was calling some other person. Again Anthony cried out to him, "To you I speak, O Eulogius, who has come from Alexandria." Then Eulogius said to him, "Master, what do you command me to do? Tell me, I beseech you." Anthony said to him, "Why have you come?"

Eulogius answered and said to him, "Let Him that has revealed to you my name, declare to you for what purpose I have come." Then Anthony said to him, "I know why you have come, nevertheless declare it before the brethren in order that they may hear." Eulogius answered and said to him, "I found this Arian in the street, and I gave the right hand to God (i.e. made a covenant with God), that I would minister to him, that I might live because of him, and he because of me. Behold I have ministered to him for the last fifteen years, and now, after all these years, he stirs himself up against me, and causes me tribulation, and I have had it in my mind to cast him out.

Therefore I have come to your holiness so that you may advise me what I should do, and that you may pray on my behalf, for I am greatly oppressed." Anthony said to him angrily in a hard voice, "If you send him away, He who created him will not send him away; if you do cast him out, God, Who is better and more excellent than you, will gather him to himself." When Eulogius heard these words he set a bridle on his mouth and was silent.

Having left Eulogius, Anthony came to chastise Arian for his tongue. Anthony cried out and said to him, "O you deformed Arian, you are worthy neither of heaven nor of earth. Will not you cease to contend against God? Do you not know that he who ministers to you is Christ? How can you dare to utter these words against our Lord? Was it not for Christ's sake that Eulogius gave himself to your service?" Then having made the man sorrowful, he ceased from Eulogius and the Arian, and spoke to all the brethren who were there, to every man according to his business. He called to Eulogius and the Arian and said to them, "Do not turn to any other place, but depart, do not separate yourselves from one another, and return to the cell in which you have lived so long a time, for behold God will send upon you your end. And behold, this trial has come upon you because the end of both of you is near, and because you are esteemed worthy of crowns. Therefore do not act in a contrary manner, and let not the angel come after you and not find you in your places, lest you be deprived of your crowns." So the two of them departed and came to their cell. In less than forty days Eulogius died, and in less than three days afterwards, Arian died.

This Chronius, who related to us the narrative of this matter, tarried for a time in the monasteries which were in the Thebaid, and came down to the monasteries which were in Alexandria. It happened that the brethren were gathered together commemorating the death of Eulogius after forty days, and the death of the Arian after three days. When Chronius heard, he marvelled, took down a Book of the Gospels, and set it down among the brotherhood. Then related what had happened; and he took an oath and said, "In all this affair, I was the interpreter for Saint Anthony because he did not know Greek; but I know both languages, and I acted interpreter for both sides, turning Greek into Egyptian for Eulogius, and Egyptian into Greek for Anthony."

DAY 50

Saint Mark, The Mourner

MACARIUS THE PRIEST TOLD US THE FOLLOWING STORY, "At the time when I was administering the Holy Offering, I took good heed to Mark the mourner, and I never gave it to him, but an angel did so from the altar. I saw, however, the palm of the hand of the angel who gave it to him."

This Mark was a young man, and he could repeat by heart the New and Old Testaments. He was meek beyond measure and both in body and in thought, he was purer than many.

Paul, the Prince of Monks and the Anchorite

CONCERNING ABBA PAULUS, THERE WERE QUESTIONS among the monks and anchorites who were living in the land of Egypt, and they asked who were the first monks who lived in the desert. Some of them remembered the saints of old time, and said, "It has been proved that the first to dwell in the desert were Saint Elijah the Prophet, and John the Baptist. It is manifest that Elijah was immeasurably superior in ascetic excellence to the other monks, yet John was proclaimed in the womb to be a prophet before he was born." There were many who contradicted this opinion and who asserted with firmness that Saint Anthony was the first, the prince of them all, and also of the order of monks.

However, if we wish to learn the whole truth, we shall discover that it was not Saint Anthony who was the first monk that dwelt in the desert, but the blessed man Saint Paul. For I myself have seen the disciples of Saint Anthony who buried him, and it was they who related to us the history of the man Paul the anchorite, the Theban, who was indeed the first monk to live in the desert. Therefore, we believe that it was not the blessed man Anthony who was the first to do this, as some men say, but Paul. For this reason, I wish to narrate briefly the history of Paul the anchorite, how he began and how he ended his career in the days of Decius and Valerianus, the persecutors, and how Cornelius made an end of the strife of his testimony for the sake of the Name of our Lord Jesus Christ in Rome.

This blessed man Paul dwelt with his sister, who was the wife of a certain man. Their parents died and left them great riches, when the blessed man Paul was sixteen years of age. He had been educated in the learning of the Greeks and the Egyptians. He was meek of soul, and he loved God thoroughly. When the persecution of the Christians waxed strong, he remained continually in one place, and he took care of himself at all seasons. The Avarice, which constrains the race of the children of men to commit evil deeds, did not cease from him, for his sister's husband, endeavoured most strenuously to give him up to the persecutors, and he neither had pity upon the tears of his wife nor did he fear the judgement of God.

He desisted not from this iniquitous conduct, but continued in his envy and sought always to give him up because he was a Christian. The wise young man, having comprehended his guilt and knowing that he was lying in wait for him, took to flight secretly. He went to a certain high mountain and changed his place of abode on account of the violence of the persecution. As he was living there, little by little he found out in the mountain a rock, in which was a large cave, which was shut in with a stone. Having lifted up the stone, he found within great repose, and he looked inside with great desire. He discovered that the cave was clean, and that the dust of the ground also was fair. He loved the place and dwelt there, and gave thanks to God who had given it to him for a dwelling-place. He lived in that mountain all the days of his life, and his food and his raiment were made of palm trees which were in the mountain. In order that no man may say, "How is this possible?" I take God and His holy angels to witness that we have seen many monks living in this fashion, and that they have brought their lives to an end in this way, and have not been afraid of Satan.

I must not, however, neglect the history of the blessed man Paul. This holy man lived a heavenly life upon the earth, in love to our Lord, for one hundred and thirteen years. Saint Anthony, who was ninety years old at the time, was living in another desert. Saint Anthony on one occasion told me the following, "I once thought within myself that there was no man living beyond me in the desert, and on the night wherein I pondered upon these things in my mind, it was revealed to me from God, by one who said to me, "Beyond you, in the desert, there is a man who is more excellent than you, and it is necessary that you should go and see him with all diligence, and with great joy."

When the morning had come, the blessed old man, Saint Anthony, took the palm branch upon which he leaned his weight, and he began to walk in the desert as his mind directed, because he did not know the way. When it was noon, although the heat of the sun was fierce and burning, the blessed old man did not turn aside from the way, but he said, "I believe that God will not withdraw His hands from me, but will show me His servant concerning whom He has sent me a revelation."

As he was thinking thus about him, he suddenly saw a man who possessed two natures, one half of him being that of a man, the other half being that of a horse, the poets call this being a centaur. Then the blessed Anthony called him and said, "I, a man of God, say to you, where do you dwell here?" The creature answered in a barbarous language with words of impurity, and his mouth was full of fear. The old man went on his journey seeking out the way. As Anthony was marvelling at this thing, the animal passed in front of him as if it were going to a broad field. Anthony knew that it was Satan who had taken the form of the creature in order that he might terrify the blessed man, and he wondered at the similitude of the form which he had seen in the animal.

Having passed on a little way further, he saw another animal, which was smaller in stature than the first one, he was standing on a rock, and had horns upon his head and on his forehead. When the blessed Anthony saw him, he put on the helmet of faith and took the shield of righteousness, and he asked him, "Who are you whom I see here?" The creature answered him saying, "I am a mortal man and one of those who are in the desert, whom the heathen call satyrs, and whom because of their error concerning them, they worship as a god." The beast having spoken these words, the old man Anthony went on his way, and his tears were flowing. But he rejoiced because of the glory of Christ, and because of the destruction of Satan, and he wondered within himself how he had been able to understand the words of the animal. He struck the ground with his staff and said, "Woe to Alexandria! Woe to the city of the heathen, in which are gathered together all the devils of all creation!"

Anthony went on his journey thinking anxiously how he could attain the end of it. He wished to find the servant of God. Whilst he was meditating what he should do and where he should go, he observed on the flat surface of the desert, the footprints of an animal, which had passed over the spot that very day. He meditated within himself, saying, "It is impossible for our Lord to forsake me." He journeyed on his way during the night with his prayers in his mouth continually. When the morning had come he saw a huge hyena, running with all its might up to the top of a mountain, and he followed in its footsteps and having ascended the mountain, he came near a cave. He saw the hyena going into it and he looked into the cave and saw perfect love, that is to say, Saint Paul, the old man. He cast away from him all fear and doubtful thoughts.

Looking into the cave, he saw that there was much light therein. He approached the door of the cave, and knocked it with a small stone. As soon as the blessed man Paul heard the sound of the knocking, he rolled the stone down quickly and closed the entrance of the cave. Anthony fell upon his face before the door of the cave and besought him to let him come in, saying, "I am alone." The blessed man Paul answered, saying, "Why have you come?" Anthony said, "I know that I am not worthy to see you. But since you received wild beasts, why do you hold the children of men in abhorrence? I have sought and have found thee, and I knocked with confidence; open then the door to me. If this may not be, I shall die here. When you see my dead body, bury it."

The blessed man Paul answered from within saying, "No man who is angry comes in, and no man entreats for admission and makes accusations." Then he spoke to him words of gladness. He opened the door to him, they met and embraced each other and kissed each other with holy kisses. Each man told his fellow his name.

After these things, the blessed man Paul made Saint Anthony sit by his side, and said to him, "Why did you cast upon yourself all this tribulation and the great labour of seeking to see an old man whose body is altogether withered and emaciated? After a short time you will see that I have become dust; but love overcomes all things. Tell me now what is the present condition of the race of the children of men, and whether they are still building houses in the ancient cities, and whether there are still kings in the world, and whether the governors of the world are still in subjection to the error of devils."

Having said these things to Anthony, the two of them looked and saw a raven sitting on the branch of a tree. Straightaway it stood up with great quietness upon the branch, and had in its beak a whole loaf of bread, which it came and laid it down between them, while both men were looking on. When the bird had departed, they both marvelled. The blessed Paul said to Saint Anthony, "Truly our Lord is merciful and pitiful in that He sends us a meal in this way. For behold, for sixty years, I have been in the habit of receiving from this bird half a loaf of bread daily, but at your coming, behold, our Lord has sent to us a double portion of food because we are His servants."

Then having given thanks to God, both men sat down at the table, and disputed with each other who should first break the bread. While they were disputing, the night came on. The two men took the bread, spread out their hands, broke the loaf in the Name of our Lord, and ate it. Having eaten, they stood up the whole night in prayer.

When the morning had come, Paul said to Anthony, "You must know, O my brother Anthony, that I have been living in the desert for a long time, and that it was our Lord Himself who revealed to me what manner of man you are. But because the time of my rest has come, and because that which I have been seeking, that is to say, that I should depart and be with our Lord, is about to overtake me, I could not go to see you. Now that my time has come to an end, and, as I believe, a crown of righteousness has been laid up for me, you have been sent by our Lord that you may bury my body in the ground."

While the blessed man Paul was saying these things, Saint Anthony was weeping with many tears and heavy sighs. Saint Anthony made supplication to him, saying, "O my beloved one, do not leave me here, but take me with you, wherever you go." The blessed Paul answered him, saying, "It is not right that you should seek your own advantage, but that of your neighbours. Therefore, O my beloved, I beseech you, if it be not a thing which is too hard for you, go quickly to your monastery, and bring here to me the cloak which Saint Athanasius the Bishop gave you." He did not speak such because he had need of any apparel, but because he wished to depart from his body whilst Saint Anthony was absent.

When Anthony heard concerning the Bishop and his cloak, he marvelled within himself. Having looked upon the blessed Paul, in our Lord Jesus, he bowed down before him, prayed and set forth to go on his journey. He approached and kissed him on his eyes and on his hands, made haste and went forth to depart to his monastery. Having made the journey and arrived at this monastery, his two disciples, who had been seeking him for a long time, met him, and they said to him, "O father, where have you been these days?" He answered them, saying, "Woe to me! Woe to me a sinner, for the name of Christian, which I bear, is only a borrowed thing. This day have I seen Elijah and John in the desert, for verily I have seen Paul in Paradise."

Saint Anthony struck with his hand on his breast, and took the cloak and went from his disciples, who besought him to reveal to them the whole matter. He said to them, "There is time to be silent, and time to speak." He departed and went forth on his way without taking any provisions with him. He made haste to come to the place where the blessed man Paul was, for he desired earnestly to see him again. He was afraid lest while he was yet afar off, Paul might deliver himself up to our Lord. He journeyed on his way the first day, but on the second day, at the time of the ninth hour, he saw along the road, in the air, a company of angels, a multitude of the Prophets, the Apostles, and Abba Paul, who was shining with light like the sun, was in their midst. He went up with them to heaven. Immediately he saw them and fell upon his face on the ground. Anthony sighed, wept, and cried out, saying, "O fearer of God, why have you left me thus? Why didn't you receive my salutation together with all the toil of this journey, which I have made as swiftly as a bird?"

Saint Anthony went on his way and arrived at the cave. He saw Abba Paul kneeling upon his knees, with his face gazing to heaven and his hands spread out. Seeing him thus, Saint Anthony thought within himself, and said, "Perhaps he is alive." He prayed fervently. The blessed Paul also stood up and prayed with him. When sometime had elapsed, he heard neither the sounds nor the sighs, which are customary in prayer, he knew that it was only the body of Abba Paul which prayed. He bowed down before God, in whom everything lives, and placed the body in the middle of the cloak, and wrapped it. He took it on his shoulders and though he sang Psalms, according to the custom of the monks, the blessed Anthony was greatly grieved because he had not remembered to bring with him a spade or some other instrument to dig a grave for the body. He meditated, saying, "What shall I do? If I go to my monastery and bring a spade, I cannot possibly return here in less than four days. O Jesus Christ let me die with Your beloved servant Paul."

As he was saying these things, behold, two lions came running along together. When he saw them, his whole body smoked with fear. When he had lifted up his mind to God and had looked at them again, they appeared to be doves flying through the air. The lions drew near and stood beside the body of the blessed Paul. They wagged their tails at the blessed Anthony, and crouched down before him in perfect tameness. They rubbed their teeth together and purred so loudly that the blessed man knew that they wished to be blessed, to be helped, and that they desired to know concerning the departure of the blessed Paul. After they had acted thus, the lions began to dig a grave, and they threw up the earth with their paws. They made the hole in the ground deep enough, wide enough, and long enough, according to the measure of the body. They lowered their ears and their tails, and bowed down their heads before Abba Anthony. They licked his hands and his feet. He knew that they wished to be blessed.

Then he gave thanks for the glory of God because even the wild and savage beasts knew how to help the good and chosen men of God, and he spoke thus, "O Lord God, without whose command not one leaf falls to the ground, and against whose will not one bird drops into the snare, do bless all of us." He brought his hand near the lions, and commanded them to depart. When the two lions had gone away, Anthony took the body and buried it in the customary way. After one day, he took the tunic of Abba Paul, which was made of palm leaves sewn together, like a true inheritance and a thing that brings privilege. Then he departed to his monastery. When he had arrived there, he related to the monks the whole matter in due order. On the feast of unleavened bread and at Pentecost, Saint Anthony used to put on the tunic of the blessed and holy man Paul, and would pray with it upon him.

I, Hieronymus the sinner, entreat all those who read this book to pray for me. In the text here comes the following note by some editor of Palladius. Concerning these histories of Paul, and of the company of Mark and of Macarius, there are some who say that they were compiled by Hieronymus because his name occurs at the end of them.

Here ends the History of Saint Paul, the Holy Man, the Firstborn of All the Desert Monks.

DAY 51

The Young Man who was an Alexandrian

THERE WAS A CERTAIN YOUNG MAN IN ALEXANDRIA, who the law of nature began to work for him, to make him possess knowledge to distinguish good from evil. He endeavoured by every means in his power to make himself a wholly stranger to things that were evil, and to cleave to those that were good. Having been trained for a long time, and proficient in the things which befit monks, he thought to himself: "Since there is no good reason whatsoever to compel me forcibly to remain in the city any longer, it is not right that I should do so." He was at all times reminding himself of the word which was spoken by our Lord to the rich man, "If you wish to be perfect, go and sell all what you have, give it to the poor, take your cross and come after Me." The young man said, "The word of our Lord is true, but it is impossible for a man to acquire that perfection which He spoke about, while living among men."

When he had made himself ready to perform in very deed this great thought, he began to journey along the road which leads to one of the deserts of Alexandria, where large numbers of monks used to dwell. He offered up prayer to God that God would prepare a way for him, and would direct him to a man who would be able to help him attain his object, and would lead him to the destiny he desires. He said within himself, "This shall be to me a sign that the Lord has prepared His way before me; the door where I shall knock, and where from shall go forth one who lives there, and shall receive me in peace, and shall urge me to go in to him, and shall receive me in love, that shall be the place, whom the Lord has prepared for the fulfilment of my thoughts concerning spiritual excellence."

He additionally said, "To the man who has been prepared by the Lord, it is right for me to be in subjection as to Christ, and I must hearken to his command willingly and unhesitatingly as to that of Christ." As he was saying these words, and was thinking deeply, he arrived in the desert into which he had set his face to go. Having gone in among the monasteries, he found himself by the dispensation of God, before the door of a habitation in which a certain old man dwelt. When, according to his expectation, he had drawn near, and knocked at the door, there came out an old man who dwelt inside. The old man opened the door, and when he saw the young man who was standing there, he saluted him gladly and entreated him to come inside.

After he had gone in and prayed, he sat down. The young man compared the things, which had taken place with those, which he had written down in his mind. Then, being full of gladness, the old man urged him repeatedly to partake of food. The young man answered saying, "My lord, I beseech your holiness to permit me first of all to speak openly, and to make known to your fatherly nature the reason for my coming. If through the working of God you will make yourself the perfection of my desire, and of my thoughts, whatever your holiness and meekness shall command me to do, I will perform strenuously."

When the old man had heard these things, he answered him, saying, "You have full power to say everything you wish, joyfully and fearlessly, as to your father who, according to his power, in great love, is ready to fulfil your desire by the help of God." Then, after these words, which the old man spoke in simplicity, the young man made clearly manifest before the old man the matters which he had marked out and decided upon in his mind from the beginning of his actions in the city even until that very hour.

When the old man heard all these things, he was greatly moved and disturbed, because he remembered his own former acts and life. The old man was held in contempt by his conscience because of the conditions and circumstances under which he was then living, and because of this, he was unable to promise to fulfil the works of which he had then no knowledge whatsoever. He was afraid and excused himself from the task. When he considered his own feebleness and the greatness of the matter concerned, the strenuousness and readiness of the young man, the many other reasons, which he called to mind, he was ashamed to reveal to the young man the true reason for his refusal. Yet nevertheless, because of these reasons, he said that he was unable to act for him. The young man dismissed his objections and made an end of them. He showed him that they all were insufficient to drive him away from the old man, and to do away the fervent desire and aim which were in his mind.

The old man felt compelled to plainly manifest before him the true reason for his refusal and to show him that it was not a mere matter of a report of words, but one which could be seen by the actual sight of the eyes. Wishing to fulfil his intention of showing that the true reason was not a mere excuse or one which was fabricated like those which he had previously given, he took the young man by the hand, led him into a certain chamber where his, the old man's, wife dwelt with her two children, and he said to him, "God has sent you here for my shame, and for the condemnation of my old age. Behold, this is my wife whom Satan, and not God, has given to me. Behold, these are the children of shame whom I have had by her, and they are the fruits of a contemptible and damnable union."

When the young man saw and heard these things, he was neither moved nor disturbed. He was not offended by the old man, and did not regard him with any contempt. After these things, the young man said to the old man, "My lord, I entreat your holiness to confirm what I am about to say to yourself. Let me have with you, even as with a real father, a wholly perfect understanding, such as it is right for children to have with their fathers and with their brethren, which shall be free, by the help of God, from all stumbling blocks. Let me have the same understanding with this woman, as with a real mother, and with your children as with beloved brethren."

Thus the old man was overcome by means of these words by a gracious defeat, and though he wished by the urging of his own mind to give the young man permission to live with him as a disciple, and to fulfil his desire according to the bent of his mind, he was driven far more by the power of the excellence of the young man himself. When these things had taken place they gave thanks to God. They occupied themselves, each one with the service and work that were requisite for their habitation, day by day with the help of God. The young man excelled in works towards the old man, according to his promise, in humility, and in great obedience, the spiritual excellence of his mind was greatly revealed.

One day the old man said to the young man, "My son, do you know that you and I are building this house with weariness and abundant toil, and that we do not have sufficient reeds to make the roof, and that the winter has drawn near? Now, in order that our labour may not be in vain, behold, I see that there are reeds in the habitation of the monk who is our neighbour, and since he is not there, that we may borrow from him and supply our need. Go down and take up from there a bundle, and bring it hither so that we may finish the roof, and may rejoice through his forethought." When the brother heard this, he quickly made ready to fulfill the command of the old man. Having gone down and brought what was necessary for them, they completed their work. Then the old man said to that brother, "Tell me truly, O brother, what did you think in your mind about what I said to you, that is to say, that you should go down, and bring reeds as it were by theft, during the absence of their owner?" The brother said to him, "As I have already told you, everything that you shall say to me, I shall receive as if it came from the mouth of Christ, and shall perform it in faith unhesitatingly.

I said within myself, "Christ said to me, you shall not steal, but now it is He who has just said to me, "Steal." I have nothing to do with the matter, and it is Christ to whom I must render obedience." When the old man had heard these words, he marvelled at the wisdom and at the integrity of his obedience. Wishing to make him to rejoice in his hope, the old man said to him, "My son, you must know that I had made up my mind that we must tell the owner of the reeds what I had done, and must give him whatever price he might require. When I sent you down to bring up that which belonged to him, I did not do so with the abominable intention of stealing from him."

After a certain time, during which the two men had lived together a correct life, full of peace and profit, the old man thought within himself, saying, "It is a great iniquity on my part, and it merits a severe penalty, that I, who has grown old in sins, and who am still in the mire of fornication, should dwell with this brother who is perfect in spiritual excellence; for it is not appropriate that darkness should live with light. But I will leave this abode in his hands, will take away this stumbling block which Satan has set in my way, and these fruits of shame which have come to me from her, I will go to the world and to those whom I resemble, whose works are like mine."

When he meditated with these thoughts, he made them known to the woman who dwelt with him. He was sent to the village which was near to them, and brought from there an animal to take away what he needed from the monastery, so that he might lead away his wife and his children, and he might go and live in one of the villages around them. When the animal had come, the old man had loaded him with whatever they needed, they, him, his wife, and his children, began to go forth. He said to that brother, "My son, we are not able to dwell in a monastery because our sins are many, and because we are not worthy to do so. It is great wickedness for us to dwell under the cloak of falsehood among monks, while our deeds are more evil than those of the folk who are in the world.

Do remain in this dwelling, O my son, The God whom you have loved, and whom you have made plans to please in everything, shall be to you a father, and a fellow monk. Pray on my behalf that the Lord may visit me." When that brother had heard these words, he answered the old man with love and great humility, saying, "O my father, I have made a covenant with the Lord that I will not be separated from you except by death. As much as my dwelling with you has been to me a source of great benefit, there is nothing, which can remove me away from you. Wherever you go, I will go and wherever you dwell I will dwell."

Then after all these things, the old man came to himself, and sighed greatly, saying, "Truly, this is a matter which can only come from God, the merciful, who desires not the death of a sinner, but that he may turn to Him and live. It is he who has remembered my former works, and has not left me to perish utterly, but has sent this young man to me so that He might again turn me to Him." Then the old man found himself able, by means of words, which were full of strong entreaty, to persuade the woman to take her daughter with her, and to go and dwell in one of the abodes of women which existed in the villages around them. After the old man had remained there with his son, and with that excellent disciple, he began to remember his former life, and to renew its habits. He excelled greatly in the cultivation of all kinds of spiritual excellences, and gave thanks to God unceasingly, that by means of the young man He had held him worthy of the end of peace. He was always saying, "Truly obedience for the sake of God not only greatly helps those who possess it, but it greatly gratifies God also. Obedience is found by others to be the cause of life, and it torments Satan sorely. On the other hand, disobedience works contrary to all these things." So after a long time, that old man died in peace, being worthy of the great measure of reward of his fathers. He departed from the world, and left behind upright heirs of spiritual excellences. May our Lord through their prayers make us worthy of their spiritual excellence and their inheritance!

DAY 52

The Old Man in Scete

THERE WAS A CERTAIN OLD MAN WHO USED TO LIVE in the desert called Scete. He had a disciple who lived with him. This latter brother was adorned with spiritual excellences of every kind, which benefit those who are in subjection to old men. The brother was exceedingly conspicuous for his obedience, which was the greatest of all his virtues. He was sent to the village continually by the old man to sell their work, and to bring back whatever was needed for their habitation. That brother, without any compulsion, whatsoever, performed every command given by the old man, with zeal and diligence. When Satan, the enemy of righteousness, the foe of the human race, especially of the orders of the monks, the opponent of all virtues, the hater of the upright life, saw that this brother was overcoming and bringing to naught all his crafty designs by the might of his simple full-of-discretion obedience, he made a plan to lay two snares for him in the path of his spiritual excellence.

It is said concerning him in the Psalm, "As it were by the mouth of those who cultivate spiritual excellence, and who walk in the way of righteousness; In the way of my steps have they hidden snares for me." The two snares were the following. The first consisted in making that brother to pursue fornication. The second was in making him fall into disobedience. The Enemy, in his cunningness, expected that the brother would not only be caught by one of these, and so become involved in both, but also that deliverance from the one would be found to be the occasion for his falling into the other, for he saw that he was being sent continually to Egypt by his master on the business of the work, of their hands and of the matter of their need.

One day, when that brother was carrying on his shoulders something he wished to sell, he was going to the market of the village according to his custom. It happened that owing to the sight of a woman, who was a virgin, who was continually coming in his way, who bought from him some of the wares which he carried; the war of fornication rose up against him suddenly by the operation of the Evil. When this thing had thus come to pass, the evil cunning of the Devil did not depart from that discreet brother. The brother meditated within himself saying, "Both matters are exceedingly difficult for me. Perhaps, if through some reason such as this, which the Enemy has prepared for me, I reject the command of the old man, and do not go up to him, I shall always be in the habit of thinking that I have treated the command of the old man with contempt; and if I do go up to him I shall be oppressed for a very long time with the war of fornication."

When that brother had passed much time in tribulation, and in such thoughts, and in doubts of mind, he did not know which course of action to choose and which to reject. He drew near a certain old man who dwelt close by them, who was great and skilled in all such matters, and made known his business to him, speaking thus, "Father, what shall I do, for the war of fornication has risen up against me? My father always sends me to the village for things that we need. Every time I go to the village I am vexed with thoughts about fornication, through which I am thrown into strife. I know not what to do. If I obey my father, and go to the village, the war is stirred up against me and becomes fiercer. If I remain here and do not go, I shall be a disobedient disciple. I beseech you to give me the advice, which shall be beneficial for me. Pray on my behalf, for I am greatly vexed."

When the old man heard these words, he answered him, saying, "My son, if I were you, I should, with God's help, obey my father, and should overcome the war of fornication." Then the brother said to him, "I beseech you, O my lord, to perform an act of grace, teach me the object of this conquest, and help me with your prayers." The old man said to him, "Know, O my brother, that Satan is not so anxious to cast you into fornication as he is to dismiss thee from obedience. To make you disobedient and rebellious, he plots always with exceedingly great care to make you thus. Satan himself has been acquainted with disobedience from the beginning and he knows that it is the cause of every kind of condemnation and wickedness.

O my son, let it be certain to you that, if he vanquishes you by means of it, you will be, as it were, stripped henceforth of the help of the power of obedience, and of your father's prayers. Whenever he casts you into the passion of fornication, he will be able to drag you down into passions of all kinds easily. If you do vanquish him, first of all, in the matter of obedience, and do abide therein undoubtingly, and do believe in the prayers of your father, God will make you prosper in every strive with a crown of righteousness. He will give you victory in every war with the Calumniator. Obedience to God is the victory over all passions. Go, therefore, O my son, and obey your father faithfully and unhesitatingly. When the war comes upon you say thus, "O God of my father, help me!"

When the Adversary saw that the brother was armed with the wise and powerful words of the old man, as with an impregnable coat of mail, and had prepared himself strenuously for the contest, he, the Adversary, changed the method of attack which he had formerly employed. Instead of vexing that brother with thoughts about the woman as he had done at first, he left him, since he was prepared and was sufficiently strong to stand up against him. The adversary went to the feeble woman who lacked both discernment and help, for it has been his custom always to run to the weak and sluggish side of the disciples, and to overcome the strenuous by means of it. Therefore when this brother, according to custom, had taken his work, and had readily gone up to Egypt, and had arrived at the village in which he was known to sell, Satan stirred up that woman to go forth to meet him as if by chance.

Having seen that brother and being inflamed, through the operation of Satan, with the fire of love for him, she drew near him by means of some crafty device, and took him and brought him to her house, with the excuse that she was going to buy something from him. After they had gone in, she shut the door, and began to throw herself upon him. The brother, with faith in which there was no doubt, cried out with a loud voice and said, "O God of my father, help me!" Immediately, by the agency of God, he found himself upon the road to Scete. By the Divine help, the Calumniator was put to shame, the war of fornication ceased from that brother. When he had come to the old man with whom he lived, he narrated to him the whole matter and what had happened. They gave thanks to God and glorified Him who had hearkened to the voice of His servants and had redeemed them out of the hand of their enemies, and had saved them from the snares of the Calumniator. May our Lord hide us beneath the wings of His mercifulness and save us from all the evil workings of the Calumniator! Amen.

The Disciple of Another Old Man, Who Dwelt Alone in a Cell

ONE OF THE AGED MEN SAID, "I have heard from certain holy men that there have been youths who have led and guided old men to life. They told me the following story: 'There was a certain old man who used to plait mats of palm leaves by day and sell them in the village at night; getting drunk with the money he received from the sale. At length there came a certain brother who took up his abode with him, and also worked at the plaiting of mats by day. The old man took his work also, sold it, and got drunk with the money which he received. He would bring home a little bread for that brother. Though the old man did this for a period of three years, the brother said nothing to him about it. After these things, the brother said to himself, "Behold, I am naked, and I only eat my bread by forcing myself to do so. I will therefore arise and depart from this place."

Again he thought within himself, saying, "Where have I to go? I will stay here a little longer, for I can live to God just as well as if I were in a monastery where many monks are." Straightaway the angel of the Lord appeared and said to him, "Do not depart to any other place, for tomorrow we are coming to you." Then that brother made supplication to the old man and entreated him, saying, "I beseech you, O my father, do not go forth this day to any place, for the angels are coming to receive my soul." When the hour had arrived for the old man to go out and sell the work according to his desire, he said to the brother, "My son, they will not come today, for they have delayed too long." The brother said, "Yes, my father, indeed they will come."

While he was talking to the old man, he died. When the old man saw what had happened, he wept and sighed deeply saying, "Woe to me! Woe to me, O my son! I have lived in faith for many years, but you have gained life for yourself through a short period of patient endurance!" From that day forward the old man led a life of sobriety and became a chosen monk."

DAY 54

The Disciple of an Old Man in the Desert

THERE WAS A CERTAIN DESERT MONK who was very anxious to find a quiet suitable place for him to dwell in. There was a certain old man who had a cell near him, and he entreated him, saying, "Come, take up your abode here until you find a cell suitable for you." He went there. The brethren used to come to him as a stranger. They brought him food in order that they might be helped by doing so. He rejoiced in them and gave them relief. The old man began to envy him, and to heap abuse on him, saying, "Behold, how many are the years where I have lived here in the strictest abstinence, and yet no man came to me. Yet to this deceiver who has only passed a few days here, many come!" This old man said to his disciple, "Go and say to him, Depart from that place, for I am in need of both the place and the cell." His disciple went and said to him, "My father, speak some words and pray for me because I am greatly vexed by my stomach." Then he came to his master and said to him, "He said to me, I see a cell and I am going forth."

After two days, the old man sent his disciple to him again, and said to him, "If you have not departed, I will come myself and drive you out with a stick." The disciple came to the monk and said to him, "My father has heard that you are sick and he is greatly grieved. He has sent me to visit you." The monk said to him, "Through your prayers, all is well." The disciple came and said to his master, "I have spoken to him, and he said to me, "Wait until the first day of the week, and I will, by the Will of God, go forth." When the first day of the week had come, the monk had not departed. The old man took a stick and was going forth to beat him, and to drive him out. His disciple said to him, "Let me go first, lest there be some stranger who will be offended at your act." Having gone before his master, the disciple said to the monk, "Behold, my father has come to entreat you to leave and to take you to his cell."

When the monk heard of the old man's love, he made haste to go out to meet him, expressed his sorrow afar off, and said, "Do not be vexed, O my lord and father, for I was coming to your holiness. Forgive me for the sake of Jesus." God saw the work of that disciple, and He opened the mind of the old man. He threw away his stick and ran to salute the monk. Having drawn near to him, he gave him the salutation of peace, and took him into his cell. The stranger had heard nothing whatsoever of the words which had been said by the old man. Then the old man said to his disciple, "Perhaps, did you say to the monk what I said to you?" The disciple said to him, "No, father, I did not." The old man rejoiced greatly, brought him in to the stranger and treated him kindly. The old man knew that what had taken place in him had been caused by the working of Satan. He fell down before his disciple and said, "Hence forward, you shall be my father, and I will be your disciple, for through your good works, after God, you have helped the souls of two men."

DAY 55

Peter, the Disciple of one of the Old Men

THERE WAS A CERTAIN OLD MAN who had an excellent disciple. On a certain occasion, the old man, by reason of his hasty temper, drove him away, turned him outside the door, his apparel with him. The brother sat down outside the door and waited patiently. When the old man opened the door, he found him sitting outside. The old man repented, saying, "O Peter, the meekness of your long suffering nature has vanquished my hasty temper. Henceforward you shall be my old man and father, and I will be your servant and disciple. By your good work you have made me old."

A Disciple of One of the Old Men

ON A CERTAIN OCCASION, THE DISCIPLE of a great age had a war of fornication. When the old man saw that his brother was vexed and oppressed in his mind, he said to him, "Do you wish me to entreat

God to make the war less fierce?" The brother said, "Father, I perceive that, although I toil and am afflicted, I am yet able to see the fruit which I possess within my soul through this strife, therefore pray not for this thing, but entreat God especially in your prayer to give me strength to endure." His father said to him, "This day I know that you have surpassed me."

Aurelius

I USED TO KNOW A MAN IN JERUSALEM whose name was Aurelius, and by race, came from the city of Tarsus. When this man arrived in Jerusalem, he walked wholly in the path of no stumbling and in that which not many have walked. He laid down for himself ascetic rules of life of new kinds, these were so severe that the devils were afraid of him, and they were unable to stand up before him. By reason of the greatness of his toil, he might have been thought to be a shadow, for he would pass the whole weeks of the Forty Days in fasting. He would spend the other days in constant vigils. The greatest of all his acts of asceticism was this.

While the brethren were gathered together each evening in the house of prayer, he would go up to the highest peak of the Mount of Olives, to the place where our Lord was lifted up, and as he stood there upon his feet, he would recite the whole Office. Whether rain, or snow, or sleet fell, he would never leave his place. When he had finished the Office according to his custom, he would take a hammer and beat a board, and rouse up those that slept, and having gone round to the doors of all the monks, he would gather them together to their places for prayer. In each place, he would recite the Office with them. He would also stand up in the midst of companies of monks, and would recite the Office. In the daytime, he would go to his cell, and in truth, on several occasions, his brethren had to strip off his clothes from him because they were completely wet, and put others on him. He would rest until the third hour of the day, and then would come to the service in the church and stay until the evening. Such was the manner Aurelius lived. In this way he brought his life to an end. He was buried at Jerusalem.

DAY 56

Abba Moses the Ethiopian, a Captain of Thieves

THERE WAS A CERTAIN MAN whose name was Moses; he was by race an Ethiopian, and his skin was black. He was the slave of a man in high authority. Because of his evil deeds and thefts, his master drove him out of his house. It is said that he even went so far as to commit murder. I am compelled to mention his wickedness in order that I may show forth the beauty of his repentance. People say that he was the captain of a band of seventy thieves.

He had as an enemy a certain shepherd, against whom he remembered certain evil things. He went to steal sheep from his flock. The shepherd was told by a certain man who said, Moses has crossed the Nile by swimming, and he holds a sword in his hand, and his clothes are placed on his head. The shepherd covered himself over with sand, and hid from him. When Moses had come and did not find the shepherd, he chose out two fine rams from among the sheep and slew them. He tied them together with a rope, and swam across the river again with them. Having come to a small village, he skinned the rams and ate the best portions of them. He sold the remainder for wine, and drank. After these things, he went back to his companions. One day, while he was associated with doing hateful things, his senses came back to him. He repented of his evil acts, and rose up and fled to a monastery. From that time, he drew near to works of repentance so closely that the devil who had made him sin from his youth, would stand before him in visible form and would look upon him. Thus he came to the knowledge of our Lord Christ.

About Moses the Ethiopian, they tell the story that thieves once came and went into his cell, because they did not know who he was. He tied them all together with cords and lifted them up on his shoulders like a bag of chopped straw. He brought them to the church brethren, and said to them, "Since I do not have the power to do evil to any man, what do you command me to do to those who rose up against me to slay me?" At that time Moses had been fasting for seven days, and had eaten nothing. After he had done this, he informed the thieves, saying, "I indeed am Moses who was formerly the captain of a band of thieves." Having heard this, they praised and glorified God. When they saw the sincerity of his repentance they also removed themselves from their evil deeds, and said within themselves, "Let us also draw near to repentance, so that we may become worthy of the forgiveness of sins, even as he also is worthy."

Whilst fasting often, and during the time of prayer and silent contemplation, the devil who brings back to the remembrance of the mind the wickedness of former habits, would come to him, and tempt him. Having come to the old man Isidore the great, who had arrived from Scete, Moses told him concerning the war of his body. The old man said to him, "Do not be distressed, for these are the beginning of the birth pangs, and they come upon you seeking what they are accustomed to receive, even as a dog which comes continually to the cook. If a man gives him nothing he will not go there again. Thus also it is with you; if you continue in fasting, prayer and silent contemplation, the devil will straightaway fall into despair and will flee from you."

From that time, he was exceedingly constant in his work of spiritual excellence. He ate nothing whatsoever, except ten ounces of dry bread daily when he was doing work. He would recite from beginning to end fifty prayers during the day. The more he dried up his body, the more he was vexed and consumed by dreams. Again he went to one of the old men, and said to him, "What shall I do? For thoughts of lust which arise from my former habits attack me." The old man said to him, "These lead you into error because you have not turned away your heart from the similitudes of them, but give your heart to watching and careful prayer, and you will be free from them." When he had heard this direction, he went to his cell, and made a covenant with God that he would neither sleep during the whole night nor bend his knees.

He dwelt in his cell for seven years, and remained standing the whole of each night with his eyes open, and never closed his eyelids. After this, he set himself other ascetic labours, for he would go out during the nights and visit the cells of the old men, to take their waterskins and fill them with water, because they lived a long way from the water. One night, he went to fill the water skins with water, according to his wish. As soon as he had bent down over the spring, a devil struck him a blow across his loins as with a stick, and departed leaving him half dead. Moses understood who had done this thing to him. On the following day, one of the brethren came to fill the water skins with water, and he saw the blessed man lying there. He drew near to him, asking, "What has happened to you?" When Moses had told him the story, the brother went and informed Abba Isidore, the priest of the church of Scete. Abba Isidore sent brethren immediately, took him up and brought him to the church. He was ill for a long time, and never thoroughly recovered from his illness.

Abba Isidore said to him, "Rest yourself, O Moses, do not fret against the devils, and do not seek to make attacks upon them. There is moderation in everything, even in the works of ascetic life." Moses said to him, "I believe in God, in Whom I placed my hope, that being armed against the devils, I must not cease to wage war with them until they depart from me." Abba Isidore said to him, "In the Name of Jesus Christ, from this time forward, the devils shall cease from you. Draw near then and participate in the Holy Sacraments. You shall be free from all impurity, both of the flesh and of the spirit, for you must not boast within yourself, and say, 'I have overcome the devils, for it was for your benefit that they have waxed strong against you.'

Moses went back again to his cell. After two months, Abba Isidore came to him, and asked him concerning himself. Moses said to him, "I never see anything which is hateful to me." He was also held worthy of the gift of Divine Grace, and he could chase away the devils from many folk who were vexed therewith, and as flies take flight before us, so did the devils depart from before him. Such were the ascetic labours of the blessed man Moses, who was himself vexed with great matters. He also became a priest, and left behind seventy disciples who were men of worth. When he was a thief, he had seventy followers who were thieves, and these became his disciples, and were perfect in the fear of God.

DAY 57

Abba Pior

THERE WAS AN EGYPTIAN YOUTH named Pior. Pior was a holy man. When he departed from the house of his parents, he made a covenant with God, with the zeal of excellence, that he would never see any of his kinsfolk. After fifty years, the sister of this blessed man, who was very old and grey, heard that he was alive. She greatly desired to see him. She was unable to come to him in the desert, and she besought the Bishop, who was in that country, to write to the fathers who lived in the desert telling them, to urge him, and to send him to see his sister.

When the blessed man saw the pressure, which came from them to make him go, he took with him some brethren, and set out on the journey. Having arrived, he sent and informed his sister's household, saying, "Behold, Pior your brother has come, and stands outside." When his sister heard his voice, she went forth in great haste. When Pior heard the sound of the door, and knew that the aged woman, his sister, was coming forth to see him, he shut his eyes tightly, and said, "So and so, I am your brother; look at me as far as you can do." Having seen him, she was relieved in her mind, and gave thanks to God. She was unable to persuade him to enter her house. He made a prayer by the side of the door, with his eyes closed tightly, and departed to the desert.

He also wrote the following wonderful thing, "In the place where he lived, he dug a hole in the ground, and found water which was bitter in taste. Until the day he died, he endured the bitter taste of the water, in order that he might make known what he suffered patiently for the sake of God. After his death many of the monks wished to abide in that place. They were not able to do so, even for one year, chiefly because of the terrible nature of the country and its barren nature."

Abba Moses the Libyan

THERE WAS ALSO ANOTHER OLD MAN whose name was Moses, who came from the country of the Libyans. He was exceedingly meek and compassionate. Through this, he was held to be worthy of the gift of healing. This old man himself related to us the following story, saying, "When I was a young man dwelling in the monastery, we dug out a large cistern which was twenty cubits wide. Eighty men were digging it out, and we set seventy men to build walls around it. They dug down according to their knowledge, passed the place where they expected to find water, and went down even one cubit more. They did not find water.

Being greatly distressed at this, we wished to abandon the well and go away. When Abba Pior came from the desert at noon, being an old man, he was covered in his head-cloak, he saluted us, and said to us, "Why has your spirit lessened, O you of little faith? For I observe that your spirit has diminished since yesterday because you have not found water." He went down by a ladder to the bottom of the well, and made a prayer with the men. Having prayed, he took up an iron tool and drove it into the earth three times, saying, "O Lord God of the holy Fathers, do not make the weariness of these men to be in vain. Send them water in abundance."

Straightaway waters sprang up in such quantity that they all became wet. Having prayed a second time, he went forth and departed. When they urged him to remain with them and eat, he would not be persuaded to do so. He said to them, "The matter concerning which I was sent, is accomplished. I was not sent to eat."

DAY 58

A Certain Distinguished Wandering Monk

THE COPYIST ADDS THE NOTE: We have found the story of this wandering monk and recluse following that of the recluse John of Lycus.

There was a certain distinguished wandering monk who (as have heard from the famous monks who dwelt by the side of the country of Antinoe, lived a life of great sanctity in the mountains. He helped many folks by word and deed. The Enemy had envy of him, and he cast into his mind thoughts, which appeared to be humble, saying, "It is not seemly for you to be ministered to and treated with honour by others, for you should minister to yourself. Go therefore to the city and sell your plaited baskets, and buy whatever you have need of, and lay no burden upon any man." The crafty one counselled him in this wisdom because he was envious of his silent contemplation and constant prayer. The monk, being convinced as it were by a counsellor of good, for he was not greatly skilled in the knowledge of cunning wickedness, went down from the mountain. The brethren marvelled, because he was a wandering monk, who was well known and famous. Thus in a short time, through want of care and converse with women, he was caught in toils and fell.

He came to the river Nile in a desolate place; now there was with him the Enemy who had cast him down and who rejoiced because of his fall. He was greatly grieved, because he forgot God was his hope. He did not know how he was to be healed, and wished to throw himself into the river flood and die. Moreover, although his body was brought exceedingly low, through the suffering of his soul, the mercy of God helped him not to die and it urged him to depart again with weeping and bitter suffering of heart, as was right, to make supplication to the compassion of God. Thus, having returned to his place and blocked up the window of his cell, he wept, as one who weeps over a dead person. He reduced his body to emaciation by means of his fasting and vigil and grief.

On several occasions, when the brethren came to comfort him, and knocked at his door, because he had no excuse to make, he would say, "Pray for me, O my brethren, for I have made a covenant to live a life of silent contemplation all my days, having everything of which I have need." Then they would go away having no hope whatsoever for him.

He would pray, "O You Merciful One, Who desire that the Barbarians and all the people who are without God should have knowledge of You, and should turn to You, and Who alone art the true Physician of souls, have mercy upon me, for I know that I have made You wroth not a little. I have obeyed the Enemy, even to my death and, behold, I am a dead man. O You Who did teach the children of men who were not merciful, to show mercy to each other, O have mercy upon me! For to You nothing is impossible, even though I be brought down as low as the dust in Sheol. But You are the Lord of hosts, and You are He Who is good to those whom You created. Answer me because my heart and body are sick, for I am overcome by fear of You and am ready to perish, and I cannot live any longer. Show compassion upon me, O Merciful One, and kindle this lamp by Your light, so that I, by means of it, may receive the encouragement of Your mercy, and may pass the remainder of my life in the way which pleases You, and may never again be unmindful to the fear of Your Commandments."

He said these things with tears on his face. He fell upon his face again and besought the Lord, saying, "O Lord, have mercy upon me, and I will confess Your goodness. I have been ashamed before the righteous angels. If it were not that it would cause scandal, I would make my confession to the children of men. Therefore, have compassion upon me, for from this time forward I will teach others that their hearts must not be outside Your fear, even for a moment; I make supplication to Your goodness." The monk prayed in this manner three times, when suddenly his lamp lit up, he found it burning brightly. He was strengthened with hope, and rejoiced, wept abundantly, marvelled at Divine Grace, and made prayer to the Lord about this also, saying, "You show compassion to him who is unworthy, and especially by the great and new sign which You have given. Yes, Lord, You always show Your compassion upon the miserable soul, and spare it." The monk continued to give simple thanks until the day dawned, and he rejoiced in the Lord, and forgot the food of the body. He tended the light of the lamp everyday, and poured oil in it. He trimmed it from above, and kept it covered so that it should not be extinguished. When he was about to yield up his soul to the Lord, he related the story gladly to the brethren who happened to be there, that it might cause them fear, saying, "Let that lamp be placed in my grave in commemoration of my repentance." We, who heard concerning the grace of God, have written down these things in order that men may be watchful in the Lord.

DAY 50

Evagrius, the Solitary Monk

IT IS NOT APPROPRIATE THAT WE SHOULD VEIL the history of this holy man in silence. We must set it down plainly in writing, both for the help and edification of those who shall come across it. For the glory of God, Whose wish is to change bitterness to sweetness, we shall, therefore, make clear the history of the blessed man from the beginning, and tell how he journeyed step by step to the goal of spiritual excellence. How he was carried onwards to ascetic life, how he arrived at purity of heart, and how he departed from this world at the age of fifty-four years. This blessed man came from Pontus, where his family lived. His father held the office of visitor. The blessed man Basil, Bishop of Caesarea, appointed him to be a reader.

After the death of the blessed man Basil; Gregory, Bishop of Nazianzus, seeing his perspicacity and his great skill in the Divine Books, and that he was free from passions, and adorned with virtues, brought him near to the grade of the priesthood. He went up to the synod, which was held at Constantinople with the blessed man Gregory, who loved him greatly. When the blessed man Nectarius, Bishop of Constantinople, met him, he was drawn to love him, because he saw that he was a man of strong character, and attached him to himself. Evagrius was beloved by all men, and was held in honour by all men. For this reason Satan was envious of him, and disturbed his understanding through the vision of his mind, which he set in a blaze through the love of a certain woman. This woman was the wife of one of the noblemen of the city, according to what he himself related to us. When, by the will of God, he was set free from these thoughts, the woman herself began to love Evagrius. She was a great lady of high degree.

Then Evagrius, setting before his eyes the reproach of fornication, prayed to God with labour that, in His Grace, He might bring this matter to naught, and that he might extinguish the mad lust of that woman. His prayer having been heard, when as yet he had not had union with her sinfully, an angel appeared to him in the form of a soldier of the prefect, who seized him, cast him into prison, and who loaded his neck and his hands with chains. He did not inform Evagrius for what reason he had to bear this ill-treatment. The thought sprang up in his mind, which said, "Perhaps that woman's husband has laid an accusation against me before the judge." Evagrius found himself in great agony of mind, because he saw that other men, who had been committed to prison for offences similar to his own, were condemned to judgement before his eyes. The angel changed his form, and appeared to him in the guise of one of his friends, and he began to say to him, when he saw that he was loaded with chains and had been placed with the malefactors, "What is this that happened to you, O brother?"

Evagrius answered him, saying, "My brother, in truth I do not know. I think that perhaps some prince of the city has laid an accusation against me before the judge, because of some vain jealousy (or envy), which has burst flame in him. I am afraid lest, through a gift of much money, the judge may issue a decree of death against me." The angel said to him, "If you will receive the words of your friend, I counsel you not to remain in this city." The blessed Evagrius said to him, "Do you think that you will see me in this city if God will deliver me from this trial? You might as well think that I am enduring these evils righteously!" The angel said to him, "Swear to me that you will depart from the city, and will have a care for your soul, and I will deliver you from these trials." Evagrius took an oath to him by the Book of the Gospel, saying, "I will not tarry here more than the one day which will be necessary for me to put my things in the ship."

When Evagrius woke up from his sleep, he thought within himself and said, "Although the words of the oaths have been uttered in a dream, it is right that I should fulfil that which I have promised." So he put his things in a ship and departed to Jerusalem, where the blessed woman Melania received him gladly. Melania had come from the city of Rome. Because Satan had made the heart of Evagrius as hard as that of Pharaoh, he failed to call to mind that which he had promised to do, and he went back to his former habits and returned to his pride. He was arrayed in filthy garments. But God, because He is in the habit of bringing to naught on our behalf, things of evil, kindled the fire of a great fever in Evagrius, and He cast him into a sickness which lasted for six months. No physician was able to bring healing to him.

The blessed woman Melania said to him, "My son, your long illness does not please me. Tell me, then, concerning it, for perhaps there is something hidden in your mind. Your illness is not like that of every other man." Then Evagrius confessed to her the whole matter. Melania said to him, "Promise me truthfully that from this time onward, you will take care of yourself in a habitation of monks, and that you will work to God. However great a sinner I may be, I will pray for you, and relief shall be given to your tribulation." Then he promised to do that which she required at his hands. Within a few days, the blessed man was healed, and he rose up from his bed, and from that day, his whole mind was changed.

He departed to the mountain which is in Egypt, called Nitria, and dwelt there for two years. In the third year, he departed to the inner desert, and dwelt there for fourteen years in a place called The Cells. He lived on one pound of bread a day, and a box of oil every three months. He laid down a rule that he should pray in the course of each day one hundred prayers. He lived by the labour of his hands, and he only accepted the bare price of his daily food for all the work he did; and his work was to write books. Before the fifteen years had passed by, he had cleansed his heart, and was held to be worthy of the grace of God. Wisdom and understanding were given to him, and he knew the power of spirits. He composed three volumes, and taught therein the cunningness of the devil's snares especially laid by thoughts.

The blessed man Evagrius related to us that the devil of fornication once made an attack upon him, and that he stood up naked the whole night long in the desert (now it was the season of winter), until his flesh was quite shrivelled and dried up. On another occasion, the devil of blasphemy made an attack upon him, and according to what he told us, he passed forty days under the open sky in winter until his flesh became like that of the beasts of the desert. He also told us that one day, three devils came to him in the daytime, in the form of three members of a religious body, and they began to discuss the faith with him. One of them declared himself to be an Arian. The second said that he was a Eunomian (i.e. a follower of Eunomius, Bishop of Cyzicus, AD 360-364). The third confessed himself to be of the seal of Apollinarius (Bishop of Laodicea; he died about AD 390). By the Divine Grace within him, he drove them away, having put them to shame.

Again he told us that one day he lost the key to his cell, but he made the sign of the Cross over the door and it opened, having called Christ to his help. He was beaten with innumerable stripes by the devils. He learned, by experience, very much concerning their cunning. He made known to one of his disciples, by prophecy, what would happen to him after a period of eighteen years.

He said, "From the time when I entered the desert, I have never washed, and I have never eaten any vegetable, fruit, or grapes." At the end of his life, that is to say, in the sixteenth year in which he departed from the world, he ate compulsorily food, which was cooked by fire. He was obliged to do this because of a weakness of the stomach, which had overtaken him. He was compelled to take cooked food because of this.

Malchus, the Solitary Monk

ABOUT THREE MILES FROM ANTIOCH IN SYRIA, there is a certain village called Maronia. In this village was an old monk whose name was Malchus. He was a wonderful and a holy man. At that time, I had travelled far away from the house of my fathers, and went to Evagrius the priest, where I heard concerning the holy man Malchus. I desired greatly to see him and to be blessed by him. I went to him, and he received me gladly, and began to tell me about the habits of life the works of the monks, and how it is right to fear the Lord. Having rejoiced greatly in the pious words of his doctrine, I besought him to confirm me especially in such things. Then he said to me, "My son, I will relate to you concerning the temptations, which, in proportion to my presumption and thoughtlessness, have come upon me, in order that they may help you, and also concerning the compassionate grace of the Lord God who took me out and redeemed me from them, and who permitted them to come upon me for the correction of many who should learn of me, and should not become disobedient to the exhortation of their spiritual fathers, because disobedience is the cause of death."

Having said these things, he began to narrate to me his history, saying, "I was born in the village of Nisibis. I was an only child and my parents were proud of me because I was the only child they ever expected to have. When I had arrived at manhood's state, they were anxious to marry me to a wife. I spoke against their wish, saying, "It is right for me to become a monk and to serve the Lord." They were exceedingly upset. My father urged me to marry and threatened me with penalties if I did not, and my mother was always inciting and counselling me to do so. Seeing that their minds were most firmly set upon this, which would be to me an impediment to my confession of the faith before God, I forsook them, and treated all the riches of this world with contempt. I took with me only a small sum of money, which was just sufficient for the expenses of my journey. I wished to go to the monasteries of the east. During that time, the Greeks had determined to make war upon the Persians. I changed my intention, and made up my mind to go to the west. While I was pondering this matter, I learned that between Keneshrin and Aleppo there was a monastery, which was situated in a peaceful spot. I gave up my former intention, and went there. I asked them to receive me, and I remained with them. I wrestled with all their ascetic habits and rules of chastity according to their godly ways of life. I made good progress therein in the Lord.

Having remained in that monastery for a certain number of years, and having lived blamelessly the life of spiritual excellence, all the brethren rejoiced at the growth of my asceticism. Because the Calumniator, that jealous and envious being, could not endure this, he cast into my mind thoughts which were apparently correct ones, saying, "Since your father is dead, return to your house, and comfort thy mother so long as she is alive. After her death, sell your possessions, and give some of the proceeds to the poor. Keep the remainder to build a monastery. You yourself shall become a father and governor of monks."

To tell you the truth, the Calumniator cast within me the passion of avarice, saying, "Keep some of the money for your old age." When the war, which was caused by these thoughts had been waged against me daily for some time, I felt obliged to reveal this sickness of my soul to my spiritual father. When the holy father heard these, he said to me, "My son, do not hearken to your feelings. This is a snare of Satan who, by means of this cunning device, has put many monks backward in their course, even as a dog goes back to his vomit, and has cast them down and has made them lose their inheritance, and who, though continually setting before them the hope of that which is good, has nevertheless brought them down into Sheol. Our Lord commands him that has laid his hand upon the plough not to turn back."

By means of such testimonies, which he brought from the Holy Scriptures, he was not able to persuade me to stay. He, thus, fell down before me and wished to swear by the Lord that I would not forsake him. Whilst that merciful and pious father was saying these things for my deliverance, the Enemy was placing in my heart the words like, "The father wishes that the whole community of the brethren may be glorified by staying here." By saying words of this kind to me, that evil adviser made me gain a victory of wickedness, and he made me come out of the monastery. Still clinging to me, as to one who was lost, the father said to me, "My son, I see that you are consumed by love of money. The sheep which goes out from his flock without his shepherd becomes a prey to wolves." I left him after he spoke these words to me.

Then I went from Aleppo to Edessa by the king's highway. Being afraid of the soldiers (i.e. bands of marauding robbers), who had already taken up their abode in the countries nearby, I remained in Edessa, hoping to find a companion for the journey, as this was my watchful fear. When we had gathered together a company of seventy men and women, we set out on the road. Suddenly a band of Arab soldiers swooped down on us, and carried us all away. I called to mind the exhortation of the holy father, and said to myself, "O my soul, such are the great riches which I went out to inherit! I am a wretched man. Such are the promises of the Enemy, the deceiver and destroyer of souls! Inherit your wealth then, O wretched one, and make yourself happy with." As I was saying these things to myself, one of the Arabs took me with a certain woman. He set the two of us on one camel, and having travelled a short distance in the desert, because we were afraid lest we should fall off the camel, we were compelled to hold tightly to each other.

Not only did this shame come to my mind, but I was also obliged to eat with her. The Arab gave us milk and camel's flesh. He carried us to his tent, and commanded me to do homage to his wife and to bow down before her, saying, "This is your mistress." Through these things I, the chaste man and monk, was becoming acquainted with the form of nakedness of these people, according to the reward, which my passion of avarice merited. The Arab ordered me to gird myself about with woollen garments and to shepherd the sheep.

This occupation became to me a source of consolation for the tribulations, which surrounded me. After a few days, I was released from the evil faces of my masters and companions. But this alone did not bring me consolation, for I remembered that Abel, the Patriarch Jacob and his sons, the holy man Moses, and king David were shepherds of sheep. I rejoiced in the desert, pastured the sheep, prayed, and sang the Psalms, which I learned in the monastery. I used to eat cheese made of goat's milk, and drank milk. I gave praise to God, that I had obtained such a light penalty for my disobedience. Remembering that the Apostle said, "Servants, be submissive to your masters, not only to the good, but also to the wicked," I took care of my master's sheep with the utmost diligence. In all these things I kept in mind always the envy of the Calumniator who hates good.

When my master saw that I was acting rightly towards him, he wished to reward me well therefore. He wanted to marry me to that woman who had been taken captive with me. Yet I spoke against his proposal, saying, "I am a monk, and I cannot do this. Besides, this woman has a husband who was taken captive with us, but has become under another ownership." Suddenly, his wrath went up, drew his sword, and set his gaze upon me. He would have killed me, but I ran and took hold of his wife's hand. Having married me to the woman, he brought me into a cave with her. When I knew that this was indeed the captor of my soul, I cried aloud and wept saying, "Woe to me the sinner! What has happened to me? For having grown old in the life of virginity, a terrible evil now comes on me.

I must become the husband of a wife! Where is my mother? Where are the possessions and riches of my fathers? I disobeyed my spiritual father, I forsook the Lord and now I must endure things of this kind! What will you do, O my wretched soul? For if you conquer by patient endurance, by the Grace of God, you will be held worthy of help. But if you are lax, severe punishment is laid up for you. Fight then mightily against sin. Turn the sword against yourself, that you may keep the testimony of chastity. Hold in contempt the fire of time that you may flee from the fire of eternity. Conquer your sin in the desert, that you may be a persecuted and chosen witness."

Then I took the sword in my hands, and saluted that woman, saying, "May you remain in peace, O wretched woman. Acquire yourself rather a martyr than a husband. I will not marry a wife, as

I fled from and forsook my parents." When the woman saw the sword which was shining in the darkness, she fell down before my feet and said to me, "I will make you swear by Jesus Christ, the Lord of praise, that you will not kill yourself for my sake. If you wish to do this, turn the sword against me. Why should you wish to kill yourself so that you may not take me to wife? Know that I am far more anxious than you are to preserve my chastity to Christ. I must guard it not only against you, but also against my lawful husband, for even if he were to come I would keep myself chaste. This is what this captivity in which I am, teaches me. For this affliction should teach us to take refuge in the Lord. Take me then to yourself as a companion of your chastity. Let us love each other in spiritual love, so that when our masters see us, they may think that our intercourse is carnal. God, Who knows hearts, recognizes spiritual brotherhood, and we can easily persuade these people when they see us together in this way, that we love each other."

Then, while marvelling at the understanding of the woman, I received her good advice gladly in Christ. I loved her as a spiritual help, and as a pure and chaste helper. I never saw her body naked, and I never approached her couch, for I was afraid lest, having been victorious in the time of war, I might receive a severe wound through the arrows of the Enemy in the time of peace. In this way, our masters left us for a long time, and they were not afraid that we were preparing to run away from them, for it happened on several occasions, sometimes for a whole month together, that I was alone with the woman in the desert. My master used to come. When he saw that I was taking good care of his sheep, he would go back to his place rejoicing.

One day, according to my custom, I was sitting in the desert. I began to meditate upon the peaceful life of the brethren who were in the monastery. I also saw the face of our holy father as if it had been an image. I thought of his perfect and abundant love for me, how anxious he was in every way that I should not be separated from him, how I would not be persuaded to stay with him by the Divine revelation, and how he bore witness beforehand concerning the things which would happen to me. While, then, I was pondering upon these things in my mind, and was greatly afflicted thereby, I saw an ants' nest. I saw multitudes of these insects working with the greatest diligence and care in their various ways. I saw how they were all making their way into the nest through a narrow entrance, without impeding each other.

Some of them were bringing seeds for their winter food; others were bringing loads which were larger than their bodies; others were carrying on their backs those which had been wounded; and others were expelling from the nest those which had settled themselves inside. Others were carrying dust, so that when the winter rains fell with violence they might be able to block up the entrance to their nest firmly. This sight was in my opinion worthy to wonder at, because everything, which these small creatures did was done in perfect order. I spent the whole day watching them, and so enjoyed some relaxation from my afflictions. I said, "Well, did Solomon counsel us to be like these creatures, for he wished to stir up our lazy and sluggish understandings to perform with a ready mind the things which benefit our redemption."

While I was pondering upon these things in my mind, and was greatly afflicted thereby. I began to have sorrow concerning myself, because my lazy and sluggish mind lacked the great sense of order and arrangement which the ants possessed. My sorrow was also because the Calumniator had hunted me down like a child, had set me in captivity, and had hurled me into such great temptations. I thought of those who were offering their souls with all their hearts to Christ, and who were being guided on their way in all the monasteries, by submission and spiritual grace, through the righteous redemption of our Redeemer. I thought of those who were anxious to preserve their souls, and who were labouring diligently, without any hindrance and with all their strength to do their work, and to minister to one another. I thought about those who possessed nothing, yet possessed everything, who enjoyed sufficiently that which they had for their daily needs and glorified Him who richly provided them with everything.

Having made my heart sad and low with such thoughts for many days, I went to that woman, who, seeing how greatly my countenance was changed, entreated me to know the cause of it. Having confessed to her my story, I told her I wished to escape and return to the monastery. She asked to come with me and be placed in a nunnery. Having together decided on this plan, we wept and entreated our Lord to help us carry out what we had determined to do.

Therefore, having firm hope in God's assistance, we started our return, and I slew two large goats, making their skins into water bottles. Having loaded their flesh upon our shoulders, I took the woman, and we departed. We travelled the whole night long, and came to an exceedingly great and wide river. I blew up the water bottles, and gave one to the woman and kept the other myself. We laid hold upon them with our hands. Sitting astride the skins, we paddled with our feet, and crossed over the river. Then, seeing that we would have to cross a desert in which there was no water, we drank plenty of water from the river. We rose up from that place and went on our way quickly. We were turning round continually to look behind us because of our horrible expectation that there would be men pursuing us.

Because of our fear of the heat of the sun, we were obliged to travel by night. Urged by this great fear, and by our great anxiety, we were looking behind us ceaselessly. After traveling for five days, we turned around suddenly, and saw our master and one of his companions, riding upon camels, holding drawn swords in their hands, and pursuing after us. Because of our fear, the sun appeared to us to become dark. Whilst we were in this terrible state of fright, we did not know where to escape. Through the Providence of Christ, the Hope of the hopeless, The Help of the helpless, we peered about in that place and found a frightful cave in the ground, where gathered numerous kinds of snakes, serpents, asps, vipers, and scorpions, which had gone therein because of the burning heat of the sun. In this cave we tottered, and hid ourselves in a corner, on its left hand side. We said, "If our Lord helps us, this cave shall be to us a house of deliverance; but if He leaves us to the sinners, it will be our grave."

When our master and his companion following in our footprints had pursued us to the cave, they alighted from their camels, and stood by the mouth of the cave. When we saw our master, such great fear laid hold upon us that we were unable to move our tongue to utter a word. Owing to the greatness of our fear we were already as dead men, before the sword stroke fell upon us. Our master stood outside the cave and called us. We were unable to speak because of our fear. He took hold of the camels, and commanded his companion to go in and bring us out, whilst he stood outside waiting for us with his sword drawn, so that he might by means of it quell his brutal madness.

When the young man had gone into the cave for a distance of five paces, he stood still because his eyes had become dazzled by the light of the sun, and could not see. We being quite near him, could see him standing there, however, because he was unable to see us he began to terrify us with his voice, saying, "Come out, O you wicked slaves who deserve death, why do you delay? Behold, your master is outside expecting you." As he was saying these words, we saw a lioness rise up on the right hand side of the cave, and she sprang on him. Whilst he was still speaking, she seized him by the throat and strangled him and then dragged him in and laid him on her lair, for she had a male cub. When we saw our enemy lying there before our eyes, we glorified God with great joy. His master, not knowing what had happened, and thinking that the young man had been overcome by us, and being unable to contain himself for rage, ran forward, holding his drawn sword in his hand, and, standing at the mouth of the cave, cried out in his wrath to the young man, saying, "Quick, quick, bring these slaves out to me that they may die an evil death." Whilst he was speaking, the lioness sprang upon him suddenly, and ripped him up, and threw his head long on the ground.

We marvelled at all these unspeakable and inexplicable wonders of the Lord, and we gave thanks to Him, and we rejoiced in the glory of Him who in this tribulation had risen up, and by Whose command the wild beast had destroyed our enemies. When the lioness turned back and passed from one side to the other of the cave where we were, we thought that she would destroy us, but, because of the wonderful thing which had been wrought, we continued to praise the Lord, and we said, "Since the Lord has delivered us from those wicked men He can, if He wills, hand us over to the lions; but nevertheless let us praise Him and give thanks to Him." Whilst we were thus thinking in our minds, the lioness took up the cub in her mouth, and departed from the cave, and left the place to us; but after she had gone, because of the state of fear in which we were, we remained the whole of that day in the cave.

In the morning we went out and found the camels that were still laden with provisions, which our master had brought for himself and his slave. We ate and drank therefrom, and for all these things we gave thanks to the Lord, Who had delivered us from our enemies. We rode upon the camels, and crossed that desert in ten days. We arrived at a Greek camp, and drew near to the Tribune who was in command of it. We related everything to him, which had happened to us. He sent us on to Sabinus, the Duke of Mesopotamia. He likewise learned all our affairs, took the camels and gave us their price. He dismissed us to depart to our country in peace. Before our return, my spiritual father fell asleep.

I placed the woman who had been my helper, who had given me excellent advice, and had counselled good actions in an abode of virgins. I returned to my own monastery and to my spiritual brethren, where at the beginning the Lord directed me. I related to that blessed brotherhood the story of all the things which had happened to me, and I confessed that it was because I had not hearkened to the admonition of that holy father that the Lord left me so that all these trials might come upon me; and He did this for the correction of many.

Therefore, O my son, all these trials, which came upon me because of my disobedience, and which I have narrated before you, are intended for the edification of your soul; get you possession of them, because, by the help of God, patient endurance and implicit obedience will deliver a man from all temptations. Obedience to the commandments of God is everlasting life, the patient endurance, which is perfect, produces everlasting life in us. "For he who endures to the end shall live." These things did the old man Mark [Malchus] himself relate to me while I was a young man, and on account of the law of brotherly love I have written them down because they benefit the chaste life of holy old men, and tend to their edification and admonition. Do then relate them to those who are young, so that they may learn that those who have drawn near to the venerable estate of pure chastity, and who have preserved the same for Christ's sake even to the end, and who are protected by His power, shall overcome all the temptations of the Enemy. Neither captivity, nor the sword, nor any temptation, shall be able to overthrow those who have preserved in all purity and holiness the temple of Christ without spot and blemish, even to death, and they shall become holy temples. The Spirit of God shall dwell in them, and notwithstanding all the words of the Calumniator, He shall bestow victory upon them, for ever and ever. Amen.

DAY 61

Two Fathers Who Went Naked

ABBA MACARIUS, THE EGYPTIAN, once came from Scete to the mountain of Nitria to the Offering of Abba Pambo. The fathers said to him, "Speak with the brethren, O father." He said, "I am not yet a monk, but have seen monks. For once when I was sitting in my cell at Scete my thoughts said to me, "Go out into the desert, and consider intently what you will see there." I remained five years struggling with my thought, and trying it, lest it might be from Satan. Since the thought continued with me, I rose up and journeyed into the inner desert, and I found there a fountain of water with an island in the middle of it.

The beasts of the desert used to drink therefrom, and I saw in the midst of the beasts two naked men. Fear took up its abode in my limbs, and I thought that they were perhaps spirits. When they saw that I was afraid, they spoke to me and said, "Do not fear, we are also men." I said to them, "Where are you from? How have you come to this desert?" They said to me, "We were once in a large monastery. The desire of both of us was the same. We went out and came here, where we have been for forty years. One of us is Egyptian and the other is Libyan." They also questioned me, saying, "What news is there in the world? Do the waters of the river come as usual? Is the world flourishing?" I said to them, "Yes'" I also asked them, "How can I become a monk?" They said, "Unless a man makes himself to be remote from everything which is in this world, he cannot be a monk." I said to them, "I am feeble and I am not able to do as you do." They said to me, "If you cannot do as we do, sit in your cell, and weep for your sins." I asked them, "When it is winter, are you not frozen? In the season of the heat aren't your bodies consumed?" They answered me, saying, "God in His Providence has made us to be so that in the winter we do not freeze and in the summer we are not burnt up." It was because of this that I said, "I am not yet a monk, but I have seen monks. Permit me to be silent."

A Certain Old Man Who Went Naked

THEY USED TO SPEAK OF A CERTAIN SOLITARY MONK who went out to the desert carrying his apparel on his shoulder. He had gone on a journey of three days, climbed a rock, and saw below him an old man who was grazing like the beasts. He came down secretly and gave chase to him. The old man was naked, and his soul had diminished to such a degree that he could not bear the smell of men. He was able to remove himself from them and to make his escape by flight. Having taken flight, that brother pursued him, and cried out to him, saying, "I am following you; for God's sake wait for me." Then the old man answered him, saying, "I, for God's sake also, am fleeing from you." Finally, casting away from him the garment, which was on his shoulder, he pursued him with all his might. As soon as the old man saw that he had cast away his garments, he waited for him. When the brother came up with him, the old man said, "As you did cast away from you the things of the world, I waited for you." Then that brother entreated him, saying, "Speak to me a word of advice that I may be redeemed by." The old man said to him, "Flee from the children of men, keep silent, and you shall live."

Naked Old Man Who Fed With the Beasts

A CERTAIN BROTHER CAME TO THE MONKS who lived in that spot where there were twelve wells of water, seventy palm trees, and where Moses and the people of Israel encamped when they left Egypt. That brother told them the following story, saying, "I once had it in my mind to go into the inner desert and see if there was any man living therein. I went on a journey of four days and four nights. I found a certain cave. Having approached it I looked inside it. I saw a man sitting there. I knocked at the door according to the custom of the monks, so that he might come out to me, and I might salute him. But he never moved, for he was dead. I did not hesitate or draw back, but I went in and laid my hand upon his shoulders. He crumbled into dust and became nothing at all. In wonderment I came out of that place and journeyed on again in the desert."

I saw another cave by the side that had traces of men. I plucked up courage, and drew near to it. I knocked and no man answered me. I went inside, found no man, then came outside. I said within myself, "The holy man will soon come here." When it was evening, I saw a number of beasts, which are called buffaloes. The servant of God was in their midst, naked; and his hair was used as a covering for his shame. When he saw me, he stood up in prayer, for he thought that I was a spirit. He was greatly vexed by an evil spirit, as subsequently he told me. I understood this matter, and said to him, "I am a man, O holy one. Look at my footprints and touch me, for I am flesh and blood." After he prayed, I answered, "Amen." He looked at me, took heart, and brought me into his cave, asking, "Why did you come here?" I said to him, "That I might be blessed by the servants of God if I come into this desert." He has not deprived me of my desire. I also asked him, "How did you come here? How do you live?" He began to speak to me.

I was once in a monastery where my work was to weave linen. The thought came to me that I would leave it and dwell by myself. My mind said, "You will be able to live in seclusion, and to entertain strangers with the results of your labour. Your wages will be more than enough for you." I agreed with my thoughts, and I carried them into effect. I built a habitation, and took up my abode therein. Men used to come to me and carry away my work. While I was doing this, giving my work for the benefit of strangers, the poor, Satan, the Enemy, cast his arrows at me. He flattered me by causing a certain virgin to come to me, with the excuse that she wished to buy the labour of my hands. I gave her what she wanted. Satan stirred her up with one excuse or the other. She used to always come to me.

When she had been accustomed to come and acquired freedom of speech with me, she began to come near me. She would take hold of my hands, and laugh. She was so bold as to eat with me. Subsequently we conceived and brought forth iniquity. Having lived with her in this fallen condition for six months I thought in my mind that whether it was today, or tomorrow, or at some future time, however far off that time might be, I should be delivered over to everlasting torment. The man who takes a wife of another man, and seduces her, is delivered over to the punishment of the Law. How much greater then will be the punishment of the man who has seduced a woman who has been betrothed to Christ? Straightaway, I was determined to come to this desert, and leave everything I had behind me. I went out secretly, and found this cave, this fountain, and this palm, which is in front of it, which produces twelve clusters of dates each year. It thus yields each month what is sufficient for me for the whole month. After some time the hair of my body grew long and my clothes wore out. My hair covered my bodily shame. I have now been here for thirty years.

I questioned him further, saying, "Was your mind disturbed about anything during the first years of your life here?" He said to me, "I was greatly afflicted at first, and I used to throw myself upon the ground because of pain in my liver. I could not stand up to say my prayers, but was obliged to make my supplications to God lying on the ground. While I was in this tribulation, I saw a man come, stood by my side, and said to me, "What is your pain?" At these words I gained a little strength, and I replied, "My liver troubles me and causes me pain." He said to me, "Show me where the place is." Having shown him, he spread out his fingers and his hands, and slit up my body as with a sword, he took my liver and showed me the sore on it. Then he removed the pain. Having made the place whole again, he said to me, "Behold, you are healed. Serve Christ, your Lord, as is appropriate for Him." I have been healed since that day and lived here without any pain.

I entreated him to permit me to live in the first cave, in which I saw the dead monk. He said to me, "You are not able to endure the attack of the devils." Knowing that what he said to me was right, I entreated him to pray for me and to dismiss me. I have narrated this story to you, O my brethren, so that we may be zealous in the spiritual life and its works of excellence. May you attain the everlasting life; may our Lord in His grace and goodness make us worthy to receive it!

Another Holy Man

A CERTAIN OLD MAN, who was held worthy to be the Bishop of a city in Egypt, told the following story (which he tried to make one think he had heard from another man, but he himself had actually done the things which he described).

Once, there came to me the thought that I would go into the inner desert which is over against Ovov, that I might see if I could find any holy men who worshipped Christ. I took with me food and water for four days. I set out on my journey. After four days my food came to an end, and I wondered what I should do for more. I plucked up courage and committed myself to God. I went on for another four days, when I became so weak that I could not stand up any longer. Through hunger and exhaustion I had no strength in me. I became sick in spirit and threw myself on the ground. A certain man came and drew his finger across my lips. Forthwith, I became so strong that I thought that neither fatigue nor hunger had ever drawn near me. As soon as I perceived that strength came to me, I rose up again and continued my journey for four more days. Once more I became weary, and stretched out my hands to heaven. Behold, that man who had given me strength before, drew near to my lips and made me strong.

I continued my journey in the desert after this for seven more days. I found a booth with a palm tree and water by the side of it. There was a man, the hair of whose head was quite white, he made clothing for himself, and his face was awesome to look upon. On seeing me, he stood up in prayer. When he prayed and I answered, "Amen" he knew that I was a man. He took hold of my hands and questioned me, "How did you come here? Does everything in the world still exist? Are the Christians being persecuted?" I said to him, "By the help of your prayers, for in truth you serve God, I have travelled and come into this desert. By the power of Christ, the persecution of the Christians is at an end."

In turn I said to him, "Father, tell me how you came here." With sighs and tears he began to say his story. "I was a bishop. During the period of the persecution, many sufferings came upon me. Finally, because I could no longer bear the tribulations, I sacrificed to idols. Having come to my senses, I recognized the wickedness, which I had committed. I made myself come to this desert so that I might die here. I have passed forty-nine years in making supplication to God for my folly, and entreating Him to forgive me. God gave me life from this palm tree. I did not receive any encouragement to hope for the forgiveness of my sins until the completion of forty-eight years."

After he said these things, he rose up suddenly and went outside the booth. He stood up for many hours in prayer. When he finished his prayer, he came to me. As I looked upon his face, fear and wonder fell upon me, for it was a face of fire. He saw that I was afraid. He said to me, "Do not fear, for the Lord has sent you to me that you may bury my body." As soon as he finished speaking, he stretched out his hands and feet and died. I took the garment, which I had on me and tore it in two, and in one half of it I rolled him up and laid him in the earth. The other half formed my apparel.

As soon as I had buried him, the palm tree dried up. The booth fell down. I made many entreaties to God, and prayed to Him to leave me the palm tree, so that I might pass the rest of my life there. This did not take place, so I perceived that it was not the will of God that I remain here. I prayed, and returned to the habitation of the children of men. Behold, that man who had given me strength before, came again to me and gave me courage. Thus I arrived and came to the brethren. Having related these things to them, I encouraged them not to be in despair about their souls, but in patient endurance they would find our Lord.

Solitary Monk Who Used to Feed on Grass by the Jordan

A CERTAIN MONK WAS FEEDING ON GRASS BY THE JORDAN. At noon, he went into a cave to rest. He found a lion there, which began to roar. He said to the lion, "What vexes you? There is room enough here both for you and for me. If you do not wish for a companion, get up and go out." Because the lion could not bear him, he rose up, and went out

Certain Holy Virgin

ONCE, A CERTAIN GROUP OF THE GREAT SAGES OF SCETE were travelling along a road in the desert when they heard a sound, like the groan of a sick person, rise up from the ground. They searched, and found a path, which led into a cave. When they descended into it, they found a certain holy virgin. They said to her, "O mother, when did you come here? Who ministers to you?" They saw nothing in the cave except the holy woman herself, who was lying on the earth. She said to them, "Behold, I have passed thirty-eight years in this cave and I have satisfied my wants with grass. I labour for Christ. I have never seen a man except this day. God has sent you to me this day to bury my body." Having said these words, she died. When the fathers saw this, they glorified God. They buried her body, prayed, and departed from the place.

DAY 63

Two Young Men who were with Macarius

ABBA BYTINIUS SAID THAT THE DISCIPLE OF MACARIUS once told me the following story:

Abba Macarius once said to me while I was living in Scete; two young men, who are strangers, have gone down there. One of them has a few hairs as a beard. The other has the beginning of a beard. These young men came and said to me, "Where is the cell of Abba Macarius?" I said to them, "What do you seek from him?" They said, "We have heard of his life and deeds. We have come to see him." I said to them, "I am he." They offered me repentance, and said to me, "We wish to abide here." Seeing that they were proud because of their riches, I said to them, "You will not be able to dwell here." The elder of them said to me, "If we are unable to dwell here, we will go to another place." I said to myself, "Why should I be an occasion of stumbling to them, for the labour itself will make them flee?" I said to them, "Come, make a cell for yourselves if you can." They replied to me, "Only show us how to do it, and we will do it."

I gave them an axe, a tool for digging up the ground, and a sack of bread and salt. I showed them a rock where they might hew stone. I said to them, "Hew your stone from here, and then bring wood from the forest and roof over the place, and then take up your abode." I thought that they would straightaway take flight, but they said to me, "What is your work here?" I said to them, "The weaving of palm leaves." I plucked some leaves from the palms in the grove, and showed them how to begin to work to plait baskets, saying, "Give them to the guardians, and they will give you bread." From that hour I left them, everything I said to them, they performed with great persistence and diligence.

They remained there for three years and never came to me. I continued to debate in my thoughts, saying, "What kind of work is theirs that they never come to me to ask me for anything?" The people that are far off come to me, but those who are close by do not come to me. They have gone nowhere else, except to the church to receive the Offering when they have leisure. Then I prayed to God and fasted for a whole week that He might show me their work. Straightaway I rose up and went to them so that I might see how they were. When I knocked, they opened the door to me, saluted me, and then held their peace. I prayed, and sat down. Then the elder of the men motioned to the younger, who went outside, sat down, and plaited ropes, and said nothing. In the ninth hour, he knocked at the door. The younger man came and made a sign to him. He went out and cooked a little food. He made another sign to him, and he prepared a table with three bread cakes upon it, and then stood by in silence. Then I said, "Arise, let us eat." They drew near and we ate. One of them brought an earthenware pitcher of water, and we drank. When the evening had come, they spoke to me, saying, "Are you going away?" I said, "No, I am going to pass the night here." Then they laid down a palm leaf mat for me on one side of their cell, and they threw themselves down upon the bare earth on the other side of the cell by themselves. When I had prayed to God to inform me concerning their toil, the roof was opened. The place became as light as it was in the daytime. They did not see that light.

Then, thinking that I was asleep, the elder man struck the younger, and they rose up, girded up their loins, spread out their hands to heaven; and I saw them. They did not know that I could see them. I saw the devils hovering about over the young man like flies, and some of them wished to settle on his eyes, and some on his mouth. Behold, the angel of the Lord was going round him, and was driving away from him the devils with a sword of fire. The devils did not dare to approach the elder man. About the time of morning, the two men threw themselves on the ground and I made myself appear like one who just woke up from sleep.

They likewise feigned to have only then become awake. The elder man spoke to me these words only, "Do you wish us to recite twelve Psalms only?" I said to him, "Yes." When the elder man stood up and recited the Psalms, out of his mouth came a rope of fire, which ascended into heaven. I could only recite the Psalms little by little. I came out and said to them, "Pray for me." They excused themselves, and were silent. I learned that the elder man was perfect, but that the Enemy still waged war against the younger man. After a few days, the elder man died. Three days later the other man died also. Whenever the fathers came to Abba Macarius, he used to take them to the cell of those brethren, and say, "Behold, the martyrium of these little strangers."

Abba Bessarion

THE DISCIPLES OF ABBA BESSARION used to relate the story of his life and deeds in the following words. The mode of life of this old man was that of the bird of the heavens, of the things, which are in the waters, and of the creeping things of the earth. He passed his whole life in peace, and tranquility. No anxiety as to the condition of his cell was ever present with him. His soul was never occupied with the desire to live in certain places.

He never ministered during the whole course of his career to the satisfaction of himself with food. He never gathered together or laid up for himself possessions in clothes or books. He was free from the care of everything, which concerned the body. He rejoiced in the hope of the good things, which were to come. He was firm and immovable in the foundation of his faith. He followed the ascetic life strenuously. He wandered here and there, like one possessed in the season of frost, he went naked.

He was consumed with heat under the fierce rays of the sun. At one time he lived among the rocks and at another, in the desert. If it happened that he came to districts, which were settled or to a place where a congregation of monks passed their whole lives together in the fulfilment of the rules of monasticism, he would take his seat contentedly outside the door of the monastery.

Once, having arrived at a certain monastery, he sat down outside the door, wept and wailed aloud after the manner of one who had been saved from a storm at sea. When one of the brethren had gone out, he found him sitting there like any ordinary poor man or beggar. Having drawn near him compassionately, he said to him, "What makes you weep, O man? If you need any of the necessaries of life, so far as in my power, I will give it to you. Rise up then, and get inside the monastery. Comfort yourself with the blessed companionship of the table with us." Then the blessed Bessarion answered him, saying, "Until I find the possessions of my house which I lost. The numerous goods of the house of my fathers, which I lost, I cannot live under a roof. For pirates fell on me at sea, and a storm rose against me. I have been short of my riches, from being a man of high degree. I have become the object of contempt."

That brother was astonished and grieved at these words. He went in, brought out some bread, and gave it to him, saying, "Father, take this. The other things, which you have mentioned, like, country, family, and riches, God shall restore to you." Abba Bessarion cried out more, with louder cries, and lifted up his voice, saying, "I do not know if I shall be able to find what I lost, and what I seek, for as far as I can see they will be removed from me even further. I am afflicted daily, and am brought near to death by the violent storm of wickednesses, innumerable, which surrounds me. I endure them and rest upon hope that, perhaps, I may be worthy of mercy on the day of judgement."

The Wonderful Things, Which Abba Bessarion Wrought

ABBA SHAOUL, (OR DULAS) THE DISCIPLE OF ABBA BESSARION, used to say, "We came once to the bank of a lake and I was thirsty." I said to Abba Bessarion, "I am thirsty." The old man prayed, and said to me, "Take water from the lake, and drink." I went, drank, and I found the water to be sweet. I drew from the lake and filled all the water vessels, which I had with me. I thought that, perhaps, I should be thirsty again when I continued my journey. Then the old man seeing me do this, said, "Why did you fill these vessels with water?" I said to him, "Forgive me, father, but I did so lest, perhaps, as we continue our journey, I may become thirsty again." He said to me, "May God forgive you, for here, and there, and everywhere, God directs us."

On another occasion, he was travelling along a road, and came to the river Chrysoroan. There was nothing to aid in crossing the river. He stretched out his hands, and prayed. He crossed over to the other side. I was astonished, and I offered to him repentance, saying, "Father, when you were passing over the river how far up did your legs feel the water?" He said to me, "I felt the water as far as my ankles. But all the rest of it was solid beneath my feet."

On another occasion, we were journeying to a certain great sage. The sun was near to set. The old man prayed, saying, "I beseech You, O Lord, to let the sun abide in his place until I come to Your servant." It was so.

Once, I came to him in his cell so that I might speak with him. I found him standing up in prayer. His hands were stretched out to heaven, and he remained standing up in this position for four days and four nights. Afterwards, he called me, and said, "Come, my son." We went out on the road. Being thirsty, I said to him, "My Father, I am thirsty." Then he moved himself from me the distance of a stone's throw. He prayed and came to me, bringing with him his garment filled with water from the air. I drank, and we travelled on our road until we came to Lycus, to Abba John. After each had saluted the other, he prayed, and sat down. He discoursed concerning a vision, which he had seen. Abba Bessarion said, "A decree of judgement has gone out from the Lord, that all the temples of the idols be blotted out." This actually happened, and all were uprooted.

There was in Egypt a certain man, whose son was paralytic. He took him on his shoulders, brought him to Abba Bessarion and left him by the door of his cell weeping. The father departed and went to a place some distance off. The old man heard the sound of the weeping of the young man. He looked out, saw him, and said, "Who are you and why are you here?" The young man said, "My father brought me here, then went away, and I wept." Then the old man said to him, "Rise up, hasten after him, and overtake him." Immediately, the young man became healed, went to his father, who took him and departed.

On another occasion, a man who had a devil came to the church. Prayer was made on his behalf in the church, but the devil did not go out, for he was difficult to cast out. The clergy said, "What shall we do about this devil, for no man can cast him out except Abba Bessarion? Let us entreat him concerning the man, and even though he does not come to the church, let us act thus. Behold, the old man comes to the church early in the morning before everyone else. Let us make the sick man occupy the seat in which the old man usually sits. When he comes in, let us stand up in prayer, and say to him, "O father, make this man rise up also." They did so. When the old man came into the church in the morning, they rose up in prayer, and said to him, "Father, restore that brother." Abba Bessarion went and struck him with his fist, saying, "Rise up and get out." Straightaway, that devil went out from the man, and the man was made whole immediately.

The Holy Man Who Possessed Nine Virtues

THE FATHERS USED TO SAY CONCERNING a certain brother who lived in a large monastery that, having contended mightily, and having been helped by God, he had made himself master of nine virtues. He was exceedingly desirous of making them ten, but that in spite of many contending's he was unable to do so. The Enemy, according to his custom, cast his arrows at him. Both by day and by night Satan vexed and troubled him in order that he might depart from the monastery in which he was. Satan advised him, saying, "In another monastery you will be able to complete the ten virtues." The brother, not understanding the cunning of the Evil, was led by his thoughts, which seemed to incite him to further spiritual excellence. He departed and went to another monastery with the expectation that he would find what he sought. Having been received into the other monastery, after a very short time, through the wrath of the Calumniator, he lost one virtue. Once again the Calumniator cast into his mind the thought that he would depart from that monastery, although he remembered his promise, and said, "You have not only found what you seek, but you have also lost what you had." Then the brother, being sad and sorry about what happened to him, departed and went to another monastery, with the expectation that he would be able to both acquire the lost virtue, and to add another virtue. Whilst the brother was working and contending to acquire that lost virtue, and the one he wished, the Calumniator, through his wicked craftiness, made him lose another. The Evil made him go out from one monastery to another, so often that the brother at length lost four virtues.

The brother wandered here and there in a state of great agitation. He arrived at a certain monastery and rested himself. He leaned against the door of it, in dejection of spirit, cried over himself, and wept because of what happened to him. Having rested a little, he was determined to go into that monastery in order to be accepted into it. He told himself of all the things, which happened to him, and all the trials, which attacked him in the previous monasteries. He passed judgement on his soul, saying, "Are you able to bear all the trials, which are in this monastery?" His soul answered, saying, "I place my trust in the mercy of our Lord who will give strength to my weakness, and that I shall endure them." Then, deciding these things in his thoughts, the brother wrote them all down on a piece of paper, placed them in his girdle, and strengthened his thoughts to go into the monastery that he might be received.

After being received, he lived in the monastery for a short time. He began to have freedom of speech with the brethren, and with the archimandrite. Temptations began to assault him. He took out the written paper, which was placed in his girdle, read it, and felt relieved. He continued to do so when temptation assailed him. The brethren marvelled because he was not perturbed when they were, for on several occasions, when the brethren of that monastery were in a state of excitement, he had not permitted himself to be agitated with them in the smallest degree. They wished to know the reason for this. One day when the monks were agitated and disturbed by a quarrel, which was so serious that the matter nearly came to a murder, that brother took the paper, and looked at it. As he was reading, one of the brethren watched him. When the tumult was over, the brethren saw that he was not agitated. They marvelled, and said, "What is the meaning of this thing? Why isn't that brother as excited as we are?" The brother who watched the monk reading his paper revealed to them the matter, saying, "He has something in his girdle. On account of it, he remains undisturbed." The brethren enquired about the matter, and found that it was as the brother had said.

They approached the archimandrite, saying, "If you do not expel this brother, we will not remain here, and we will go forth, because he is a sorcerer. Behold, his sorceries are in his girdle." The archimandrite promised to expel him. The archimandrite delayed the expulsion of that brother. One night, while he was asleep, the archimandrite went to him and took the paper from his girdle. He read it and rejoiced with great joy. After reading the paper, he put it back into the girdle of the brother. Neither that brother nor any other man knew what happened. After a short time, the brethren, through the agency of Satan, were greatly disturbed by a very serious quarrel. That brother was in no way agitated. When they saw that he was not disturbed at all and wholly tranquil, they rose up against the archimandrite, saying, "If you do not expel this brother we will all depart from here." Then the archimandrite called the brother and said to him, "What is this that your brethren are saying against you? They are bringing an accusation against you." The brother expressed regret, saying, "Yes, father, all their words are true. Permit me to repent." The archimandrite replied, "But they say that you are a sorcerer." The brother said, "Yes, I am even as they say, but I beseech your piety, O father, that you will allow me to repent here." The archimandrite said to him, "But they say that the sorceries are in your girdle."

The brother, being unwilling to reveal his spiritual excellence, fell upon his face before the archimandrite, took hold of his feet, made supplication to him, and wept with groans and sighs, saying, "Do not expose me, O father. Forgive me for this once only. I will repent with all my soul." The archimandrite, who knew that great advantage would accrue to the whole brotherhood, would not be persuaded by him, but commanded that his girdle be loosened. He himself took it and brought out the paper from there. He then ordered that all the brethren be gathered together, and that the paper be read in a prominent place, so that all of them might hear. After the paper had been read the brethren repented, and fell upon their faces before that brother. They entreated him, saying, "Forgive us, O father, for we have sinned against you." Thus that brother benefited the whole brotherhood, and they regarded him as a father.

DAY 67

Blessed Woman Maria

THERE WAS A WORLDLY MAN WHO WISHED to become a monk. He had a little daughter whom he thought to take with him to the monastery. She was a maiden. He entreated her, saying, "If you wish to become a nun, let me take you to a house for virgins." She said to him, "I cannot be separated from you." She wept night and day and begged that she might not be separated from him. The father, being much distressed, made up his mind to take her with him. He changed her name to conceal her identity as a maiden. Her name had been Maria, but her father gave her the boy's name of Maryana. He committed the matter to God. He took her and went into a monastery without anyone perceiving that Maryana was a girl. After several years Maryana's father died after performing the excellent works of monastic life. The archimandrite saw that Maryana was working hard and excelling in spiritual excellence. He rejoiced in him, not knowing that he was not a boy. He commanded that he should not be sent out on the highways to beg because he was a child. The brethren were envious of Maryana because he did not go out on the highways with them.

When the archimandrite saw that the brethren were envious against Maryana because he did not go out on the highways as they did, he called to Maryana and said to him, "Since the brethren are envious of you because you do not perform the work on the high roads as do they, I command you to do so." Maryana fell down before the archimandrite and said to him, "Whatever you command me to do, I will do gladly, O father." The brethren of the monastery who lived with Maryana, whenever they went out on the high roads, they visited a certain believer, in order to rest a little and to refresh themselves. Since Maryana was sent out, even according to what had been ordered by the archimandrite, the believing man whom the brethren visited saw him, (for he knew all the brethren of the monastery because he used to go to their monastery continually).

The believing man saw Maryana in the evening. He took him and brought him to his house to rest there for the night. The believing man had a daughter. On the night where Maryana stayed with him, a certain man seduced her. He, then, commanded her, saying, "If your father said to you who has seduced you, say to him, it was Maryana the monk." As soon as Maryana had departed from them, the father knew that his daughter had been seduced, and asked her, saying, "Who has seduced you? She said to him that Maryana, the monk, has seduced me." Then the father rose up straightaway, and went to the monastery.

With tears, he spoke before the archimandrite and the whole brotherhood, saying, "What offence have I committed against you that you seduce my daughter?" When the archimandrite heard this he was greatly moved, and he said to him, "What are you saying? Who has seduced your daughter? Tell me who he is so that I may expel him from the monastery." The man replied, "It is Maryana who has seduced my daughter." The archimandrite commanded that Maryana should be sent out from the monastery. Maryana could not be found. Then they knew that he was on a journey outside the monastery. The archimandrite said to the father of the maiden, "There is nothing further which I can do except this. When Maryana returns back, I will not allow him to enter the monastery." He gave orders to all the brethren of the monastery, saying, "When Maryana returns, he is not allowed to enter the monastery."

When Maryana came back from the road, they would not allow him to enter the monastery. He wept at the door of the monastery, saying, "What is my offence that I am not permitted to enter the monastery?" Then the doorkeeper said to him, "You are not permitted to enter because you have seduced the daughter of the believing man whom the monks visit." Maryana entreated the doorkeeper, saying, "For the Lord's sake go in and persuade the archimandrite to permit me to enter the monastery. Whatever he orders me to do because of my fall I will do." So the door keeper went in and told the archimandrite everything which Maryana had said. The archimandrite said to him, "Go and tell Maryana, saying, because you have done this thing, you shall never see my face again. Get away to whatever place you please." When Maryana heard these things, he was greatly afflicted, and sat by the door of the monastery night and day. Maryana wept because of what happened to him. He besought those who went in and those who came out to entreat the Archimandrite on his behalf. Although many folks did so, begging the Archimandrite to let Maryana come into the monastery, the Archimandrite would not be persuaded to do so.

After that daughter, through whom Maryana had been trodden in the dust, had given birth to her child. Her father took the born boy and brought him to Maryana, saying, "Behold, here is your son. Take him and rear him." Maryana took the child, saying, "Glory be to God who can endure and bear with sinners like myself." Daily, Maryana took the child and went up the mountain to the goats of the monastery, and fed the boy with goat's milk. When the child was suckled, Maryana returned to the door of the monastery. He never left the door of the monastery except when he went to give the child milk. He besought those who went in and those who came out, with tears, to unite with him in making supplication to God to forgive him his sin. He sat by the door of the monastery for four years, with tears never absent from his eyes, neither by night nor by day.

Everyone who heard the sound of his weeping was grieved for his sake. After Maryana had suffered affliction by the door of the monastery for four years and had shown the child to every man, saying, "Pray for me, for I fell into fornication. This child is the result of my fornication." God moved the mind of the Archimandrite to bring Maryana into the monastery, for His mercy was revealed on him. He commanded the Archimandrite to bring Maryana inside.

As soon as Maryana heard that they were going to bring him into the monastery, he rose up straightaway, and fell down before the Lord, saying, "Glory be to You, O Lord, Who has not been unmindful of such a great sinner as I am! I give thanks to you for all the goodness which you have shown me. What have I to give to you in return? For you have brought me into the monastery, by the door of which I had decided in my mind that I must die." As soon as those who had been sent to bring Maryana into the monastery had done so, Maryana fell down before the Archimandrite, and before the whole brotherhood of the monastery. He was carrying the child and was weeping, sighing, groaning, and said to them, "Forgive me, O masters and fathers, for I have angered God with my evil works, and you I have afflicted greatly. Pray for me, that God may forgive me the fall wherewith I fell."

After many years of great labours of spiritual excellence, Maryana delivered his soul to our Lord. None of the brethren had ever seen him laugh or smile. To the contrary, he mourned all the days of his life. When he died, the brethren drew near to anoint him with oil according to the custom. Then they discovered that Maryana was a woman. The brethren ran quickly and called the man who made the accusation against Maryana. When he had come and seen Maryana, a great wonder laid hold upon him, and besought

God to forgive him the great sin and wrong which he had done to Maryana. All those who heard and saw this, glorified God that His saints fight so bravely for His Name's sake.

DAY 68

A Certain Sage and of the Watching of the Mind

THERE WAS A CERTAIN OLD MAN who lived in his cell and performed mighty ascetic works. Whenever the brethren of the Cells gathered together for the vigil of the First Day of the week, he would come to the general assembly, and act in such a way as to make the brethren despise him. Indeed, they regarded him as a man who had gone out of his senses, although he did everything with discretion. God, the Good and Compassionate, did not wish the labours of the old man to be hidden. God revealed and made some of them known for the benefit of the community. God also sent angels, in the forms of rich and honourable men, to the priest of the Cells, to salute him.

When the priest saw them, he ran forward to meet them, for he thought that they who appeared to him were great and wealthy men. He rose up immediately and saluted them. After they had sat down and conversed with the old man, they besought him, saying, "O father, we beg you to allow us to go round the Cells so that we may be blessed by the Fathers." He accepted their petition, and permitted them to do whatever they wished. They asked him to send one of the brethren. Then the priest called one of the brethren, and commanded him to go with them, he said to him secretly, "Take heed lest you take them to the cell of that mad old man, for when they see that he has lost his senses, they will be sorry they have met him."

When they had come out to the Cells, the honourable men fell down before the priest of the Cells, and said to him, "O Father, give our brother orders to take us to see all the fathers." The priest said to them, "I have commanded him to take you to them all." Having gone to the fathers of the Cells, and visited them, they returned to the priest in his cell, and he said to them, "Are you gratified now that you have seen the fathers?" They said to him, "O father, we are gratified, but we are sorry about one thing, that is to say, because you did command the brother that we should not see all the fathers." Then the priest called the brother who had gone with them, and said in their presence, "Did not I tell you to take the brethren to all the cells?" The brother said, "Yes, father, you did tell me to do so, and I took them to all the cells, and they have seen all the brethren." Then the honourable men said to the priest, "Forgive us, father, but there are some of the fathers whom we have not seen, and we are greatly grieved by that. Say a prayer on our behalf so that we may depart."

After the priest had prayed over them, they departed from him. He called the brother who had gone with them, and said to him, "How did these men know what I ordered you to do? Did you, perchance, reveal it to them?" The brother made repentance, and said, "Forgive me, father, but I did not reveal your orders to them." Then the priest knew that the matter was from God.

He rose up straight away and went to that old man whom he thought to be out of his mind. He fell down on his face before him, and laid hold upon his feet. He also besought him to reveal to him his ascetic works and labours. He swore to the old man that he would not rise up from the ground and would not let go of his hold until he had done so, saying to the old man, "That I should come to you and that you should reveal your labours to me; are matters from God."

The old man was unwilling to reveal his works, because he did not wish to be held in honour because of them. Nevertheless, he was compelled to do so as the priest had told him that the matter was from God. He promised the priest to reveal one thing to him. When the priest heard the promise of the old man, he rose up from the ground. While seeing the old man in a gentle and tranquil frame of mind, he marvelled, because he had never before seen him as he was at that moment. Then the old man said to the priest, "I have by my side two baskets, one on my right hand, and one on my left.

For every good thought which springs up in my mind I take a pebble and throw it into the basket which is on my right hand. For every hateful thought which rises in me, I also take a pebble and throw it into the basket which is on my left hand. I did this every day. When the time for the evening meal has arrived, I take out the pebbles, and count them. If the number of those which are in the basket of good thoughts do not exceed those in the basket of evil thoughts, I do not take any supper that evening. If they do exceed, then I eat, and rejoice. Sometimes, several days passed without my eating at all, because the pebbles of the good deeds do not exceed the pebbles of the bad ones. Whenever an abominable thought comes to me, I pass judgement on myself, and say, "Take heed, for you will not eat today!" Having heard these things, the priest praised God, the Lord of the universe. He marvelled how the old man could perform such works of righteousness and yet keep them hidden from every man.

DAY 60

Two Brothers Who Dwelt in a Persian Monastery

A CERTAIN HISTORY, WHICH IS FULL OF PAIN AND PROFIT, O my beloved, came to me by chance, that is to say, through conversation and speech with the brethren. I have thought much about it, and have determined that it is right for me to narrate it, and to set it down in writing, so that many may acquire spiritual profit. Watch against the enmity, be at peace with all others, forgive each other so that we may remember the words of our Lord, and God, and Redeemer, Jesus Christ.

There were two brethren who dwelt in one abode in a certain Persian monastery. It happened that one of them had a dispute with the other, and they separated from one another, one leaving the monastery altogether, and the other remaining in the abode where they lived together. It happened that he who remained behind was seized, bound, and shut up in prison, for giving testimony concerning our Lord. He was brought before the judge, and was questioned by him once, twice, and a third time. He bore severe stripes and did not deny Christ. He was again fast bound in the prison house. When his companion heard this, he repented in his soul, and thought, "It is right that I should go and be reconciled with my brother, for perhaps he may depart from the world, each of us keeping wrath against the other, and through this we both shall suffer no small loss, and probably I more than he." When the brother had meditated this, he came to the prison and enquired for his companion who was imprisoned there. He went into his presence and fell down at his feet, and besought and entreated him to be reconciled to him. The brother who was in fetters would not be persuaded to do this, and continued in his wrathful condition. When the brother saw this, he left him and departed in sorrow.

On the following day, the judge commanded the presence of the man who was bound and in prison. He asked him if he would be persuaded to deny his God and to worship the sun but he would not agree. The judge gave orders that he be laid out and beaten and smitten with rods. They laid him out and as the strokes were being laid on by two men, he denied Christ. When the judge saw this, he commanded the men to stop beating him, and called him. He asked him, saying, "What ails you? I caused you to bear severe stripes on three previous occasions, and you were neither overcome nor played the coward's part. Yet now, while they are coming near you, you deny your God." The brother said, "I have acted thus because I have sinned and treated the commandments of the Lord my God with contempt, God who commanded us to forgive each other.

I once had a brother in our Lord, and we lived together in one monastery, and it happened that anger rose up between us. We separated from each other in enmity. Yesterday he came to me in prison, fell down before me and begged for peace from me. I would not consent to be reconciled to him. Therefore, I was deprived of the goodness of God. God did not help me this day as He has always done before. I denied Him. During the stripes which I received formerly I used to see Him spread out a hand's breadth above me. He did not permit me to suffer. But today He forsook me. With a small amount of pain, I was terrified and I denied Him." When the judge heard these things, he commanded that his fetters be loosened off him, and he be dismissed. The brother, feeling disgrace and shame at the fall which had come upon him, went out from the presence of the judge. He went straight to his companion, and fell down on his face at his feet. He wept and cried out bitterly. He entreated for mercy and peace. When his companion looked at him, he suffered in great grief, and received him. They were reconciled. He prayed for him, although the experience of their separation from one another was bitter for both.

Then the brother who denied God straightaway returned to the door of the judge. He began to cry out and to curse the king, so that they might bring him again before the judge for examination. The judge did not wish to say anything to him. When the brother saw this, he departed from there, and through penitence and grief for what happened to him, and through the pain and anguish of his soul, he threw himself into a fire temple. He began to cast dust and everything else which came to his hands on the fire. He cursed the king mightily, saying, "God will receive those who have been tripped up and have fallen if they repent and turn to Him." He departed from there, and wandered about, and threw stones at every magician or pagan whom he met. He never ceased reviling the king. He never ceased or kept silent concerning the compassion of our Lord, which is laid out for those who repent. He cried out, saying, "Verily, there is no god except our Lord Jesus Christ. I, through my sins, and my negligence of His mercy, have denied Him."

When the judge heard these things, he feared lest he would suffer a penalty and be condemned to death. The judge straightaway sent forth a decree concerning him, ordering that his head should be cut off quickly with the sword. When they had seized the monk, they took him outside the city. He cried out with a loud voice, saying, "Blessed are You, O our Lord Jesus Christ, for ten thousand times ten thousand sins are too few for your mercy to forgive in one hour." Having said this, they made him kneel down and smitten him by the sword. Glory is to the Power Who makes His saints strong to do His Will. May we have mercy shown to us through their prayers. Amen.

A Certain Virgin Who Grew Old in the Works of the Fear of God

A CERTAIN OLD MAN RELATED THE FOLLOWING STORY: There was a virgin who was far advanced in years. She had grown old in the fear of God. Having been asked by me to tell me the reason why she left the world, she began, with sighs, to speak to me the following. She said, "Great and marvelous things have happened to me. My father was a peasant man. He was modest in his disposition. He was a delicate man in health and was always suffering from some kind of sickness. He lived entirely to himself, and never interfered in the affairs of other people. It was the greatest difficulty to induce him to see the people of his village. When he was in good health, he devoted his attention unceasingly to the care of his estate, and occupied himself at all

seasons with the cultivation of his fields.
He finally was obliged to pass many long days of his life laid out on a bed of sickness.

He was so quiet that those who were not acquainted with him would have thought that he was deaf. My mother was the opposite of my father in all her ways and manners. She used to do things, which were beyond her capacity. She was very talkative. Her words to everyone were useless. She talked so much that everyone imagined that her body was composed wholly of tongues. Moreover, she had quarrels with her neighbours continually, and was always in a state of drunkenness. She drank shamelessly at all times with wanton folk. She managed the affairs of her house badly, in the manner of a harlot. At length, though the house was well furnished with goods of every kind, it was with the greatest difficulty that the people could find enough to supply our wants. She was very lax in the care for the things which my father required in his illness. She displayed the utmost attention in providing for her own body in a disgraceful manner. The people of the village at length fled before her shameless appearance. No illness ever came to her and she had never been ill in the whole course of her life, from the day she was born. She was healthy until her death.

When I, a wretched girl, lived for some time in circumstances such as these, it happened that, after struggling against a long illness, where my father was obliged to pass every day of his life in the infirmity of sickness, he departed from the world. At the very moment of his death, the weather changed. The rain poured down in torrents. Lightning and thunder were tearing through the air, disturbing it violently. It was impossible to tell whether it was day or night. My father, for this reason, lay dead on his bed for three days, as the weather did not permit us to bury him.

Moreover, it made the people of the village shake their heads, and wonder, saying, "Perhaps great wickedness was committed by this man secretly, and he may have been found to be an enemy of God, that even the earth will not permit his burial. But, in order that his body might not corrupt, even though the weather was gloomy and threatening, we carried him to the grave, and laid him there. My mother, as one who had found great relief, fulfilled her lusts to the utmost. She straightaway turned my father's house into an abode of harlots. She lived there in such a state of luxury and lascivious pleasure. Then with difficulty death came to my mother. In my opinion, death was afraid to approach her, for great worms grew in her. With much trouble she was buried; the weather by its serenity and the sun by its splendour helping in the work.

After the death of my mother, I was still a little girl. I left the world. During the period when I was a young woman, the lusts of the body were stirred up within me, and goaded me severely. I used to wake up in the evening (or night) so that I might lie down again and find a little relief from the disturbance of my mind. A struggle went on in my thoughts, for I wondered what manner of life I should choose for myself; how I should end the days of my life, and whether they would be passed in quietness and happiness, and fair chastity, as during my father's lifetime. Then my thoughts spoke to me, "Behold, in this world your father did not enjoy any happiness whatsoever. He passed all his life in sickness and wretchedness. He departed from this world of trouble under the same circumstances. Even the earth was unwilling to receive his body. What does man do to receive such a life as this? God, why did my father deserve such treatment? On the other hand, supposing I chose to lead a life like that of my mother, will it be better to deliver my body over to fornication, and lasciviousness.

What is the gratification of my lusts? For, behold, my mother left no kind of abominable wickedness she did not commit. She destroyed her whole life with her depravity. Yet she departed from this world having enjoyed health and prosperity every day of her life! What then? Isn't it right for me to live even as she lived? For it is better that I should believe with my own eyes, and that they should see for themselves the various endings of such matters. There is nothing better than to thoroughly understand what we see openly before our eyes." I, the wretched girl, vainly imagined that such thoughts were the thoughts of truth. For this reason, I determined to prepare myself to live as my mother lived. When the night had overtaken me, I slept thinking thoughts of this kind. During my sleep I dreamt, a certain man, of huge stature, stood up above me. His appearance was frightful, and his form trembled and terrified me. His face was hard. In a stern voice he asked me, saying, "Tell me, what are these thoughts in your heart?" Because I was terrified by his appearance and form, I scarcely dared to look at him.

In a voice sterner than before, he commanded me to reveal to him the things, which I settled in my own mind to do. Being stupefied with fear, I forgot all my thoughts and I said to him, "My lord, I do not know what you are saying." Denying that I knew, he reminded me of everything which was in my mind, one after the other. Therefore, having rebuked myself, I turned, begged and entreated him that I might be held worthy of forgiveness. I related to him the reason for such thoughts. He straightaway said to me, "I am about to show you both your father and your mother. You will see the different manner of life which they lead, the things each does, and you shall choose which life to lead." He took me by my hands, drew me away, and carried me to an exceedingly great plain. There were many paradises, and thick trees heavily laden with fruits. Their appearance and beauty surpassed description. When I had entered into that plain, my father met me, embraced and kissed me. He conversed with me and called me 'my daughter.' While I was in his embrace, I besought him to remain with him. He said to me, "At present it is impossible. If you desire to walk chastely in my footsteps you shall come here after no great time."

I was then lifted up and the man said to me, "Come and see your mother also in the fire which is blazing fiercely, so that you may know how to choose what is good, and what manner of life is useful and beneficial for you." I saw a fiery furnace which was burning fiercely. Every kind of cruel wrath surrounded the furnace. I heard the sound of weeping and gnashing of teeth coming from there. Having looked down into the furnace, I saw my mother sunk in fire up to her neck. She was weeping and gnashing her teeth. She was being consumed in the fire, and was being gnawed by a multitude of worms. When she saw me, she cried out with tears in a loud voice, saying, "My daughter, Woe is to me. O my daughter, for these things have happened to me because of my evil deeds. I ridiculed the things, which were said to me concerning chastity, fornication and adultery. Behold, in return for my lascivious pleasure, I have to suffer torture because I did not think that vengeance was laid up therefore. The momentary gratification of my desire, is an everlasting punishment I have to endure. What penalty am I not compelled to pay?

Consider, moreover, that in return for the short-lived happiness, I, the wretched woman, have to pay a prolonged penalty. All these things have overtaken me because I behaved rebelliously, but behold, this is the time for helping me, O my daughter. Remember with what anxious care and attention, your bringing up was carried out, the helpful things which I brought you, all the good things which I did for you. Have mercy upon the woman who burns in the fire. Have mercy upon the woman who is cast into tortures as these. Have pity upon me, O my daughter, stretch out your hand, and lift me up out of this place." I excused myself from doing this on account of him that stood by my side. She wept and cried out to me, saying, "O my daughter, help me.

O my daughter, have pity upon me, and come to me. Do not neglect your mother who gnashes her teeth in pain. Do not treat her with indifference, for she suffers torment in Gehenna."

I felt pain because of her tears and mournful voice. I began to cry out loudly, to sigh and moan bitterly. Then all those who were sleeping in our house awoke. When they had risen up, I told them the reason for the outcry and disturbance. I narrated to them everything, which appeared to me. By the rich mercy of God, I chose to follow the life and works of my father.

These are the things, which we heard from the virgin who is worthy of blessing. From them we may know what delights are laid up for those who wish to live in a state of spiritual excellence, and what punishments are prepared for those who choose to live a wicked life. Because of these things it is necessary that we should strive to the utmost to live a life of virtue, and to excel, so that, by the help of God, we may merit the happiness of heaven. Amen.

Stephana, a Man who Fell into Filthy Shamelessness

THERE WAS A CERTAIN MAN IN SCETE whose name was Stephana, who dwelt in the desert for twenty-nine years. His apparel was made of palm leaves. He lived in a strict state of self-denial, and persisted to such a degree in ascetic abstinence that he never had the least inclination for meat, which are usually desired and pleasant to the taste. He greatly condemned those who, because of sickness, either ate cooked food or drank milk. The gift of healing had been given to him to such a degree that he could cast out devils by a word. It happened that on one occasion a man with an unclean spirit came to Scete, and wished to be healed. When the monk saw that the man was vexed sorely by the devil, the monk made a prayer and healed him. At length, this monk was rejected by Divine Providence because of his immeasurable arrogance and haughtiness. He imagined himself to be more excellent in his life and works than the other fathers. First of all he separated himself from the brotherhood, and went to become an archimandrite in one of the Alexandrian monasteries. He said in his pride, "Am I to be in subjection to Macarius? Isn't my life and work better than his?" This man arrived at such a state of madness that he went to Alexandria, and gave himself up to gluttony, drunkenness, eating of more flesh than rational beings need to eat. Finally he fell and settled down into the pit of the lust for women. He had always been going about in the houses of harlots, and in the ill-famed taverns. He hung closely to the whores, and gratified his lusts in a filthy manner without shame. He became a laughing-stock to all who knew him. He himself said, "I do not act thus because of passion and fornication, neither do I do anything which is abominable, for it is not a sin to go with women, for male and female were created by God."

It fell out that one day, the blessed man Evagrius went to Alexandria on some business. We had four brothers with us. As we were passing through the city market, that monk met us accidentally, and he was talking with a harlot about his filthy lust. When the blessed Evagrius saw him, he wept, and fell down at his feet. The man did not incline his head in the smallest degree. With infinite arrogance and haughtiness he made answer to him, saying, "What do hypocrites and deceivers seek here?" Then the blessed Evagrius entreated him to go with us to the place where we were lodging. He did not by any means wish to go.

When, with the greatest difficulty, he had been persuaded to go with us, so soon as we had entered in and prayed, the blessed Evagrius fell upon his neck, kissed him, and with tears said to him, "Verily, O my beloved, from all that divine service of angels you have been brought down to this depth of wickedness. You have turned yourself from converse with God to converse with harlots. Instead of the life and service of angels you have chosen the life of devils! But I beseech and entreat you, do not cut off the hope of your redemption. Arise, and come with us to the desert, for by my hands, God the Merciful is able to restore you to your former grade." His understanding had been so blinded by Satan that he did not know how to listen to what was said to him, nor did he know what he answered. He said to Evagrius, "Up to the present I have certainly been wandering about. But now I have found the path of truth." He began to make a mock of the fathers, saying, "You certainly wander about and dwell in the desert under a false character, for the sake of men, and not for the sake of God. You are to the spectators as idols whom men decorate, and to whom they pay worship." Thus, being full of the pride and boasting of Satan, he spurned the fathers, went forth and departed. The blessed Evagrius and the brethren wept and groaned over him greatly.

Then that man carried off a certain virgin, who was an orphan and a nun living by herself, with a foul design to his monastery. Though he did this with the excuse that he was going to help her by means of alms of which she was in need, it was in reality that he might fulfil his wanton desire. Having lived with her in this degraded state for about two years, thieves, at length, came to him by night. They first tied him with cords, and then struck him with hard and cruel blows until he brought everything he had in his dwelling and laid it before them. Last of all, they shut him up with the woman with whom he used to work out his wantonness, in a house full of straw. Both of them were bound with cords. The thieves set fire to the house, and the two were consumed and died a bitter death.

In them was fulfilled what was spoken by the teacher of the Gentiles, who said, "Because they did not decide within themselves to know God, God delivered them over to the knowledge of vanity, that they might disgrace their bodies therewith, and they received the reward which befitted their error in their own persons." That is to say, the burning of the fire which is here, is a pledge of that fire which tormented all the wicked. Now the things, which happened to Stephana took place because he separated himself from the brotherhood, was unduly exalted in his mind, and because he imagined that he was perfect.

DAY 72

Eucarpus

THERE WAS ALSO IN THE DESERT A CERTAIN MAN named Eucarpus. He spent eighteen years shut up in his cell. Necessary food was brought by others. He had lived in seclusion for fifteen years, and never spoke to any man during that period except when he was in need of something. He used to write on paper what he wished to say, and would give it to those who ministered to him. He has done this when any man asked him a question or spoke to him. His food consisted of vegetables soaked in water, and pounded garden herbs. He carried out his rule of life with infinite labour. Finally, however, the devils made him a laughing stock also, because of the vain opinion, which he had concerning himself. First of all, he separated himself from mingling with the brethren and conversing with them. Next, he ceased to meditate on the Holy Scriptures, and he did nothing except pray continually; for he was proud and haughty in his mind. He thought that he was perfect. One night Satan appeared to him in the form of an angel of light, saying to him, "I am Christ."

When Eucarpus saw him, he thought that the appearance was a real person. He fell down, and worshiped him, saying, "Master, what do you command your servant to do?" He who had appeared to him said to him, "Since you have excelled much in your works, and have kept all my commandments, I desire greatly to make my abode with you. Since you are perfect, it is not necessary for you to shut yourself up. It is no longer right that you should live in seclusion. You must teach all the brethren not to destroy their souls with the reading of the Scriptures, and the reciting of the Psalms. They must not labour in the toil of the body, and must not vex their souls with fasting, hunger, and thirst. They must labour with the labour of the soul, for by these means they shall be able speedily to be lifted up to the highest grade. They must always look at me with their minds, and I will show them my glory. As for you, since you have raised yourself above all the monks by your works, behold, I make you this day a chief and a governor over all the monks who dwell in Scete. Macarius is not as useful a governor as you are." Then Eucarpus was more lifted up in his mind than before. He was more proud, and truly believed the error of the Crafty One.

On another day there was a congregation in the church. Satan appeared to Eucarpus a second time, and said to him, "Go this day, for all the brethren are gathered together, and teach them everything which I commanded you yesterday in the night season." Eucarpus opened the door of the house where he secluded himself, and departed to go to the church. It happened that Abba John was sitting by the side of the church. The brethren were round about him, and were asking him about their thoughts. When Eucarpus came, and saw John with the brethren surrounding him, he was filled with envy of him. He answered and said to John with haughtiness and wicked wrath, "Why do you adorn yourself and sit down, like a whore, who wishes to multiply her friends? Or, who commanded you to be a corrector of others, seeing that I am the governor of the monastery?" When the brethren heard these words, they were greatly moved, and said to him, "Who made you the governor of Scete?" Eucarpus said to them, "Yesterday in the night I was made governor by Christ. Therefore turn to me, and I will teach you the way with which you shall easily ascend to the high grade of the vision of glory. Do not go astray after the writings of Evagrius, neither hearken to the words of John, for you have wandered far enough into error already."

Then he began to revile the fathers, and called Macarius a painted idol, whom those who err worship, for he does not know how to lead the brethren on the path towards heavenly things. He called Evagrius a hewer of words and made him cease from spiritual service. The devils made a mock of Eucarpus until they were able to lift him up and to dash him down on the earth. All these things that fell upon him took place because he condemned the brethren, and, through his pride and arrogance, he held them in contempt. Finally, when the fathers saw that he was smitten in mind, they threw iron fetters on him and bound him with. The holy fathers offered prayers on his behalf for eleven whole months. Then his mind returned to him, and he was so thoroughly cured of his pride that he perceived his weakness. He recognized his disease and how he had been made mockery by the devils. In him was fulfilled what was said, "Old blains (or wounds) are cured by burnings, and, You who did exalt yourself to heaven shall be brought down even to Sheol." Eucarpus lived after being cured of his arrogance, one year and one month. The fathers commanded that he should minister to the sick, and wash the feet of strangers, till his death.

Famous Deacon who dwelt in a Coenobium in Egypt

A CERTAIN BROTHER ASKED AN OLD MAN and said to him, "If it should happen that a man fell into temptation, by the permission of God, for the benefit of his soul, what is right for those who are made to stumble by the same temptation?" The old man answered, saying, "If he repents in every truth, with all his heart, and makes confession to God in his repentance, saying, I have been rightly humbled, God is able to heal the consciences of those who have already offended Him." The old man spoke and narrated the following story.

There was a certain deacon in a coenobium in Egypt, and a rich man, who had been driven out from the presence of a governor who had dominion over him, came with his household to that coenobium. The deacon stumbled and fell into adultery with the wife of one of those who were with him. He became a laughing stock to every man. He went to a certain man who was his friend, and revealed to him the matter, saying to him, "Let no man know where I am; for he hid himself in a secret part of a cell and he said to him, 'Here bury me during my lifetime.' Having gone down into the darkness of that hidden place, he repented to God in truth. After a certain time, the river, which was near to the place where the deacon had hidden himself, did not rise according to its measure. The people of the country prayed and made supplication. It was revealed to one of the saints that, unless that deacon who is hidden comes out, the waters will not rise. So they went and brought him out from the place where he was hidden. When he had come, he made a prayer, and straightaway the river rose. Those who had been formerly offended by him were now edified the more. They profited through him greatly and glorified God.

Bishop Who Fell into Fornication

THERE WAS A CERTAIN BISHOP IN ONE OF THE CITIES, who through the working of the Calumniator fell into fornication. One day when the congregation was in the church, although no one knew of the Bishop's sin, he voluntarily confessed it before all the assembly, saying, "I have fallen into fornication." Then he took off his vestments, and laid them upon the altar, saying, "I cannot, henceforward, be your Bishop." All the people cried out with tears, saying, "Let this sin be upon us; only remain in your episcopate." He answered and said to them, "If you wish me to remain in my episcopate, do what I shall say to you." He commanded all the doors of the church to be shut with the exception of one. He threw himself down upon his face, saying, "The man who goes out from the church without walking upon me, shall have no portion with God." They did according to his word. When the last man had gone out, a voice was heard, saying, "Because of his great humility, I have forgiven him for his sin."

Brother who was a Neighbour of Father Poemen

WHEN ABBA POEMEN CAME TO EGYPT to dwell there, he took up his abode by the side of a brother who had a wife. Though the old man knew this, he did not rebuke him. When the time had come for the woman to bring forth, he cried out to a younger brother, and said to him, "Arise, take this jar of wine and carry it to our neighbour, for he will have need of this day." The matter was not known to that brother, but he did as commanded. The brother who had a wife groaned and repented in his mind. After a few days, he dismissed the woman. He came to Abba Poemen, and said to him, "Behold from this day onwards, I repent, O father. I entreat you to pray to God on my behalf so that He may receive my repentance." Abba Poemen said to him, "If you repent with all your heart, I believe that God will bestow forgiveness to you. Do not despair of your redemption." The brother went and built for himself a place of retreat. He made an entrance through which he used to come to visit the old man. He would go to Abba Poemen and he profited spiritually. The brother laboured in fasting and in prayer. He wept, sighed, and grieved sorely for his sin. At length, it was revealed to the old man, on behalf of the brother, that God had accepted his repentance.

Brother Who Denied Christ

ONCE, A CERTAIN BROTHER WAS ENGAGED in a war against fornication. He happened to pass through a village in Egypt where he saw the daughter of a heathen priest. He loved her, and said to her father, "Give her to me as a wife." The priest answered him saying, "I cannot give her to you before knowing the will of God in the matter." He went to his devil, and said to him, "Behold, a certain monk wishes to take my daughter to wife. Shall I give her to him or not?" The devil answered, saying, "Ask him if he will deny his God, and his baptism, and the vows he made before entering the monastic life." Having gone to the brother the priest told him that he would accept him as his daughter's husband if he would deny these things. The priest also said to him, "Will you deny the baptism wherewith you were baptized?" The brother answered and said, "Yes, I will." Straightaway, he saw the Spirit of God go forth from his mouth in the form of a dove, and ascend into heaven. Then the priest went to the devil and told him what the brother had said. Behold, he has promised to deny all three things. The devil answered him saying, "You shall not give him your daughter, for his God has not departed from him. God is still helping him, and will accept him if he repents." The priest returned to that brother, saying, "I cannot give her to you, for Your God is with you. He will not leave you, but will help you." When the brother heard this, he said within himself, "So God keeps such great grace for you, and will still help you!"

Then the brother came back to his senses. He made his mind strong, fortified his will, and went out to a certain old man in the desert. He related the matter to him. The old man answered and said to him, "Sit down here with me in this cave, and fast for three weeks, only eating once every two days, and I will make supplication on your behalf to God." The old man laboured with the brother, and made entreaty and supplication to God, saying, "I beseech You, O Lord God, to grant me the soul of this brother, and to accept his repentance." When the first week was completed, the old man came to the brother, and asked him, saying, "Have you seen anything?" The brother answered and said, "Yes, I have seen a dove flying about in the heights of heaven, and standing before my head." The old man said to him, "Take heed to yourself. Pray to God with groans and sighs." The following week he came again to the brother, and asked him the same question, saying, "Have you seen anything?" The brother answered, saying, "I saw a dove, which came and drew near my head." The old man admonished him, saying, "Arise and pray to God with abundant supplication." When the third week passed, the old man came to the brother and said to him, "What have you seen?" He answered and said to him, "I saw a dove which came and stood upon my head. I stretched out my hand and took hold of it. But it fled away and entered into my mouth." Then the old man gave thanks to God, and said to the brother, "God has accepted your repentance. Watch yourself and take heed to yourself." The brother answered and said, "Behold, from this day onwards, I shall live with you, O father, even to the day of my death."

DAY 75

Old Man in Scete

THERE WAS A CERTAIN OLD MAN IN SCETE who became very sick indeed. He was ministered to by the brethren, and thought in his mind that they were tired of him. He said, "I will go to Egypt, so that the brethren may not have to labour on my account." Abba Moses said to him, "You shall not go, for if you go, you will fall into fornication." The old man was grieved and said, "My body has long been dead, and you say these things to me?" He went up to Egypt, and men heard about him. They brought many offerings to him. A certain believing virgin came in faith to minister to him. After some time, when the old man had been healed, the young woman laid with him, and conceived. The folk asked her, saying, "Where had you conceived?" She said to them, "From the old man." They did not believe her. When the old man heard that they would not believe her, he said, "Yes, I have done this thing; protect the child which shall be born." When the child was born and weaned, there was a congregation in Scete. The old man went down carrying the child on his shoulder, and went into the church before all the people. When they saw him, they all wept. The old man said to the brethren, "Observe, O my brethren. This is the child of disobedience. Take heed, then, to yourselves, for I have committed this act in my old age. Pray for me." The old man went to his cell, and dismissed the things where he had lived. He returned to his former deeds. After a time, he arrived once more at his old measure of ascetic excellence.

The Harlot Who Serapion Converted

ABBA SERAPION CAME AND PASSED through a certain village in Egypt where he saw a harlot standing in his cell. The old man said to her, "Remain here until the evening, for I wish to come with you, and to pass this night with you." The harlot said, "It is well, O father." She prepared her bed, and awaited the old man. When it was evening, Abba Serapion came, but he brought nothing with him. He went to her cell, and said to her, "Is your bed ready?" She said to him, "Yes, father." They shut themselves in. The old man answered her, saying, "Wait a little, because I must perform a certain thing which is a law to us." He began to recite the Book of the Psalms of David from the beginning. With every Psalm he offered up a prayer on her behalf, and made supplication before God that she might repent and live. God hearkened to him. The harlot stood up in fear by the side of the old man and prayed too. When Abba Serapion finished all the Psalms, she fell down upon the ground. He began to repeat many verses from the books of the Apostles. When he had finished his service, God opened the heart of that woman, and knew that Abba Serapion had not come to her for the purposes of sin, but to redeem her. She fell on her face before him, and said, "Perform an act of grace for me, O father, and take me to any place wherever I can please God." He took her to an abode of nuns and placed her there. He said to the abbess of the convent, "Take this sister, O mother, and do not lay on her the rules that bind the other sisters. Whatever she requires, give her; and in proportion as she finds rest. Let her submit to be led." When the woman dwelt in the nunnery for a few days, she said, "I am a sinful woman, and wish to eat only in the evening." After a few more days, she said, "Many sins lie to my charge, and I therefore beg that I may eat once every four days." She did so. After a few days more, she besought the mistress of the nunnery, saying, "Do an act of grace for me. Since I have made God exceedingly angry, take me into a cell and wall it up. Through a small opening therein give me a little bread and work for my hands to do." The abbess of the nunnery hearkened to her, and did thus, and in this wise that woman pleased God all the days of her life.

DAY 76

The Harlot Whom a Subdeacon Drove out of Church

A CERTAIN OLD MAN SAID, there was a harlot who was so beautiful and so rich that all princes flocked to her. One day she went into the church and desired to pass inside the gates, but a subdeacon who was standing at the door would not allow her to do so. He said, "You are not allowed to enter the house of God, because you are an unclean woman." While they were striving together, the Bishop heard the sound of the noise. The Bishop went to see what was the matter. The harlot said to him, "The subdeacon would not permit me to go into the church." The Bishop said to her, "You are permitted to do so because you are unclean." Having repented within herself, she said, "I will never play the whore again." The Bishop said to her, "If you strip yourself of all possessions, I know for certain that you will repent." She brought her possessions. The Bishop took the possessions and divided them in the fear of God among the needy. The woman went to the church, and wept saying, "If it had happened to me thus in this world, what would have happened to me in the next?" She repented, and became a chosen vessel.

Abba Apollo, who was in Scete

THEY SAY CONCERNING ABBA APOLLO, who lived in Scete, that he was originally a rude and brutish herdsman, and that he once saw in the field, a woman who was with child. Through the operation of the devil, he said, "I wish to know the condition of the child which is in the womb of this woman, and that he ripped her open and saw the child in her belly." Straightaway he repented, and he purged his heart. Having repented, he went to Scete, and revealed to the fathers what he had done. He heard them singing the Psalms, and saying, "The days of our years are threescore years and ten, and with difficulty we come to fourscore years." He said to the old men, "I am forty years old today, and have not yet made a prayer. If I live for forty years more, I will never rest, nor cease, nor refrain from praying to God continually that He may forgive me my sins." From that time onwards he did even as he had said, for he never toiled with the work of his hands, but he was always supplicating God, and saying, "I, O my Lord, like a man have sinned, and You, like God, forgive me." He prayed this prayer both by night and by day instead of reciting Psalms. A certain brother who used to dwell with him, once heard him say his prayer. As he spoke, he wept, groaned from the bottom of his heart, and sighed in grief of heart, saying, "O my Lord, I have vexed You, have pity on me. Forgive me so that I may enjoy a little rest." Then a voice came to him, saying, "Your sins have been forgiven, so is the murder of the woman. But the murder of the child is not yet forgiven." One of the old men said, "The murder of the child was forgiven, but God left him to work because this would prove beneficial to his soul."

DAY 77

Cosmas, Who was in Mount Sinai

A CERTAIN BROTHER ASKED AN OLD MAN, saying to him, "How is it that Satan brings temptations on holy men?" The old man said, I have heard that there was a holy man whose name was Cosmas, who used to dwell in Mount Sinai. Behold, a certain man went to the tabernacle (or tent) of a husbandman. Finding his daughter by herself, he lay with her, and then said to her, "When your father comes, say to him, Abba Cosmas, the monk, has laid with me." When her father came, she told him thus. Then he took his sword, and came against the old man. When he had knocked at the door, the old man had gone out, he lifted up his sword to slay him. His hand withered straightaway. He went to the church and told the people there what the old man had done.

The fathers sent after him and brought him there. Having upbraided him, and beaten him with many stripes, they wished to drive him out of the monastery. He entreated them, saying, "Allow me to stay here so that I may repent, for God's sake." They separated him from the brotherhood for three years, and they laid down the command that no man was to go to him. He spent three years coming to the church every Sunday for repentance. He besought the fathers always to pray for him. At length, the devil entered into him that had committed the act of which the old man had been accused. Being urged by him, he said, "I committed the act." Then all the people gathered together, went to the old man and expressed their penitence, and said to him, "Forgive us, O father." He replied, "I have indeed forgiven you, but it is impossible for me to remain with you." He departed from them. Behold, how temptations come upon holy men!

DAY 78

Abba Macarius

ABBA MACARIUS USED TO TELL A STORY ABOUT HIMSELF, and to say that when he was a boy, he dwelt in a certain cell in Egypt, and that the people came and made him the priest in the village. He did not wish to receive the office of priest so he fled to another place, and took up his abode in a cell not very far from the habitations of man. A certain young man who feared God used to come, take away the work of the hands of the blessed man, and minister to him. It came to pass that, as a result of a temptation, a certain virgin in the village fell into iniquity, and conceived a child. The folk said to her, "By whom is this child?" She said, "By that monk who lives in the desert." They went out, and brought him to their village, and struck him sorely. They hung round his neck black pots and handles of empty pans. They made him go round through the markets of their village. They mocked him and buffeted him, saying, "This is the monk who has seduced our daughter! Let him be hanged! Let him be hanged!" They beat him nearly to death.

Then came one of the old men of the village and said to them, "How long will you go on beating this monk who is a stranger?" The man who ministered to him came after him. He was ashamed and pained because of his disgrace. The people fastened their gaze on him, saying, "Behold, the monk who you say was a holy man. Consider what he has done," said the parents of the young woman, "and unless he gives us a surety, we will not release him." He said to the man who ministered to him, "Give a pledge on my behalf, saying, I will provide for that child." He gave a pledge for him, and then the monk went to his cell and gave him all the palm leaf mats of it, and said to him, "Sell these and give the money to my wife that she may eat." For Macarius said in his mind, "Behold, you have found for yourself a wife. It is necessary for you to work little or much so that you may feed her." He worked night and day, and sent the proceeds of his toil to her.

It happened that when it was time for the woman to deliver her child, she suffered very severely for many days; and although she was in great tribulation, she did not give birth to the child. When her parents saw this, they said to her, "What has happened to you?" Then the woman, by reason of her pains and sufferings, said, "This has happened because I told a lie and falsely accused a monk who never touched me. It was such a youth who had done this thing to me." When the man who ministered to Macarius learned this, he came to him with gladness, rejoiced and said to him, "The virgin was not able to bring forth until she confessed and said, the monk had never touched me. Behold, all the village is preparing to come to you with repentance so that you may forgive them." Macarius, in order that they might not trouble him, rose up straightaway, and fled, and departed to the place in which he had his abode at that time.

An Old Man Who Thought Melchisedek was the Son of God

ABBA DANIEL TOLD A STORY OF ANOTHER OLD MAN who used to live in the lower towns of Egypt. He said in his simplicity that Melchisedek was the Son of God. When this became known to the blessed man Theophilus, the Archbishop of Alexandria, he sent a message that the monks should bring the old man to him. When he saw him, he perceived that he was a seer of visions, and that everything, which he had asked God for, He gave him. He perceived that he spoke these words in his simplicity. The Archbishop dealt with him wisely in the following manner, saying, "Father, entreat your God for me, because my thoughts tell me that Melchisedek was the Son of God." He said to him likewise, "It cannot be thus, for the high priest of God was a man. And, because I had doubts in my mind concerning this, I sent for you that you might make supplication to God that He may reveal to you the matter." Then, because the old man had confidence in his labors, he spoke to him boldly, saying, "Wait three days, and I will enquire to God. Then I shall be able to inform you who Melchisedek was." So the old man departed, and came again after three days, and said to the blessed Archbishop Theophilus that Melchisedek was a man. The Archbishop said to him, "How do you know, father?" The old man said, "God showed me all the Patriarchs, one by one. They passed before me one after the other, from Adam to Melchisedek. Also, an angel said to me, 'This is Melchisedek.' Know then that of a truth the matter is as it has appeared to me." The old man departed, and he himself proclaimed that Melchisedek was a man. The blessed Theophilus rejoiced greatly.

DAY 70

Abba Macarius the Egyptian, the Disciple of Saint Anthony

ABBA MACARIUS USED TO DWELL BY HIMSELF IN THE DESERT. South to him, there was another desert where many dwelt. The old man was watching the road one day, and saw Satan travelling on it in the form of a man. He came along with the intention of passing him. He was arrayed in a garment full of holes, and various fruits were hanging from him. The old man Macarius said to him, "Where are you going?" He said, "I am going to visit the brethren, to make them mindful of their work? The old man said to him, "What is the purpose of the fruits on you?" Satan answered saying, "I am carrying them to the brethren for food." The old man said, "All these?" Satan said, "Yes. For if one does not please a brother, I hand him another. If that does not please also, I give him another.

One or other of these must certainly please him." Having said these things, Satan went on his way.

Then the old man continued to watch the road until Satan returned. When he saw him, he said to him, "Have you been successful?" Satan said, "Where am I to obtain help?" The old man said, "For what purpose?" Satan said, "They have all forsaken me, and rebelled against me. Not one of them will allow himself to be over persuaded by me." The old man said, "Have you no friends left there?" Satan said to him, "Yes, I have one brother, but one only who will be persuaded by me, although whenever he sees me, he turns away his face as if from that of an adversary." The old man said to him, "What is the name of this brother?" Satan said, "Theopemptus." Having said these things he departed and went on his way.

Abba Macarius rose up and went down to the lower desert. The brethren heard of his coming, brought palm leaves, and went out to meet him. Every monk prepared and made his abode ready, thinking he would come and dwell there. The old man only asked for the brother whose name was Theopemptus, and he received him joyfully. When the brethren began to speak among themselves, the old man said to him, "What do you have to say, O my brother, and how are your own affairs?" Theopemptus said to him, "At the present moment, matters are well with me." He was ashamed to speak. The old man said to him, "Behold, I have now lived a life of stern asceticism for many years, and I am held in honour by every man.

Nevertheless, even though I am an old man, the spirit of fornication disturbs me." Theopemptus answered, saying, "Believe me, father, it disturbs me also." The old man, like one who was vexed by many thoughts, made a reason for talking. At length he led the brother to confess the matter. Afterwards he said to him, "How long do you fast?" The brother said to Abba Macarius, "Until the ninth hour." The old man replied, "Fast until the evening and repeat passages from the Book of the Gospels, and from the other Scriptures. If a thought rises in your mind, do not let your mind look downwards, but always upwards. The Lord shall help you." Thus having made the brother reveal his thoughts, and having given him encouragement, he departed to his own desert. He travelled along the road and watched according to his custom.

He saw the devil again, and said to him, "Where are you going?" He answered, saying, "I go to remind the brethren of their work." Having departed and come back again, the holy man said to him, "How are the brethren?" The devil said, "They are evil cases." The old man said, "Why?" The devil said, "Because they are all like savage animals, and they are rebellious. But the worst thing of all is that even the one brother who used to be obedient to me, has turned, for a reason I do not know, and he will not in any way be persuaded by me. He is the most savage of them all against me. I have on this account taken an oath that I will never go again to that place, at least, only after a very long time."

Abba Macarius was marvelous in his life and deeds. Once as he was travelling along in the inner desert, he looked, and, behold, there was an old man coming towards him. He was arrayed in very old apparel. Over his whole body there were hung very many things which were like pots, each one being provided with rings. He was covering them over as it were with a covering. He drove his staff into the ground. Though he was as timid and as terrified as a fugitive slave, he pretended to be bold, and stood up like a brave man. He spoke to the blessed Macarius, face to face, saying, "What are you doing in this wilderness, and why are you wandering here and there?" The blessed Macarius answered him, saying, "I wish to find God, for I am fleeing from sin. But who are you, O old man? Tell me, for I observe that your raiment is very different from that of the children of men. Tell me, what are these things which you have on you?" The old man, though unwilling, confessed and said, "I am he whom you call by the name of Calumniator. I fulfill the work of sin. By means of lusts, I turn people away. I have great happiness in those who, through my crafts and wiles, stumble and fall."

When the blessed Macarius heard these things, he plucked up courage, and said to Satan, "By Christ, Who caused you to make a mockery of the holy angels, explain to me, one by one, each and all of the things which you earn. For by this you shall be revealed, and a man may see the insidiousness of your crafts and wiles. A man may learn your hidden snares, may recognize the multitude of the burning arrows of your error, and may flee from the performance of your will." The Calumniator answered and said, "I must reveal to you my craftiness, even though I am unwilling to do so. It is impossible for me to hide from you any of the things which you see. If I find a man who meditates continually on the Law of God, I pour out on him from the pot, which is on my head, dizziness and headache, and restrain him from this work. On the man who has chosen to watch by means of the recital of prayers and psalms, I pour out from the pot which is on my eyelids, a disposition to sleep, and I drive him along by main force into slumber. These, which you see that I have on my ears, are prepared for disobedience, the transgression of the Commandments. By their means, I trap those who wish to lead a good life to disobey the word of truth.

From those, which hang from my nose, I sprinkle on the young the sweet smell of happiness, and lead them into fornication. From those which are on my mouth, I throw out flowers and I incite the ascetic by means of blandishments, and I make to sin those who live a life of abstinence and self-denial by means of such dainty meats and foods according to my desire. By means of those, which are in my mouth, I draw many into the utterance of calumnies, and filthy talk. To speak briefly, in each one of these pots is the seed, which is most useful for increasing the fruits which are worthy of me, and which may be gathered from the labors of the husbandmen who labor in my vineyard. From the pots, which are hung about my neck, I pour out pride, and enclose with my nets those who are haughty in their minds. By means of all these, I possess in the world multitudes of subjects who love the things, which are mine, that is to say, worldly praise and wealth, which are things remote from God. The pots which you see hanging from my breasts are full of my imaginings, and with some of these I water the hearts of the children of men, and by means of the drunkenness of the passions, I dissipate and destroy the mind which fears God; and through my error I confound the memory of those men who wish to meditate upon and to think about the things which concern the world to come. Those which hang upon my body are full of want of feeling and perception, and by them, I prepare those who are without understanding to live in a savage and animal manner, a life which is characterized by various kinds of brutish habits.

In the pots, which are below my body are all things which are useful and suitable for union with women in fornication, and for filthy wantonness. Those which are on my hands, are useful in the committal of murders. The pots which you see hanging from my neck and back have in them the thick darkness of my temptations, where with I am able to vanquish those who are so bold as to contend against me. I lay ambushes behind me, and I rush out to overthrow those who depend upon their own strength. The pots which you see hanging on my loins and thighs, and downwards to my feet, are full of the snares and nets which I pour out, to make crooked and confound the ways of those who wish to journey in the narrow path. By these pots, I impede the goings of those who cultivate ascetic excellence, and make them journey on my way, which is easy to travel.

I strengthen them and I make them valiant so that they may go forward easily in my paths. When they are bowed down and labor under my yoke, I sow evil and abominable vices among them like thorns and brambles. But you, O Macarius, have never once inclined yourself to obey me. By your obedience, I might be able to find even a little consolation but you burn me up wholly by means of the mighty armour of humility which you bear. For this reason, I haste to depart to my own subjects. For you possess a good Lord, and you have mighty companions, who tranquilly and happily serve God, and who protect you as a beloved son."

When the chosen athlete had heard these things, he made the sign of the Cross over himself, and said, "Blessed be God, Who has made those who have put their hopes in Him to make you a mockery and a laughing stock, and Who has preserved me wholly and completely from your craft so that while turning aside from the same, I was able to advance in the good fight. Having fought and conquered I shall receive a crown from the good Lord Whom I possess. Flee then, and get afar off, O you who are envious of the things, which are good, for Christ will make an end of you. You may not dare to attack any of those who worship Him. For sufficient for you are those whom you have drawn to yourself by flattery, through your evil wiles, and their own sluggish will."

When the blessed man said these things, straightaway the Calumniator disappeared. The holy man Macarius bowed on his knee, prayed saying, "Glory is to You, O Christ, You who are the Refuge of those who are overtaken by storms. You who are the straightway of those who sin. You who are the Redeemer of those who flee to you for refuge, now, always, and for ever and ever! Amen."

Abba Mark the Less, the Disciple of Abba Sylvanus

THEY USED TO SAY CONCERNING ABBA SYLVANUS that he wished to depart to Syria. His disciple Mark said to him, "Not only I do not wish you to depart from this place, O father, but also I will not permit you to go now. Wait then here for three days more" On the third day Mark died in peace.

Abba Paul the Simple, the Disciple of Saint Anthony

THE BLESSED MAN, PAUL THE SIMPLE, the disciple of the holy man Anthony, used to relate to the fathers the following matter, reciting: I once went to a certain monastery that I might visit the brethren for profit spiritually. After some conversation on the matter, they went into the holy church that they might form a congregation as usual, and perform the service of the Holy

Sacraments. The blessed Paul looked at and scrutinized each one of them, so that he might see in what frame of mind he was going, for he had the gift, given to him by God, of looking into the soul of every man, and knowing what that man's soul was like. He saw that every man was going in with a glorious soul and with a face full of light. Also, the angel of each man was rejoicing in him, with the exception of one, whose face was sick and afflicted. This very one's whole body was in darkness, and devils held both of his hands. They were lifting him up, dragging him towards them, and they had put a ring in his nose. He saw that the holy angel of this man was a long way from him, and the angel followed after him sadly and sorrowfully.

When the blessed Paul saw these things he wept, and struck himself upon the breast many times. He sat down before the church, and cried unceasingly for the man who had appeared to him in this state. Those who saw the old man became greatly astonished, especially at his swift change from happiness to weeping and tears. They asked him, entreated, and begged him to tell them what he had seen. Paul sat outside the church, held his peace, cried aloud and groaned loudly concerning that which had appeared to him.

After a short time, when the service ended, all the fathers were coming out. Paul carefully scrutinised each one of them again, so that he might see in what manner they would come out and whether it would be of the same countenance as they had gone in the church with. He saw again that man whom he had seen go in, and whose body before had entered into the church in darkness. Behold, he came out from the church with a face full of light and with a white body. The devils followed him at a distance and his guardian angel was close to him. Saint Paul was glad and rejoiced over that man. Paul cried out blessing God, saying, "Hail overflowing mercy of God! Hail to the immeasurable goodness! Hail to His rich treasuries! Hail to His pleasure, which is beyond measure!" He ran up and stood upon a lofty platform, and cried with a loud voice, saying, "Come, and see how awesome are the works of God, and how greatly they are worthy of admiration! Come, and see Him Who wishes that all the children of men should live, and should turn to the knowledge of the truth! Come, let us kneel and worship Him, saying, "You are He who alone can forgive sins." Therefore all the fathers ran diligently so that they might hear what he was saying. When they had all gathered together, the holy man Paul related to them the things, which he had seen. When each one of them came out, they entreated that brother to tell them what the reason for that complete change was, and of the gladness which God bestowed upon him so quickly.

The man, being afraid lest he might be rebuked by the blessed Paul, related the following things concerning himself, before all of them. Without any concealment whatsoever, he said, "I am a sinful man, and for a long time past, even to the present day, I lived in fornication. When I went into the church, I heard the Book of the Prophet Isaiah read, that is to say, I heard God speaking and saying, 'Wash, and be clean, and remove your evil deeds from before my eyes. Hate the evil things, learn to do good, seek out judgment, and pass righteous sentences upon those who are afflicted. If your sins are red like crimson, they shall become white as snow. If you are willing to hearken to Me, you shall eat of the good things of the earth.'

When I had heard and read these words from the Prophet, as having heard God speaking, I immediately repented in my soul sincerely. I was sighing in my heart saying, "You are the God who did come into the world to make sinners live. Make manifest in me the things, which you have promised in Your Prophet. Fulfill them in me, even though I am unworthy for I am a sinner. For behold, I promise, and I enter into a covenant with you. I will thrust this promise down into my soul. I will acknowledge that from now onward, I will never commit such wickedness but will keep myself remote from all iniquity. I will serve you from this day onwards with a clean conscience. O My Master, from this day, and this hour, accept me, for I am penitent. I will make a supplication to you. I will remove myself from all sin." Therefore, with such promises and covenants, I came out from the church determined in my soul that I would never again do anything which would injure my fear of Him." When all the fathers heard this, they all cried out with a loud voice, saying to God, "O Lord, how great are Your works! You have created all of them in wisdom."

Therefore, O Christians, we know from the Holy Scriptures and from divine revelations how great is the grace, which God dispenses to those who truly seek Him for refuge. He blots out their former sins using repentance. Let us not be in despair of our lives. For, even as He promised by the hand of Isaiah the Prophet, He will make clean those who have toiled in sin. He will make them bright and white like clean wool and snow. He will make them happy with the blessings of heaven. Moreover, God asserts with oaths by the hand of the Prophet Ezekiel that He does not desire their destruction, for He says, "As I live, says the Lord, I do not desire the death of a sinner, but that he should turn from his evil way and live."

Scan the QR code to go to our website where you will find

- Book reviews
- Great deals
- Our full library of books

www.ingramcontent.com/pod-product-compliance
Lightning Source LLC
Chambersburg PA
CBHW031309150426
43191CB00005B/141